LAW
WITHOUT
A LAWYER

Fenton Bresler has been a practising barrister since 1951, but also works in newspapers, magazines and television, specialising in legal and criminal matters. He was legal correspondent for the *Daily Mail* and the *Sunday Express*, and now contributes to the *Daily Telegraph* and the *Daily Express*. He is the author of several books, including *The Murder of John Lennon* and *Interpol*.

LAW
WITHOUT
A LAWYER

Fenton Bresler

SINCLAIR-STEVENSON

First published in Great Britain in 1995
by Sinclair-Stevenson
an imprint of Reed Consumer Books Ltd
Michelin House, 81 Fulham Road, London SW3 6RB
and Auckland, Melbourne, Singapore and Toronto

Copyright © 1995 by Fenton Bresler

Reprinted 1995

The right of Fenton Bresler to be identified as author
of this work has been asserted by him in accordance with the
Copyright, Designs and Patents Act 1988.

A CIP catalogue record for this book
is available at the British Library
ISBN 1 85619 320 9

Phototypeset by Intype, London
Printed and bound in Great Britain
by Mackays of Chatham PLC

For my brother,
Harold Bresler

Contents

Part Five   YOUR LEISURE

Part Six   YOUR PURCHASES

Part Seven   YOUR SPECIAL PROBLEMS

Part Eight   YOUR DEATH

INTRODUCTION

What This Book Is All About

This book is for the articulate, the determined and those who believe that knowledge is power. Never before in our history has the law been allowed to creep so deeply into almost every nook and cranny of our lives. Governments have become bullies, and they have many imitators in our everyday existence.

The consequence is that never before have lawyers been so necessary; but ironically never before have they been so expensive or inaccessible to so many people. State legal aid has become meaningless to most people in this country who want to fight or defend their case in the civil courts (criminal cases are in a different category) – and this book is aimed at them.

The notion behind the legal-aid scheme when it was first introduced in those heady days following World War Two was noble: 'to provide a charter of the little man to the British courts of justice', as Sir Hartley Shawcross, then Labour Attorney-General, put it. The cost of going to law would no longer be a barrier to obtaining justice.

But that was back in 1949. Today the story is very different. Subsequent governments, of both major parties, failed to let the scheme keep pace with reality. The income and property limits, within which legal aid is available, were not allowed to keep pace with the rising rate of inflation and the sinking value of money. Then in April 1993, as part of the Major government's determination to reduce public spending, sometimes at seemingly almost any cost, the Lord Chancellor, Lord Mackay, plunged his dagger into the very heart of the scheme with slashing cuts in eligibility of a scale never before even attempted.

Pressure groups such as Age Concern, Shelter and the Consumers' Association warned that up to 12 million people would be disqualified.

Mr Mark Sheldon, then President of the Law Society representing some 60,000 solicitors in England and Wales, said it was 'the most serious attack on legal aid since the scheme began over forty years ago'. Lord Taylor, the Lord Chief Justice, called the cuts 'draconian, deplorable and wrong in principle'.

No matter. They are now firmly in place. Nearly a year later, in March 1994, Lord Mackay tried to alleviate the situation a little by raising the income qualifying limits by 3.8 per cent, a pitifully small amount which made almost no difference to the overall picture. As Sir Thomas Bingham, the Master of the Rolls, wrote in the magazine *The Lawyer* in the following month, 'It is a very serious thing indeed when one gets to a position where the ordinary citizen simply cannot go to court to get a dispute resolved.'

Civil legal aid has become like so many other things in modern British life: a class issue. If you are working class or really substantially in need, you are adequately protected by the courts. If you are upper middle class or truly wealthy, you are in the same position as you have been ever since men and women first began stamping their rulers' heads on pieces of gold and silver: your money will cosset you and keep you warm. But, if you are in the middle, the cold blasts of economic – and legal – reality hit you the hardest.

Civil legal aid is simply not available to most middle-class people. All legal aid eligibility figures are subject to minor adjustment every April but, as I write (in December 1994), anyone earning more than £7,080 a year after deductions for tax, National Insurance, rent or mortage, etc. (i.e. £136 'disposable income' a week) is now considered too 'rich' to qualify for any form of legal aid at all, even if willing to pay a sizeable contribution towards the costs. *Free* legal aid is available only to those with a staggeringly low 'disposable income' of £45 a week. If this rises to between £45 and £136 a week, you are in theory eligible for 'assisted' legal aid; but the contribution you will be asked to pay towards your costs is generally so high that *The Times*, hardly a militant left-wing publication, has estimated that about 20 per cent of those offered legal aid on this basis have to turn it down on the grounds of expense.

Even if your income is low enough to qualify, the notional amount of your capital (including the value of your home, except in cases where its ownership is the matter in dispute) will almost certainly take you out of the scheme. No one with capital of more than £6,750 (with a slightly higher level for pensioners and an £8,560 limit in accident cases) is eligible for civil legal aid.

The problem is made more acute by the fact that, although there are many solicitors and barristers who do not earn large fees and undertake work as much for social good as for private profit, the legal profession as a whole is extremely expensive, and I write as a lawyer!

Local Citizens Advice Bureaux and neighbourhood law centres undoubtedly do valiant work; but they primarily do not get involved with litigation and the kinds of case that they tackle are generally more for lower-income groups. In any event, most middle-class people would feel happier consulting a solicitor: the problem is that so many cannot afford them.

The amount you will be asked to pay depends on where you live, the size of the law firm you consult and how high ranking your solicitor is. A partner in a central London firm will charge about £155 an hour plus VAT in a typical civil case (partners in the best London firms charge top rates of up to £350 an hour for complex cases), although in Wales or the Midlands it would probably be nearer £100. In the North West of England or East Anglia you could expect to pay about £75–£80 an hour for a non-partner. All that many people want is 'a strong solicitor's letter' to state their point of view, but such a letter, and the necessary visit to the solicitor's office beforehand, can easily cost £75–£125 in London and £50–£75 elsewhere. That does not come cheaply out of taxed income.

But these figures are only the basic amounts. Solicitors are not restricted to their hourly rates. They can, and often do, add a given percentage, which can be as high as 50 per cent, for what they call 'mark-up', like restaurateurs charging extra for their wine. In theory, this is supposed to reflect any special features of the case. In reality, it is all too often an amount plucked from the air to help the solicitor's cash-flow problems.

In any given case, the amount of this blatantly commercial item will depend on how much the solicitor thinks the case is worth to the client or how much he thinks the client will be prepared to pay. French stall-holders use a colourful phrase in their street markets: '*Le prix est à la tête du client*' (The price will depend on the 'head' of the client).

3

Many solicitors use the same none-too-edifying principle in their dealings.

Furthermore, this does not include the extra cost of briefing a barrister, if you want representation in court or seek counsel's opinion on a question of law or your prospects of success.

No wonder that Mr Tony Holland, an ex-President of the Law Society, has admitted: 'If a solicitor had himself for a client, he would not be able to afford his own fees.'

Solicitors are not even required by their disciplinary body, the Law Society, to tell their clients at the outset of the likely cost of their work and their basis for charging. The Law Society merely 'encourages' them to do so. At a Law Society conference in Oxford, Mr John Taylor, Parliamentary Secretary at the Lord Chancellor's Department and Lord Mackay's Number 2, has complained that too many solicitors are in effect asking for a 'blank cheque' from their clients.

The way round this is, before you go ahead, always to ask a solicitor for a written estimate of how many hours' work will be involved and how much it will cost; and do not be afraid to negotiate. Even so, your final bill may still be much more than the estimate, although you have a right to query it with the Law Society. In cases not involving court work, you should ask your solicitor to obtain 'a remuneration certificate' from the Law Society that his fees are 'fair and reasonable', although in November 1994 the law was changed so that you now can only do this if you have already paid half his costs and all the VAT plus disbursements. In all cases involving litigation, however, you can ask for the bill to be 'taxed': i.e. assessed by the court itself.

If all else fails, you can telephone the help line staffed by the Solicitors Complaints Bureau on 01926–822007/8. The Bureau, set up in 1986, is an independent arm of the Law Society that provides a free service to complainants, mainly by way of voluntary conciliation. It cannot guarantee results but its track record is not unimpressive.

Yet, of course, the fact remains that, even with these safeguards, the cost of going to law or even seeking skilled legal advice can be prohibitive. Hence, the need for this book.

Primarily its purpose is to help you to be your own lawyer, although recognising the necessary limitations, the occasions when you inevitably have to seek expert help. It is aimed at an audience of reasonable intelligence and reasonable education who have the desire – and the ability – to stand up for themselves. If you have never firmly but politely queried a bill in a restaurant, or think that you would not like to because it would be too embarrassing or demeaning – or because you do not have the courage – please do not bother to read on. This book is not for you.

But in countless situations in everyday life today people need to know what the law is in order to be able to protect their own legitimate interests.

This is not a manual: that would be boring and unreadable. This is, I hope, a readable book, which will give you the knowledge to enable you whenever possible to battle for yourself.

I have practised at the Bar for over forty years and also been a legal journalist for most of that time. An elderly barrister once dismissed me with a perceptible sniff as 'a populist'. I happily accept the title.

But this book is not comprehensive. That is a will-o'-the-wisp in a single book of this length. I have chosen instead those sections of law which I think will be of most value to my readers: there is no section on 'Squatters' Rights' but you will read about how to get rid of squatters. You will find no reference to the legal problems of the homeless or the complex laws dealing with social security. But you will read about birth and death, divorce and marriage, landlords' rights, holiday problems, motoring law, wills, schools, employment law, maternity rights, coping with the police, jury service, etc., etc., and all put in their historical and social context, with true-life cases, so that you can understand them better.

The aim is to give readers the particular kind of information that they require – which, at the moment, they cannot easily find elsewhere. I have two main rivals, both much more expensive and at times inaccurate in important matters of detail, perhaps through trying too hard to cover every point. These are the Reader's Digest's *You and Your Rights* (10th Edition, 1991), with its thirty-three contributors, at £26.95 in hardcover for 768 pages, and the *New Penguin Guide to the Law* (3rd Edition, 1992), with twenty-two contributors, at £20 in hardcover and £12.99 in paperback for 955 pages.

There is also the *Daily Telegraph Guide to Everyday Law* (May 1994) at a more reasonable price (£8.99) but utterly unreadable as a book: it is like a law student's detailed textbook and, as with the other two, is not one person's work but the product of several people's efforts.

5

What I claim for my 'one-man-band' effort is that it presents one person's view of the law. I have written only on subjects that I know about myself, often from practical experience at the Bar or in legal journalism, and which I believe to be of special interest to the sort of person likely to pick up this book and turn over its pages.

I also believe immodestly that it is more readable, more reliable and more up-to-date than the others.

In general terms, the law is stated as of 1 January 1995. It will vary in some respects for Scotland but I have done my best to make it as accurate as possible for England and Wales, although I can accept no liability to anyone if unwittingly I have erred in any specific instance. Halsbury's *Laws of England*, the semi-official statement of the law found in every lawyer's office and on the shelves of most public reference libraries, runs to fifty-six volumes.

Part One
YOU AND
YOUR FAMILY

ONE

Pre-Birth

The law – and medical science – used to be simple. You were born and your life was said to start, both legally and factually, when you left your mother's body and, kicking and perhaps screaming, you started an independent existence taking in your own air and your own food. As Mr Justice Brett told a jury back in 1874: 'A child is born alive when it exists as a live child, breathing and living by reason of its breathing through its own lungs alone, without deriving any of its living or power of living by or through any connection with its mother.'

His Victorian lordship never had to consider the legal ramifications of a newborn babe going straight on to a ventilator or of an 'unborn' child aborted late in pregnancy by the prostrogland injection method who, small but perfectly formed, manages to survive, struggling for breath for minutes or even hours. It is impossible to speculate what the learned Mr Justice Brett, now long lying dead in his coffin, would have thought of the first-ever coroner's inquest in April 1979 on an aborted baby: a 23-week-old girl foetus who survived for thirty-six hours at a hospital in Barnsley, South Yorkshire, and was actually given a name – Emma.

Medical science has not stood still. In recent years judges, lawyers – and Parliament – have had to rethink many of the concepts involved in the whole complex gamut of rights and legal situations brought about by the modern hi-tech phenomenon of birth: from conception through to delivery.

In fact, we have to start even before conception. It is a truism that not every couple who have sex want to have a child: rarely do those who have had a 'one-night stand' or a brief affair want to complicate their lives by the birth of a child and nowadays all married couples and long-term partners, except those whose religious principles forbid it, use modern scientific methods to try to select when they have children.

What is the law on contraception?

It takes two forms: birth control and sterilisation – and the law on both has changed very much in recent years.

Birth control

Birth control is almost as ancient as mankind. No one knows when the first coupling pair used any of the 'natural' methods of contraception. But tattered fragments of Ancient Egyptian papyri tell us that, about 1,850 years before the birth of Christ, upper-class Egyptian women were trying to stop themselves becoming pregnant by using – of all things – crocodile dung as a primitive vaginal pessary, while Egyptian men some five hundred years later were putting on ill-fitting, uncomfortable, handmade sheaths.

Nowadays, of course, it is all very different. Condoms are readily available, slickly packaged and, so we are assured, a pleasure to wear. You can even get them free on the National Health Service: in July 1993, for instance, a woman in Dorset claimed that forty condoms a month was not enough and her local family planning clinic duly gave her more, free of charge.[1] Men can buy them with no legal difficulty (regardless of age) in most chemist's shops – and if they find that too embarrassing, as, according to a survey in October 1993 by Exeter University, 80 per cent still do, there is the comforting anonymity of vending machines in the lavatories of countless public houses, motorway cafés and discos.

But how 'safe' does a condom, wherever bought, have to be in law? According to a report in October 1992 in, of all places, *The Times*, an average purchaser uses 102 condoms a year. Yet there still is no specified legal standard. The British Standards Institute issued its Kitemark quality standard for condoms (No. 3704) in 1989 but, like most Kitemarks,

---

[1] There is a nice twist to this: only women can obtain free contraceptive devices on the NHS and they can only ask their doctor for female contraceptives: a supply of pills, the coil or a cap. If they want to get their men free condoms, they must ask their local family planning clinic.

it has no legal effect. In August 1993 the Consumers' Association warned that they had recently tested condoms produced by thirty-four different manufacturers – and nine makes had leaked or split in use. Disturbingly, three of those nine carried the British Standards Kitemark. Moreover, according to the World Health Organisation, over a third of penises exceed the Kitemark dimensions: 52 mm wide when flat.

The truth is that there is no legal guarantee of complete security and, if you read the small print on the pack, you will see that no manufacturer is so foolhardy as to give any such assurance. The result is that no one can sue if a condom fails and a baby is born – or a sexual disease is contracted.

The only legal protection for users is that extravagant claims should not be made. The 1968 Trade Descriptions Act says that *all* retail goods must not bear a 'false trade description' – and this equally applies to condoms:

The case of the 'supersafe' condoms

In 1987, trading standards officers in the London suburb of Greenwich, alerted by complaints about foreign-manufactured 'Supersafe (Ribbed) Condoms' on sale locally, found that nineteen out of a hundred had holes in them. In the first prosecution of its kind, Greenwich Magistrates' Court fined the importers £1,000 and £500 costs for selling goods with a false trade description. Whatever the quality of the condoms may have been, they were most certainly not 'supersafe'.

Most men probably prefer women to take the precautions against pregnancy and, with the first contraceptive pill going on the market in the United States as far back as May 1960, it is estimated that today at least three out of four women in England, both married and single, choose it as their preferred form of contraception. At present there are about thirty-five brands, but, again, no legal guarantee is given.

What about the young? Nearly half the girls and a third of the boys in a survey by *Cosmopolitan* magazine in May 1993 claimed to have had sex before they were sixteen, as against only 2 per cent of girls and 6 per cent of boys back in 1964. Some may find this perfectly acceptable and readily identify with the mothers whom a journalist in the *Sunday Times Magazine* has described as 'practically packing condoms in their children's lunchboxes'. Others may find totally unacceptable the current state of the law where a doctor or family planning clinic may prescribe the pill or other contraceptive device to a child under sixteen without insisting that she first obtains her parents' consent – or even tells them.

That was decided in the famous case of *Gillick* v. *West Norfolk Area Health Committee and the DHSS* in October 1985 when a devout Roman Catholic mother, anxious about the future welfare of her four young daughters under sixteen, went to court for a declaration that her local area health committee had acted unlawfully in refusing to promise her not to give them the pill without her prior knowledge or consent. The case went up to the House of Lords, the ultimate court of appeal, and Lord Templeman would have granted the declaration:

> I doubt whether a girl under the age of sixteen is capable of a balanced judgement to embark on frequent, regular or casual sexual intercourse fortified by the illusion that medical science can protect her mind and body and ignoring the danger of leaping from childhood to adulthood without the difficult formative transitional experiences of adolescence. There are many things a girl under sixteen needs to practise but sex is not one of them.

But the four other law lords disagreed. Lord Scarman's judgment was typical of their philosophy: 'Parental right yields to the child's right to make her own decisions when she reaches a sufficient understanding and intelligence to be capable of making up her own mind.' All four law lords said that doctors should normally seek parental consent but unanimously ruled that it was not legally necessary so long as their young patient was, in the words of Lord Fraser of Tullybelton, 'capable of understanding what is proposed and of expressing her wishes'.

To comply with this majority decision, the British Medical Association laid down guidelines saying that a doctor must first decide if an underage patient understands the risks of taking contraception and having sex. He should then 'encourage' her to tell her parents but must take into account whether she is likely to have sex without protection if help was refused. Finally he must determine whether contraception is likely to have any harmful effect on her physical or mental health and must 'consider' whether making it available without parental consent is in her own best interests.

12

But under no circumstances must he himself tell the parents that their young daughter has asked for or been given help with contraception.

That seems clear enough; but doubts about confidentiality persisted among young people and in November 1993 the BMA announced it was sending leaflets to every surgery in the land stressing its importance. 'All the evidence shows that concern about confidentiality is the main reason that prevents underage girls from seeking advice,' said the BMA's Dr Fleur Fisher. 'There is general confusion among the public but we are quite clear in the medical profession that confidentiality must be regarded, whatever the age of the patient.'

Not every parent would agree. Or be happy with the fact that the same largesse seems to apply to schoolteachers. But in October 1994 it was announced that three teaching unions and the National Children's Bureau had obtained an opinion by a leading QC that, although the matter had never been tested in the courts, teachers could, in his view, safely ignore recent Education Department guidelines on sex education limiting teachers' discretion to give contraceptive advice to children under sixteen without telling their parents. The opinion said that the guidelines had 'no special legal status' and teachers need not comply with them if, in their professional judgement, a child's best interests were better served by confidentiality.

Yet whatever the rights and wrongs of the moral debate, in practical terms the law is quite clear: parents do not have to be told and birth control for girls under sixteen is obtainable virtually on demand.

There are umpteen examples. In early 1992, for instance, there was a great furore in the press because a school doctor at Marlborough, one of the country's most prestigious co-ed establishments, had prescribed the pill to a fifteen-year-old girl unbeknown to her parents and she had been found in her seventeen-year-old boyfriend's bedroom. The headmaster expelled them both but maintained vehemently that his school had been 'unfairly picked on'. He protested: 'There is nothing that happens here that doesn't happen in many other schools.'

Yet there is a disturbing paradox: despite this legal availability of contraception for children, Britain still has the highest teenage pregnancy rate in Western Europe. In fact, about 8,400 girls under sixteen become pregnant each year in England and Wales: the equivalent of two for each secondary school. In July 1993, a fifteen-year-old pregnant schoolgirl near Bristol got legal aid to challenge in the courts her proposed exclusion from school because of her condition – and, in the current state of the law, she was so likely to win her case that Avon County Council promptly settled out of court and rescinded its ban.

Sterilisation

Unlike birth control, this is primarily a modern phenomenon. It really only began to be medically possible on any large scale in the Seventies; but already the law is well established, evolved by the judges themselves in several precedent-making cases. Parliament has had little to do with it.

Sterilisation is legally just like any other operation: the surgeon must ensure that the patient understands and agrees to what is going to happen. Any surgery without consent is 'trespass to the person' and the patient could recover substantial damages from the surgeon or the NHS authorities. With sterilising a man, there is usually no problem: he will have chosen quite deliberately to have his vasectomy and signed the normal consent form without demur. With women, the situation can be much more delicate – and doctors overlook the need for consent at their peril.

Two doctors who went too far

In 1980, a 33-year-old married woman who already had four children and whose religion forbade sterilisation entered hospital for a minor gynaecological operation. During the operation the surgeon saw that her womb was ruptured and sterilised her there and then. She won £4,000 damages for the loss of her ability to conceive again and £2,750 damages for her distress at what had happened to her.

In 1978, a 35-year-old Roman Catholic woman was about to be wheeled into the operating theatre to give birth to her second child by Caesarean section, for which she had already signed a consent form, when she was asked to sign a second form for a sterilisation to take place at the same time. She understood what that physically meant but, in her trauma, no one sufficiently explained the psychological implications to her. She won £3,000 damages.

Does a surgeon have to satisfy himself that the spouse or live-in partner of his patient also consents to the sterilisation? After all, they are intimately involved. The British Medical Association recommends this as a courtesy – but there is no legal obligation.

What happens if the operation fails? The risk of natural reversal of a male vasectomy is lower than that of a female sterilisation; but there is still no absolute guarantee that any sterilisation will work for all time. Yet, if the operation fails and a child is born, you can, in this increasingly materialistic world, still sue for damages if (a) the surgeon did not warn you there was a risk, however slight, of failure or (b) you can prove he was negligent in carrying out the operation. This second possibility will require expert evidence from other medical men which, because of the professional freemasonry of doctors, is not always easy to obtain.

Back in the early Eighties some judges objected on moral grounds to this sort of litigation but now it is clear that parents are entitled to recover reasonable damages for what Mr Justice Brooke called in January 1992, in *Allen* v. *Bloomsbury Health Authority*, a mother's 'discomfort and pain' in carrying and bearing an unwanted child, and much more substantial damages for the cost of bringing up the child through to adulthood. This can, in appropriate circumstances, include the mother's loss of earnings in not going back to work for a while – and the cost of private education. As Mr Justice Brooke said: 'If an unplanned child is born after a failure by a hospital doctor to exercise the standard of care reasonably to be expected of him and the child's parents have sent all their other children to expensive private boarding schools for the whole of their education, then it appears to me that a very substantial claim for the cost of private education of a healthy child of a reasonably wealthy family might have to be met from the funds of the health authority responsible for the doctor's negligence.'

Attempts to prevent conception with birth control or sterilisation in this imperfect world sometimes fail. Now let us look at what the law says about that other main form of preventing childbirth:

Abortion

For more than half this century, most abortions in England and Wales were sordid, illegal, back-street affairs with large quantities of gin and a hot bath or knitting needles as the principal tools to hand. The only abortions legally allowed were medical terminations of pregnancy performed by a doctor when the child was not capable of being born alive or when necessary to save the life of a pregnant woman who would otherwise have died or, as Mr Justice MacNaughten said in a classic 1939 case, 'have become a physical or mental wreck'. By 1967, about fifty thousand abortions were estimated to be taking place every year – of which more than thirty thousand were illegal.

Then the 1967 Abortion Act, introduced as a Private Member's Bill by David Steel, MP (now Sir David), revolutionised the law. A woman could thenceforth obtain a medical abortion within the first twenty-eight weeks of pregnancy if two doctors signed a certificate on the basis that:

(i) continuing the pregnancy would involve risk to her life or to her physical or mental health or to that of her other children; or

(ii) there was substantial risk that the child would be born with a serious physical or mental handicap.

Subsequent decisions in the courts have made clear that, once a woman obtains those two vital signed certificates, it is only *her* decision that counts. A man cannot stop his wife or girlfriend having an abortion, even though he admits the child is his. And (except with a girl who is mentally backward or ill, where the courts decide the issue) parents cannot obtain an injunction to stop their teenage daughter from having an abortion. She has the legal right to do what she likes with her own body.

How many abortions do you think took place in England and Wales in the over twenty-three years between April 1968, when the Abortion Act came into effect, and December 1991? According to figures released by the Office of Population, Censuses and Surveys in July 1993, the staggering total was 3.5 million, of which 2.9 million (81 per cent) were performed on women living in this country: the other 600,000 came from abroad to profit from more liberal laws than in their homeland. Although Sir David Steel has always denied that was his intention, his Act effectively created legal abortion on demand – at least, within the first twenty-eight weeks of a pregnancy.

That time limit has since changed. In 1990, Parliament amended the 1967 Act and reduced the period to twenty-four weeks – but only when the woman's physical or mental health or that of any of her existing children is involved. In fact, today a legal abortion can take place well beyond twenty-four, or even twenty-eight, weeks if, even at that late stage, it becomes apparent that there is a substantial risk of a seriously handicapped child being brought into this world. In such cases, unknown to many people, there is now no time limit whatsoever.

The other side of the coin – modern methods of assisted conception

What about those people who, far from not wanting a child, passionately want one even though God seems to have decreed otherwise? It is estimated that as many as one in ten couples, perhaps more, have difficulty in conceiving naturally and seek medical help. What are their legal rights to use modern science to conceive and deliver a child against all the natural odds?

Within the past twenty years 'reproductive medicine', as it is called, has grown out of all recognition to form a whole new section of science – for which a whole new set of legal rules has had to be created. The subject is highly complicated and the law is still evolving and extremely complex.

Only those cursed with a natural blight on their ability to have children can truly understand the yearning and the anguish. As the journalist Joanne Glasbey, who has a fine healthy young daughter thanks to 'reproductive medicine', wrote in *The Times* in January 1994:

> It remains a huge gamble, born of a biological imperative so strong that couples will try after seven failed attempts to conceive, if they can afford it; if the frustration, disappointment and emotional battering has not disfigured their relationships and their lives drastically; above all, if they are prepared to accept that the odds are stacked against them as they were against us.

So let us examine the situation. It takes two main forms:

1. *Artificial insemination*

Back in the Sixties, this was the only kind of assisted conception available. An estimated 1,700 children are still born this way every year. It can be done if the problem is with the man, not the woman: i.e. if for some reason he cannot have normal sexual intercourse and

17

penetrate the woman naturally with his penis so that his sperm can travel within her body, mingle with her eggs and bring about fertilisation.

It is, however, a comparatively simple procedure to start the fertilisation process by artificially inserting his sperm into her. If necessary, this can even be done without medical assistance. In fact, animals have been artificially inseminated for more than two centuries: the first recorded instance of a puppy being born to a bitch from a dog's sperm inserted artificially into her vagina was back in 1780. The process has for many years been extensively used in rearing farm animals, especially cattle; and there are several statutory regulations on the subject with such marvellous titles as the 1964 Artificial Insemination of Pigs (England and Wales) Regulations and the 1984 Importation of Bovine Semen Regulations.

By the 1960s artificial insemination was also becoming available for humans.

There are two kinds: DI ('Donor Insemination') where the sperm does not come from the woman's husband, and AIH ('Artificial Insemination by Husband') where it does. AIH has seldom caused any legal complications: a child conceived in this way is as much the couple's legitimate child as any other and generally no outsider even knows it has occurred.

With DI it is different, and for one obvious reason: a third party is necessarily involved. Orginally the Church condemned the process as adultery, although in January 1958 the Court of Session held that was not so – at least, in Scottish Law. But up to 1987 a child born as a result of DI was still born into a legal limbo. Even if husband and wife had agreed to the wife being impregnated by another man's sperm (as nearly always happens), the child was treated as *their* illegitimate child and not the child of the married couple. That has now changed. The 1990 Human Fertilisation and Embryology Act says that, if the woman is married and has the treatment with her husband's consent, the baby is the legitimate child of their marriage, and the husband, not the donor, is the legal father. If the couple are unmarried but seek treatment together, the child is illegitimate just as if it had been born naturally, but the male partner is recognised as the father and can obtain full parental rights by seeking a 'parental responsibility' order in the courts under the 1989 Children Act, just like any other unmarried father.

Unmarried couples can now use DI without having to worry about undesirable legal consequences.

2. Test-tube babies

This is the generic term for all babies produced with the help of modern science – other than by artificial insemination.

In its simplest form it is designed to aid a woman who can produce eggs normally from her ovaries but whose Fallopian tubes are, for some reason, blocked so that she cannot conceive naturally because her eggs cannot travel through the tubes to meet male sperm entering her body and so be fertilised. Mrs Lesley Brown was just such a woman. In November 1977 Dr Patrick Steptoe implanted direct into her womb one of her own eggs after it had been fertilised – in a test-tube – by her husband's semen. Nine months later, in July 1978, she gave birth at a hospital in Greater Manchester to the world's first test-tube baby: a perfectly normal, healthy baby called Louise. The Latin for 'glass vessel' is *vitrum* so the new process was formally named *in vitro* fertilisation (IVF for short).

Immediately hope was given to thousands of couples around the world. 'Yet,' as Professor Margaret Brazier has commented, 'for every man and woman who rejoiced at what the doctors could now do, there were as many who condemned the technical advances as unnatural and contrary to the will of God.'

Improvements and refinements of the technique soon followed and, in answer to continuing public disquiet, Mrs Thatcher's government established an official Committee under Dame Mary (now Baroness) Warnock to draw up legal guidelines for the future. Its Report was published in the summer of 1984 and six years later, in the summer of 1990, after vitriolic debate in Parliament and two further Government reports, its somewhat modified recommendations became law as the 1990 Human Fertilisation and Embryology Act – which even today many people know little about.

The Act came into effect in August 1991 when its creation, the Human Fertilisation and Embryology Authority, began functioning. Based in London's East End, the 21-member Authority includes doctors, a geneticist, a psychiatrist, a lawyer, a bishop, a rabbi, an actress (Penelope Keith) and lay members. It is responsible for inspecting and licensing all clinics, whether private or NHS, which provide any form of fertility treatment where any part of the fertilisation process takes place outside a woman's body (with the one exception of artificial insemination by her husband) and all clinics which store human embryos or carry out research on them. No such clinic can operate lawfully without the Authority's licence and its staff and procedures are strictly monitored and controlled. In July 1993, for instance, it intervened to ban clinics from providing treatment which would allow parents to choose the sex of their offspring unless there was a risk the child could be born with an inherited disease.

The Authority has licensed some 107 establishments, and anyone wishing to know the address of the nearest clinic can telephone the Authority on London (0171) 377 5077.

It has to be said that, even today, fertility treatment carries no guarantee: legal or otherwise. Every year in Britain, 10,000 women attempt to have a test-tube baby but only 1,500 births result. It is believed that IVF pregnancies are perhaps more likely to end in a miscarriage than normal pregnancies because women undergoing IVF tend to be older or are more likely to have other fertility problems.

Free treatment is available on the National Health Service but, as ever, funding is limited. Joanne Glasbey has estimated that, of all IVF-assisted births in Britain, only 10 per cent have been achieved through the services of the NHS.

But nowadays test-tube babies are no longer supplied only by 'traditional' IVF methods. Even more advanced technical refinements are available:

Surrogacy

This is a further stage on from normal DI. It applies when a woman gives birth to a child through ordinary artificial insemination – but she is not intended to be the 'real' mother once the child is born. She is merely 'lending' her womb to another couple to help them bring into the world their child, even though genetically half the child may be 'hers' with her own egg fertilised by the would-be father's semen.

Kept within the family and with no money changing hands, surrogacy usually causes no major legal problems. It often takes place between sisters, one of whom may have had her womb removed by hysterectomy, or even, as happened recently in the United States, between a 53-year-old grandmother and her daughter-in-law when the grandmother gave birth to her own grandson.

But back in January 1985 the first known English case of *commercial* surrogacy occurred – and the courts at once became involved. Mrs Kim Cotton, a 28-year-old housewife from north London, with a husband and two other children of her own, gave birth to a baby girl after she had 'leased' her womb for £6,500 through a professional agency to another married couple to carry the husband's child. They had no form of sexual relations. She never even met him. As Mr Justice Latey later clinically explained in the High Court: 'He had come to England for the sole purpose of providing seminal fluid for insemination of the surrogate mother. The semen was introduced into the mother by a qualified nurse. The father and surrogate mother never met. Conception resulted from the insemination. It was agreed that at birth the baby would be handed to the father and his wife.'

Using the traditional legal yardstick in all cases dealing with children of what is best for the child, Mr Justice Latey ruled that the couple should bring up the baby and look after her – although Mrs Cotton was undoubtedly her genetic and legal mother.

Parliament has twice intervened since then. The 1985 Surrogacy Arrangements Act outlawed all commercial arrangements negotiated through an intermediary – but not many people realise that the Act still allows a married couple to negotiate direct with a surrogate mother *and* even to pay her, so long as no 'middle man' is involved.

And the 1990 Human Fertilisation and Embryology Act laid down that no surrogacy arrangement can be enforced in the courts. A mother cannot be made to hand over the child; nor can a commissioning couple be made to accept it. Even today the surrogate remains the child's lawful mother and a married couple can only become the child's legal parents by adopting it or (since November 1994) by obtaining a 'parental order' under the 1990 Act. But this latter course is only available if they are married and the child is genetically related to at least one of them. If unmarried, their best hope is to persuade a court to make a 'parental responsibility order' or a 'residence order' under the 1989 Children Act – which will give them somewhat lesser rights.

The girl who lost a child to her own mother

A teenager in Lancashire agreed to bear a baby for her own mother because the older woman was eager for a baby after remarrying but had suffered two miscarriages and been told another pregnancy was dangerous. The daughter handed over the child at birth but some six years later changed her mind after quarrels about how the little girl was being raised. She applied to Fleetwood magistrates' court for the child to be handed back to her. The result was a Solomon-like decision whereby she withdrew her application and the child's grandmother – for that was her legal status! – obtained a 'residence order' saying the child should live with her but the daughter won a 'contact order' giving her contact at certain weekends.

As Andrew Bainham says in his book *Children – The Modern Law*, 'English law is ambivalent about surrogacy. On the one hand it is seeking to discourage the making of agreements, whilst on the other it is providing mechanisms for giving effect to a proportion of them.'

Hormone treatment, egg donation and embryo transplants

Sometimes intensive hormone treatment can help a women who does not ovulate naturally to start ovulating and so release her eggs into her reproductive system with the result that a child may be conceived. Since this treatment is all internal and within the woman's own body, it does not have to be supplied in an establishment licensed under the 1990 Act and there are no national rules or guidelines.

It all depends on where you live. For instance, couples wanting treatment in south Cumbria must be in a stable relationship for two years, while in west Essex the period is four years. In May 1993, in Grimsby, sextuplets were born to a single woman to whom a local NHS hospital had chosen to give drug fertility treatment, although she already had one child and did not even live with the father who already had three children of his own by someone else.

But, if hormone treatment does not work, infertile women may be helped by egg donation, which is a later variant on 'normal' artificial insemination and is within the Human Fertility and Embryology Authority's remit. Eggs are taken from a fertile woman, fertilised in the laboratory with male sperm – usually but not always (as we shall see) from her husband – and the resulting entire embryo is implanted in her womb. One cycle of treatment costs between £2,000 and £2,500 and couples have been known to remortgage their homes and sell their cars just to try it.

But there is a limit to the lengths to which the Authority will permit a couple to go in their search for a child. There are no legal restrictions on the age of a woman who can be offered fertility treatment under the 1990 Act, but, in July 1993, when commenting on a case reported widely in the press where a 58-year-old Englishwoman had gone to Italy for fertility treatment denied to her in Britain, Professor Colin Campbell, the Authority's chairman, said it did not 'encourage' treatment of women over the age of menopause but did not actually forbid it. In December 1993 the Authority allowed a licensed clinic in Cambridge to make a black woman pregnant using eggs from a white donor but said the reason was that the black woman's husband was of mixed race – and so the child would have been born of mixed race anyway. Mrs Flora Goldhill, the Authority's chief executive, commented that they would not have followed a recent Italian example where a black woman was helped to have a white baby solely because she felt it would have a better life. 'That smacks of social engineering and the creation of a designer baby which would not be acceptable to the Authority,' she said. Within a fortnight it was announced that a licensed clinic in Nottingham, operating under the Authority's control, had refused an Indian couple's request for a donor egg implant from a white.

At much the same time the Authority published a detailed written questionnaire to which the general public was asked to send in its replies over the next six months on the subject of whether women should be allowed to become pregnant using eggs from aborted foetuses. That will sound appalling to many people but the Authority explained that the shortage of donor eggs was so great that clinics had waiting lists of three to four years for women whose only chance of becoming pregnant was to receive a viable donor egg – from some source or other.

'The use of donated adult, cadaveric or foetal ovarian tissue could provide many more eggs than are currently available,' said its somewhat chilling press release in January 1994. In July 1994, after having considered 10,000 responses from the public to its questionnaire, the Authority announced that it was banning the use of eggs from aborted foetuses to treat childless women but that they could be used for research purposes. In November 1994, the Criminal Justice and Public Order Act went further: it made it a criminal offence to use eggs from aborted foetuses for fertility treatment in Britain.

One final question: should fertility treatment be available to women who are not married to their sexual partner?

Section 13 (5) of the 1990 Act says not too helpfully:

A woman shall not be provided with treatment services unless account has been taken of the welfare of any child who may be born as a result of the treatment (including the need of that child for a father), and of any other child who may be affected by the birth.

What does that legal mumbo-jumbo, hurriedly cobbled together while the Act was going through Parliament (it was not in the original version of the Bill), actually mean? In practice, not very much: it was a sop to the traditionalist lobbies in Parliament. You do not have to be married to qualify for fertility treatment. It is available to both unmarried women in stable relationships and to single women living on their own. In 1991, there was even a much publicised 'virgin birth', in which a single women who said she had never had sex with anyone lawfully gave birth to a child assisted by DI.

Doctors in the Britain of the Nineties rarely make moral judgements about candidates for fertility treatment. And who is to say they are wrong? A quarter of the children born this year will see their parents separate before they are sixteen and, when families break up, almost half of all fathers lose contact with their children. So is lack of a father necessarily a good reason for denying a woman the right to have a child?

In reality, if the staff at a clinic or hospital licensed by the Authority believe that a single woman without a partner, let alone a stable one, has the right to a child and will probably do a good job of bringing it up, they will treat her. As Dr Jack Glatt, medical director of the Infertility Advisory Centre in London, told a *Daily Express* journalist in May 1993:

The Human Fertilisation and Embryology Act encourages clinics not to discriminate against single women. If you don't deal with single women, you have to justify yourself. We see single women in stable unions, single women who live with a man and single women without a partner. We treat each case individually. If we are satisfied by her special circumstances we go ahead.

The law doesn't say much. It's how you interpret it. It says you must not discriminate, and that includes against lesbians.

We don't treat lesbians because our staff object. Our Birmingham clinic doesn't treat single women because the staff object. But our London clinic does.

A baby has somehow managed to overcome the hurdles of birth control, sterilisation and abortion. Now one last question has to be asked:

What are the legal rights of the unborn child?

Lying in its mother's womb, it has no legal rights at all. In 1989, a young Liverpool woman had just nine days of her pregnancy to go when a drunken motorist drove into her on a pedestrian crossing. The impact threw her across his car bonnet and into the road. Her baby girl was stillborn after an emergency Caesarean section. Despite a string of previous motoring convictions, the driver was jailed for only three months for reckless and drink driving. He could not be charged with the more serious offence of causing death through reckless driving because, as defence counsel explained in words that he may afterwards have regretted, 'in law, of course, the unborn child does not count'.

Indeed, it has no separate legal existence – and therefore no legal rights until at least it is born. In January 1993, an eighteen-weeks-pregnant woman in Leeds lost her unborn baby when stabbed in the stomach while struggling with a street mugger and the police had to admit that the attacker, if caught, could be charged with attempted murder of the woman or grievous bodily harm upon her – but not with any offence concerning the 'death' of the unborn baby. Six months later, in June 1993, a woman driver three and a half times over the alcohol limit was jailed at Winchester Crown Court for three and a half years on charges of causing the deaths of a heavily pregnant mother *and* her child – but the baby, delivered by Caesarean section, had survived for thirty-six hours.

This governing principle that an unborn baby has no legal rights until actually born was first set out by Sir George Baker, then Family Division President, in the High Court in May 1978. A Merseyside steelworker, whose pregnant wife had just left him, had applied for an injunction stopping her from going ahead with an abortion without his consent. But he lost his case – on two grounds. Sir George ruled that he had no legal right, merely because he was the woman's husband, to prevent her from having an abortion *and* that he had no such right as a spokesman for the unborn child itself. Indeed, Sir George rejected the idea out of hand, saying somewhat tersely: 'The foetus cannot in English law, in my view, have any right of its own – at least until it is born and has a separate existence from the mother.'

This doctrine has been developed in subsequent decisions. In January 1988 the Appeal Court specifically ruled that a child, while still unborn, has no legal rights as against its own mother. There is a limit to legal intervention in the miracle of childbirth. No woman can be ordered to behave in such a way that no harm comes to the foetus within her. This was in the case of *Re F (in utero)*:

> London social workers had applied to the High Court for an unborn child to be made a ward of court (and therefore protected by the full authority of the Law) because its mother, a mentally disturbed 36-year-old drug addict, had gone missing, not for the first time, and they considered she was a danger to the foetus, now only a few weeks off its expected date of birth.
>
> Mr Justice Hollings refused the application and the Appeal Court ruled he was quite right.
>
> Said Lord Justice Staughton: 'This court is in no position to inquire into the problem of mothers who may neglect or harm their children before birth or to decide in what circumstances and with what safeguards there should be power to restrict the liberty of the mother in order to prevent that happening. The court cannot care for a child or order that others should do so until the child is born; only the mother can.'

But, once a child is born, the House of Lords has said that a court can rightly take into account events that happened while it was still in its mother's womb. This was in December 1986 when five law lords ruled that Berkshire County Council had been right to take into care a baby girl born prematurely to a heroin addict and suffering from heroin withdrawal symptoms caused by the mother's addiction – even though that inevitably meant taking into account what had occurred before the child had been born.

Similarly, once born, a child can sue for damage sustained through someone else's negligence while it was still in its mother's womb, as when a negligent driver smashes into a car in which the pregnant woman is a passenger, or when a doctor or nurse is negligent while the child is actually being born. In May 1992, a six-year-old boy made legal history by winning £700,000 damages against his own mother (but paid by her insurance company) after he had been born disabled because, while pregnant, she had negligently crashed the car she was driving.

This is a rapidly developing part of the law. In October 1992, a thirty-year-old 'born-again' Christian was in labour with her third child. The baby was lying transverse with its elbow through the cervix. There was a high risk of rupture of the uterus and, unless a Caesarean section was performed, it would be impossible for the baby to be born alive.

But the woman, supported by her husband, refused the operation.

After the woman had been three days in labour, her gynaecologist applied to the High Court for a declaration that the operation could be performed lawfully without the mother's consent. Within eighteen minutes – and with no one in court to argue the mother's case – Sir Stephen Brown, then Family Division President, granted the declaration. 'The surgeon's evidence is that we are concerned with minutes rather than hours and that it is a life-and-death situation,' he explained.

The operation was performed – but the baby still died. Two days later, Alexander McCall Smith, a Reader in Law at Edinburgh University, wrote forcefully in *The Times*:

> Pregnant women should be afforded the normal courtesies when they make decisions about their health. They must be entitled to refuse treatment, even if their refusal is dangerous to them and to the foetus they carry. If their conduct causes the death of the foetus, then that is a matter for their consciences, and it should weigh very heavily indeed.
>
> The consequences of allowing compulsory treatment, though, are just too unattractive to accept.

What will be a judge's ruling when the situation arises – which assuredly it will – that an operation is required which would certainly save the life of the unborn baby but might kill the pregnant mother? I would not wish to hazard a guess. It would all depend on the individual judge and how the law has developed by then.

But sometimes one can try and be too legally watertight, cross too many 't's and dot too many 'i's, lay down too many wide-embracing principles in advance.

There is often a simple way round most legal problems. When over thirty years ago my wife's gynaecologist, whom I knew to be Roman Catholic, arrived to deliver our first child, with my wife already in labour, I said to her: 'If there is any problem, any question of risk, you are to save my wife's life – even it it means the baby dies. I want you to agree that now, before you go into the delivery room' – and she did.

That vital exchange formed a legal contract between us. If she had then gone back on her word and saved the baby at the cost of my wife's life, I could have sued her. Whether I would have chosen to do so is a different matter.

TWO

Birth

Even being born can have legal complications nowadays. It was reported in *The Times* in May 1993 that the number of babies born by Caesarean section had more than doubled in the past fifteen years. And why? One reason advanced was that doctors and midwives were frightened of being sued if something went wrong during childbirth.

Such cases used to be extremely rare. Even so, lawsuits involving claims of medical negligence in childbirth trebled during the late Eighties to about two hundred in 1990. In that year the process was accelerated because legal aid was for the first time made available to young children and teenagers under eighteen irrespective of their parents' financial status. The result is that more young people can now sue if something goes wrong when they are being born. Ironically, today many middle-class children have better access to the courts than their allegedly too wealthy parents.

Caesareans are less risky than natural childbirth. Therefore there is less risk of being sued. So many doctors and midwives, forced to practise what they call in the United States 'defensive medicine', nowadays prefer, if at all possible and there is any likelihood of complications, to advise their patients to have a Caesarean. In the US, it is even worse: one in four babies are now born by Caesarean and exorbitant premiums for medical malpractice insurance have driven many doctors out of maternity care altogether. One can only hope that this is one instance where we do not too slavishly follow the American pattern.

Thankfully most parents do not have to think in these terms. Their child is born healthy and with no problems. Their only legal need is to choose a name and register the birth.

Naming and the birth certificate

Some young couples panic because they still have not agreed on a name even after the child has been born. They need not worry. The 1953 Births and Deaths Registration Act gives parents up to six weeks in which to supply all the details – including the name – and register the birth at the local Register Office. Only then is it crunch time and you actually have to commit yourself: when TV star Anne Diamond's latest baby son aged three days appeared on his mother's BBC *Good Morning* show in May 1993, his parents still had not agreed on a name. 'We haven't decided what to call him yet but for the TV show he will be introduced as Jake,' she explained.

You can call your child anything you like. There is no law about it. 'Coloured parents often call their babies "Prince" or "Princess",' a helpful official at a London Register Office has told me, 'and we raise no objections. Why should we? It would only become a problem if in later life they became con artists and tried to pass themselves off as royalty. In the same way, we would not object to registering "Lord" or "Lady" as a first name. But we do object to profanity. I would refuse to register a newborn babe as "Little Bleeder" or "Bloody Awful" – but I cannot actually point to any legislation which gives me the right to do so.'

She actually knew of a baby named Little Joy – but 'Little' was legally the first of the baby's two first names, as stated on the birth certificate. A Christian name is, of course, only a child's baptismal name. Only someone who has been christened bears a true Christian name.

In any event, whatever name you register, you can always afterwards change your mind and get the birth certificate altered. If you do so within a year, the Registrar cannot question your decision. After that he will need to be satisfied that you have in fact been calling the child by a different name from that stated on the certificate. In later life, the child, when grown to adulthood, can change his own name – but we will come to that later.

Who can register the child? Here immediately we run into one of the few remaining – but important – differences between children whose parents are married when they are born and those who are not. The 1987 Family Law Reform Act which came into effect on 4 April

1988 is supposed to have removed the unfair stigma associated with illegitimacy and to have put the two kinds of children on virtually the same legal basis.

But it has not fully happened.

'Illegitimate' is no longer a politically correct word and the fashionable term nowadays for children born to single mothers is 'non-marital'. Yet, as we shall soon see in the section on illegitimacy, this bland phraseology masks a still-imperfect reality.

It is popularly believed that having the short version of a birth certificate shows that a child is illegitimate. Unlike the full certificate, this does not give full details of the parents. But many people, both legitimate and illegitimate, only have a short certificate: it is provided free at the time of registration whereas the full one costs £2.50.

The truth is that, irrespective of short or full certificate and despite everyone's good intentions, an unmarried mother can all too soon discover that the law puts her and her child into a different category from others. This is how it works:

(1) If the couple are married, either she or the father can register the child and sign the birth certificate. In practice, the birth certificates of legitimate children usually have only one signature: that of the father or mother who happened to register the birth. It does not matter which.

And please note that a baby is born legitimate if his parents are married to each other *when the baby is born*. It does not matter that they were not married to each other when the baby was conceived – or even if at that time one or both were married to someone else. It is their marital state at birth which counts – except (and there is all too often in the law a sentence beginning with 'except') if a couple are married to each other when their child is conceived but, by the time the child is born, they are divorced or the father has died. Then the child is still born legitimate and can be registered as such. In that specific instance, the law takes account of the couple's marital state when the child is actually conceived.

(2) If the couple are not married to each other (and never have been) at the time of the birth, only the mother can register the birth by herself and her signature alone will appear on the birth certificate. The father cannot register the child by himself and the only way in which his signature can appear on the birth certificate is alongside the

31

mother's if they both go to the Register Office and register the child jointly.

It is unusual for both parents to register a child's birth, if they are married, so both parents' signature on the certificate is often a sign of illegitimacy: it tells the world even today what your child in later life may not wish everyone to know.

(3) Even without his signature, an unmarried father's name can still appear on a birth certificate – but only if both father and mother consent *or* the mother asks for it and produces a written statutory declaration signed by him (i.e. a statement sworn in front of a solicitor) declaring that he is the father *or* she produces a court order to that effect, which is rare.

Sometimes a problem arises when a pregnant woman lives with her boyfriend and has adopted his surname but, for some reason, he is still married to another woman when their child is born. Can the child be registered in his name, even though he is still married to someone else and the child is not his wife's? The answer is 'Yes'. The child is undoubtedly illegitimate but his mother has chosen to use her lover's surname, so there is no legal reason why she cannot register her child in that name. If the father thereafter becomes free to marry and marries the mother, that will automatically – ever since the 1926 Legitimation Act – legitimise the child with retrospective effect as from birth and either parent can then, as a married parent, go to the local Register Office, re-register the child and obtain a new birth certificate with that tell-tale solitary signature.

One last matter: a baby can legally be given *any* surname, not necessarily that of either parent. You could call your child John Windsor, if you liked, giving him a spurious air of bearing the royal family name and perhaps being a distant cousin of the Queen.

Illegitimacy

In October 1989, Marina Ogilvy, daughter of the Queen's cousin, Princess Alexandra, announced that she was expecting a baby. She was single and said she had no intention of marrying her boyfriend, Paul Mowatt. Overnight a bitter feud erupted between her and her parents, duly reported in loving detail in certain sections of the press. At first,

Marina claimed that her parents had tried to trick her into an abortion and that her father had cut off her trust fund allowance. Then, within a month, she and Paul changed their minds and announced they would marry after all.

'They said if I had the baby without getting married, it would change history and bring disgrace on the monarchy,' said Marina. She was exaggerating. In Britain at the turn of the century just one in twenty-three babies was born illegitimate. But by 1978 the proportion had increased to one in ten and in June 1994 the Office of Population Censuses and Surveys reported that almost one in three of all children was being born outside marriage. Furthermore, the number of illegitimate births registered by both parents, a sure sign of a stable non-marital relationship, has doubled since 1961.

Since World War Two there has been a constant process of legal change to keep pace with this sustained development in moral and ethical values. It culminated in the 1987 Family Law Reform Act, which is virtually the Bible of illegitimate children's rights. Before the Act there were still considerable, if somewhat bizarre, injustices. For example, if someone died without making a will their illegitimate child shared in the estate in exactly the same way as a legitimate child, but that did not apply if grandparents, brothers or sisters died: in that case, the illegitimate grandchild, brother or sister was ignored.

But the 1987 Act proclaimed roundly the general principle that in future all references in statutes or private legal documents to 'any relationship between two persons shall be construed without regard to whether or not the father and mother of either of them, or the father and mother of any person through whom the relationship is deduced, have or had been married to each other at any time'. What could be simpler? The Act means what it says: legitimate and illegitimate children are now, as a general rule, treated by the law in exactly the same way – except (and I warned you earlier of 'except'!) that an illegitimate child is not entitled as of right to British citizenship and still cannot succeed to a hereditary title.

But many people do not realise that it is possible to contract out of the Act: it only applies 'unless the contrary intention appears'. This means that if, for example, you want to ensure that only the legitimate children of your children living at your death benefit from your estate, you state in your will that the bequest is 'to my legitimate grandchildren living at my death' instead of simply 'to my grandchildren living at my death'. The result would be different if you did not make a will and your estate was shared out between your family on the basis of the 1952 Intestates' Estates Act. Then *all* your grandchildren living at your death, illegitimate as well as legitimate, would inherit.

So old-fashioned grandparents should take note: to ensure that your wishes prevail, you should seek expert advice in making a will – which, as we shall see later, is true of everyone anyway.

But the 1987 Act not only gave a new sense of legal equality to illegitimate children. It also bestowed new rights on their parents. For the first time, unmarried mothers were put in the same position as wives to make claims for the financial support of their children. Until then, unmarried mothers could claim only in their local magistrates' court, whose austere and often depressing atmosphere is generally more appropriate for minor criminals and shame-faced motorists on drink-driving charges than for women with an unpleasant problem in their personal life. Now such women have the option of also going to their local county court or High Court, which provide a far more agreeable atmosphere.

But it is not only the setting that has improved: under the old law, a mother claiming maintenance had to take the baby's father to court within three years of the child's birth. Now there is no time limit. Previously, mothers had still to be single to claim. Now they can already be married to someone else. In the old days, they could not obtain a lump sum order from the father of more than £1,000. Now there is no limit on the amounts that a man can be ordered to pay on top of his monthly or weekly payments.

This is all very well and fine. But not every father of an illegitimate child happily admits that he is the father. How does a mother prove it in court? Until recently blood tests were never conclusive: they were able to establish that a man could not be the father rather than prove positively that he was. But now the blood is submitted to modern DNA testing methods and the results are claimed to be virtually 100 per cent accurate.

The ex-policeman who was proved to be a liar

In the late-Eighties, a former policeman swore in court that he had
never had sexual intercourse with a baby girl's mother. The magistrates
believed him and she lost her case. But later DNA testing became
available – and proved he was the father. At Gloucester Crown Court
in May 1989, he was jailed for six months for perjury.

But the court always has a discretion to grant or refuse a test in what
it considers to be the child's best interests. What happens if a man
refuses to take a test ordered by a court? The worst is presumed against
him and he can be made to pay for the child as if he was, indeed, the
father. This course of action was approved by the Appeal Court in July
1993 when a wealthy Midlands businessman, who had always denied
that a young girl was his daughter but refused DNA testing, was ordered
to pay maintenance plus a £1,000 lump sum. The mother claimed that
she had given birth to the child after a brief office fling nine years
earlier.

Normally, of course, it is the woman who asks for the alleged father
to be tested but he has the right to ask to be tested to prove that he
is the father – when she is denying it! However, in such cases, the
court is generally wary.

The end of the affair

A woman had been having an affair with another man while still
sleeping with her husband. She became pregnant but insisted that it was
her husband's child. The affair ended and several months later a baby
girl was born. She and her husband (whom she had told about the affair)
believed it was their child and intended bringing her up as such, but
the ex-lover still insisted it was his and in July 1992 asked the High
Court to order DNA testing to prove he was right. The baby was then
eight months old. Judge Callman refused. He said that, in the
circumstances, it would disrupt the family unit and not be in the child's
best interests. In February 1993, the Appeal Court upheld his decision.

Formerly, only the unmarried mother had legal rights over her child.
She had sole legal control: she alone had the legal right to decide its
name, its school, its religion, where it lived – in fact, its whole general
upbringing. The father's only effective 'right' was to ask a court to be

allowed to see the child – at risk of being ordered to pay towards its maintenance.

Nowadays an unmarried mother still starts off with sole legal control – now called 'parental responsibility' – but a father who wants to act like a father (even though not marrying the mother) also has substantial rights. As Lord Justice Balcombe recognised in the Appeal Court in November 1990 in *Re H (No. 2)*: 'The position of the natural father can be infinitely variable. At one end of the spectrum his connection with the child may be only the single act of intercourse (possibly even rape) which led to conception. At the other end of the spectrum he may have played a full part in the child's life from birth onwards, only the formality of marriage to the mother being absent.'

Parliament has acknowledged that reality and the 1989 Children Act gives every unmarried father the right to acquire *joint* parental responsibility along with the mother. They can either agree this amicably between themselves or he can go to the High Court or nearest family hearing centre (via the local county court) and ask for it. A judge will order joint responsibility, if he considers it in the child's best interests – which will, of course, depend on all the circumstances. As Lord Justice Balcombe also said in *Re H*, 'The court will have to take into account a number of factors of which the following will undoubtedly be material, although there may well be others: (1) the degree of commitment which the father has shown towards the child, (2) the degree of attachment between them and (3) his reasons for applying for the order.' He does not have to be living with the mother: in *Re H*, for instance, the Appeal Court made the order although the parents were living apart.

In fact, the Children Act so encourages unmarried parents to function, at least in this respect, as if they were married that couples can easily give themselves joint parental responsibility without even going before a judge. All they need do is ask a clerk at their nearest county court office for a Parental Responsibility Agreement form. Its wording is extremely simple. They merely fill it in, sign it and post two copies to the Principal Registry of the Family Division, Somerset House, Strand, London WC2R 1LP. No fee is required.

My only word of warning is that they should do this only if they are sure – at least, as sure as anyone can be of anything in this world – that they will stay together during the child's early years. A parental responsibility agreement lasts until the child comes of age on his eighteenth birthday. It should not lightly be entered into.

But not everyone can have children or is prepared to undergo artificial methods of reproduction. Ever since the original 1926 Adoption Act, the law has provided a widely used alternative.

Adoption

Until they actually get involved in trying to adopt, most people do not realise that the factual basis of adoption has changed fundamentally in recent years. This is inadequately reflected in the current legislation, which is still based on the old 'total transplant' idea, as enshrined in the most recent Adoption Act dating from 1976: this assumes that adoption irrevocably transfers a child from one family to another. It does this by vesting joint parental responsibility in the adopters and by extinguishing the parental responsibility of the natural parents. In March 1993, Mr Justice Thorpe went so far as to rule that the natural mother of an adopted five-year-old boy was no longer legally his 'parent' and so required the leave of the court before applying to see him again after having handed him over for adoption four years earlier – which leave he refused.

An adopted child is treated in law in almost every way as the adopters' child with exactly the same rights of inheritance and nationality as their blood child. One so-called exception trotted out by most law books is that it does not apply to the 'prohibited degrees of relationship' within which two people cannot marry, so that, for instance, an adopted woman can marry her adoptive brother but not her genetic brother.

But this, of course, is hardly a practical problem, since most adopted people will not know who are their genetic brothers or sisters. In fact, a case in August 1993 highlighted a tragic loophole in the law:

The young mother killed by the pill

When a 22-year-old Birmingham divorcee, who already had one child, decided to go on the pill to help beat period pains, her doctor asked her the usual family medical history questions. But the doctor did not know that she had been adopted and she herself did not know that her natural mother had suffered from thrombosis. If the doctor had known about the thrombosis, she would never have prescribed the pill – which killed the young woman with a massive blood clot. 'Accidental death' was the jury's verdict and afterwards her adoptive mother told a reporter: 'There should be a way of checking if a patient is adopted and find out if the natural mother had suffered from thrombosis.'

But, as the law now stands, that is impossible. An adoption order virtually amounts to a legal rebirth. The Registrar General enters the adoption in the Adopted Children's Register. This is kept at the Office of Population Censuses and Surveys' headquarters at Titchfield, Hampshire, and certified copies may be obtained, for a small fee, either in person at the Office's London address at St Catherine's House, 10 Kingsway, WC2B 6JP, or by post from Smedley Hydro, Southport PR8 2HH. An entry states the child's sex, date of birth and new name and gives the adopters' names and occupations plus date and place of the adoption order. Although each entry has a number linked secretly to the original registration of birth, it does *not* give the natural mother's or father's name or address.

This is effectively the child's new birth certificate. The new parents can even request a short-form certificate which makes no mention of the adoption.

This legal framework seems very enlightened. The problem is, as shown by the sad story of the young divorcee who did not know of her natural mother's thrombosis, that it is largely out of date. It relates back to a time when, as Professor Stephen Cretney says in his book *Elements of Family Law*, 'Adoption was primarily seen as a method whereby a healthy, white (and usually illegitimate) baby would be placed with a childless couple who would bring him or her up as their own child with preferably no contact at all with the child's birth mother or natural family.' In practice, adoptions of this kind are no longer typical: in 1986 only 452 adoption orders were made in respect of illegitimate children aged under six months where one adopter was not the parent. Nowadays, candidates for adoption are much more likely to be older children who often already know at least one of their parents or family background (in 1989, 26 per cent of all adoption orders were in respect of children aged ten or over and more than half were aged five or over) or they are stepchildren or close relatives of at least one adoptive parent. Also many adopted children are now of mixed race, handicapped or with emotional or behavioural problems where it can sometimes be useful for some kind of monitored link to be maintained with their previous existence.

The result is that silence about antecedents is no longer the sacred cow it used to be. As far back as 1975 an earlier Children Act tried to remove some of the secrecy by providing that all adopted persons over eighteen who want to trace their natural parents can apply to the Registrar General for the information needed to find their original birth entry – which would, of course, give their mother's name and her then address and possibly also that of their father. If adopted before 12 November 1975, an applicant had first to see a counsellor because until that date parents were assured their offspring would never know their names. If adopted later, counselling was optional.

But, because the details given were only those on the original birth registration, in practice it proved difficult for people to trace their genetic parents. So the 1989 Children Act instituted an alternative streamlined process. It set up an Adoption Contact Register, also kept by the Registrar General, on which parents and other relatives (including anyone related by blood or marriage to the child) can inscribe their names and current addresses. These updated details can then be passed on to adopted children who apply to be registered; but, as the Registrar General emphasised in an official leaflet when the scheme began, this will happen only if both parties want it: 'Birth parents and other relatives who have decided that they would prefer not to have contact with an adopted person need have no fear that the introduction of the Register will put them at greater risk.'

We still are a long way off from a thoroughly thought-out modern law of adoption. As Andrew Bainham says in his *Children – The Modern Law*, 'There has been a growing realisation that the "exclusivity" of adoption, perhaps the cardinal feature of English adoption law, would have to give way to a more flexible concept which admitted greater "openness".'

So, after all this, what is the actual process of adoption? Only 7,000 children are adopted each year in Britain – with 100,000 couples wanting to adopt. They face a virtual obstacle course.

The first hurdle is to get accepted by one of the 200 authorised adoption agencies: all forbidden by law to exact a fee for their services. Most are run by social services departments of local authorities but some are independent voluntary agencies. Since the law was changed in 1982 (by an amendment to the 1976 Act), 'private' adoptions are no longer legally possible: even adoptions within a family must first be vetted by the local social services department and require, like all others, an adoption order by a court.

Adoption law is somewhat two-faced. The Act itself lays down only the most minimal qualifications for adopters: they must usually be at least twenty-one but there is no upper age limit. Most adoptions are joint, in which case the Act specifies that the couple must be married; but single people, whether unmarried, widowed, separated or divorced, may apply. Contrary to popular belief, there is no law that says the adoptive single parent and child cannot be of the same sex. Heterosexual unmarried couples and homosexual couples cannot jointly apply – but a sole application by one (with the other in a sort of legal limbo) is technically possible, although in practice unlikely to succeed. Lesbian couples (with one as the actual adopter) are sometimes successful but male gay couples almost never – whatever the sex of the child.

In fact, the law of supply and demand is more rigorous than the law of the land. Just because, in this age of extensive birth control and unmarried mothers, there are many more would-be adopters than children available for adoption, the agencies have wide scope within the law to pick and choose those they accept.

There are no hard-and-fast rules: acceptability, like beauty, is in the eye of the beholder. All agencies require would-be adopters to submit to medical examination and regular 'assessment' home visits by social workers. Most set an upper age limit of thirty-five for the wife and forty for the husband. Couples do not have to be particularly well off but they must all be able to show they can afford to take on a child.

Some agencies will not accept people who have been divorced and most insist that the marriage is at least three years old. All agencies accept people from all kinds of different ethnic origin or religious background but some only allow them to adopt children of similar origin or background. Believe it or not, smoking can be a reason for refusal: several social services refuse to accept couples one or both of whom smoke as candidates to adopt children under ten, while the coordinating body, British Agencies for Adoption and Fostering, has told all social services and voluntary agencies that children *under two* should not generally be adopted by people who smoke. When the British Agencies announced in March 1993 these new national guidelines, Tim Yeo, then Junior Health Minister, commented: 'It would be wrong for a child to be denied the chance of a loving home solely because there is a smoker in the household. There is no room for dogma or ideology in any aspect of adoption. Each case has to be judged on its merits, using common sense and compassion.'

Few people would argue with that but, in the same month, the British Agencies gave two reporters from the *Daily Telegraph* this revealing profile of ideal candidates:

> Non-smoking, heterosexual couples under the age of thirty-five, with a comfortable home, plenty of friends and no criminal convictions.
> There is only one factor which absolutely rules anyone out for adoption – a conviction for child abuse or molestation.

In July 1993, one particularly disturbing case was picked up by the media: a white Englishman and his Asian-born wife were told by Norfolk social services after three years of 'assessment' by social workers that, because they lived happily in the country far from any under-deprived inner city, they were 'too racially naïve' to be accepted as adoptive parents for a youngster of mixed race. The furore prompted Peter Thurnham, a backbench Tory MP, to tell the *Sunday Times* of his own experience of the adoption process:

The MP's story

In 1983, Mr Thurnham and his wife, who had four children of their own, wanted to adopt a child with special needs. 'The social workers thought our house was too neat and tidy. They didn't like the fact that we sent our children to boarding school and, because I am in a Tory marginal, they thought my job was insecure,' he said. But they persevered and six years later they succeeded in adopting a boy who was severely mentally handicapped.

The position will eventually change for the better. In November 1993 the Government published a White Paper, *Adoption – the Future,* which proposed several important reforms. Children aged twelve or more will have to agree to their own adoption. Couples over forty will no longer be barred as adopters and it will be made easier for step-parents. Above all, 'common sense' is promised as the watchword of the selection process.

Unfortunately, even if implemented, the proposals in the White Paper will not become law for quite some while.

Until then, under the present set-up, acceptance by an agency remains only the first stage in the long, drawn-out process towards adoption. After acceptance comes the agonising wait to be tried out for a specific, available child – and that too has its problems, as witness this letter published in the *Sunday Times* in July 1993:

The adoptive parent is the lowest of the low

We are a white, middle-class married couple. We have a large, tidy house in the country with a good-sized garden. I am a university lecturer, aged 49, and my wife (48) is a teacher. We have lived and worked in Africa; we have fostered a Mauritian boy for eight years and we have three children of our own (two grown up, and a 10-year-old son at home). We want to offer a home to a disadvantaged child or children.

We are approved as adoptive parents and have been receiving visits from various social workers over the past three years without success. Many reasons have been given as to why we were not suitable: we are too old; we live in the country, which is not suitable for town children; we will have too high an expectation of children academically; etc., etc.

Recently we were short-listed for a group of three children and then we were dropped because 'the other two couples dropped out and so it was not possible to offer the selection panel a choice'.

We fully appreciate the principle that the child's welfare is paramount and we have no argument with it. However, we feel that the system has gone overboard in its search for ideal parents. Time and money seem no object as social workers search for months for the end of their rainbow. In this regard the best is so often the enemy of the good. Prospective adopters are just a commodity to be used as and when convenient.

The position of the adoptive parent is the lowest of the low. Judgements are made about your suitability by social workers who visit you for two hours, and there is no right of reply. There is no way they will allow you to present your case at their panel discussions. Someone described to us the rejection you feel as having a psychological miscarriage. We can vouch for that feeling, as I am sure many others can.

So much for would-be adoptive parents. What about the rights of the adoptive child's natural parents?

The fear of many adopters is that at some time in the future the child may be taken away from them, reclaimed by its natural parents. They read cases in the newspapers such as that of two-year-old Jessica DeBoer in the United States and wonder: 'Can that happen to us?'

The adoption girl taken from the only parents she knew

Cara Clausen in Iowa was twenty-eight and single when she waived her parental rights on the birth of her unnamed daughter and put her up for adoption. She had broken up with her boyfriend Dan Schmidt, and felt unable to cope as an unmarried mother. Mrs Roberta DeBoer, who had a hysterectomy after a honeymoon illness, heard of Cara's plight through a friend, drove through a snowstorm to see the baby and a private adoption was agreed. Cara wrote to Roberta and Jan DeBoer: 'I know you will treasure her and surround her with love. God bless and keep you all.'

Then she had second thoughts and filed a court motion to reclaim her baby, exactly a month after the birth. The news devastated the DeBoers. They argued they should retain custody as they were the only parents Jessica (as they called her) had ever known. By the time the case eventually came to court, Cara had married Dan Schmidt and had another child. So the judge ordered their first baby must be returned to complete their family.

In August 1993, the Iowa Supreme Court upheld that ruling and Jessica, now two years old, was carried in tears from the only home she had known and handed over to the Schmidts. They at once said they would rename her Anna and refuse all visits to the DeBoers.

In fact, that could never happen here. It is a fundamental rule of our adoption law, enshrined in the 1976 Adoption Act, that natural parents must 'freely, and with full understanding of what is involved, agree unconditionally to the making of the order'. If the parents are

LAW WITHOUT A LAWYER

married, both must give their consent; if unmarried, only the mother must – unless a court has granted the father an order sharing parental responsibility or (most unlikely) a residence order saying the child must live with him. In all cases, the baby must be at least six weeks old for the mother's consent to have any legal validity and the actual adoption can only take place when the child is at least nineteen weeks old: two vital differences between the law in this country and that in the US.

Generally, the agreement takes the form of a properly executed and witnessed document but it can also be by word of mouth. But, whether written or oral, it can be withdrawn at any time before the adoption order is made. The only major exception is that, if consent is withdrawn too late in the process, a judge may rule the parent has unreasonably withheld consent to the adoption – and overrule it.

Unreasonable refusal of consent to adoption by a natural parent is one of the few instances envisaged by the 1976 Adoption Act when consent can be dispensed with. But the courts do not lightly come to that conclusion. In one case, a young mother changed her mind after she and the child's father decided to marry and bring up the child with the help of her family. A judge ruled this was reasonable – and the adoption did not go through.

As Judge Stephen Willis said in a 1991 case, 'Many adopted people start looking for their roots, particularly in adolescence ... adoption should only be the last resort where no one in the wider family is available and suitable to look after a child. Parentage is not always perfect but parentage in the family is preferable to the unknown risks of adoption.'

The 1976 Adoption Act says that a child must be placed with its prospective new parents for at least thirteen weeks – in practice, usually much longer – before they can apply (usually to a circuit judge at the nearest family hearing centre) for an adoption order. But even this formal 'placement' does not guarantee success: if the agency believes that things are not working out satisfactorily it can, on giving the would-be adopters fourteen days' notice, remove the child and 'place' it elsewhere.

The last stage in this long process is, of course, when the prospective parents ask a judge to make an adoption order in their favour. The 1976 Adoption Act states:

In reaching any decision relating to the adoption of a child a court or adoption agency shall have regard to all the circumstances, first consideration being given to the need to safeguard and promote the welfare of the child throughout his childhood; and shall so far as practicable ascertain the wishes and feelings of the child regarding the decision and give due consideration to them, having regard to his age and understanding.

In practice, the would-be new parents have been so thoroughly vetted and the child already have lived happily with them for so long that the decision is almost a formality. The adoption will nearly always be approved. A new life will begin for both child and parents.

THREE

Childhood and Growing Up

To many a parent you remain a child, however old you are: 'Small children small worries, big children big worries,' is an old Jewish saying. That is almost the view of the law, for the legal line between childhood and adulthood is extremely blurred. Indeed, the word 'adult' has no precise legal significance. When the law treats you as 'grown up', which again is a concept with no precise legal meaning, will depend on what aspect of life one is looking at.

If it is the criminal law and your responsibility to be held to account for your criminal acts, the 1933 Children & Young Persons Act says you are a 'child' until you are fourteen, when you become a 'young person', which you remain until you are eighteen. In divorce and family law, the 1989 Children Act keeps you a 'child' right up until you are eighteen. With contract and general business law, the 1969 Family Law Reform Act says you are not a 'child' but a 'minor' until eighteen, when you legally come of age: it used, of course, to be twenty-one.

But even these divisions are far from watertight. The age at which you can and cannot do things legally is a jigsaw with some very odd little pieces tucked away. Here is a guide to the puzzle:

As soon as you are born You can sue or be sued in the civil courts but, until you are eighteen, an adult will need to act as your 'next friend', if you are suing, and as your 'guardian *ad litem*', if you are being sued. A bank or building society account can be opened in your name and you can claim the single person's tax-free allowance so that, if the interest is less than £3,525 a year (as from April 1995), you will not have to pay income tax. You can also open a National Savings bank account but normally the money cannot be withdrawn until you are seven. You cannot hold shares or unit trusts in your own name but an adult, usually a parent or grandparent, can buy them and hold them as your trustee until you are eighteen, when they can be re-registered in your name and an income tax refund claim made to recover the tax credits.

When you are five   This is the first major legal stage in growing up. You are no longer entitled to travel free on buses, trains and the London Underground (although only two youngsters under five are allowed free per adult) and a reduced 'child fare' becomes payable until you are sixteen. You still cannot go into the bar of a public house except when *en route* to some part of the premises which is not a bar (garden, restaurant, etc.) and 'there is no other convenient means of access or egress'; but you can now drink alcohol in private, although up to this age any adult giving you an alcoholic drink, however small, could have been fined up to £200 except if doing so on doctor's orders, in sickness or 'for other urgent cause'. You can go to the cinema – but, if the film is PG rated, you must be accompanied by an adult. Most important of all, you must start going full-time to school.[1] No law says that you must first go to a nursery school, although they usually are available from about three; but the 1944 Education Act states that any parent not ensuring that his child of five years old or more receives 'efficient full-time education suitable to his age, ability and aptitude ... either by attendance at school *or otherwise*' can be fined up to £1,000.[2] By 'or otherwise' the Act means that a suitably qualified adult can teach you at home – but I warn you that it is not easy.

When you are ten   Until now you have enjoyed complete immunity from criminal prosecution: in *Walters v. Lunt*, in 1951, the parents of a seven-year-old boy were charged with receiving a stolen tricycle from their young son but, since he was legally incapable of theft, the tricycle

---

[1] The actual date of your compulsory first school day is the first day of the first term after your fifth birthday, although some schools may be prepared to take you before.
[2] This is more theory than reality. The law lacks rigorous enforcement. Department of Education figures in November 1993 showed that school truancy was a disgrace nationwide – and not only in socially deprived inner-city areas.

was not 'stolen' and they were acquitted. But at ten, although still legally a child, criminal responsibility starts: you can be convicted of any crime, even of a sexual nature, although until a recent landmark decision in the Divisional Court the prosecution had specifically to prove that you knew it was 'seriously wrong', as for instance, Mr Justice Morland told the jury in the tragic case of the two eleven-year olds convicted in November 1993 of Liverpool toddler James Bulger's murder;[3] but in C (a Minor) v. Director of Public Prosecutions in March 1994 Lord Justice Mann ruled that this ancient Common Law principle was totally out of date ('unreal', 'contrary to common sense', 'conceptually obscure', 'divisive' and 'perverse' were some of the adjectives he used) and 'was no longer part of the Law of England'. A similarly discarded Common Law principle was that a boy under fourteen could not be convicted of rape or any other sexual offence involving penetration because he was conclusively presumed to be physically incapable of sexual intercourse, although as far back as 1839 there is a case in the Law Reports where a twelve-year-old had shown that was nonsense: the 1993 Sexual Offences Act abolished that doctrine and there have since been several cases of under-fourteen-year-olds being charged with rape. I suppose that some people might call that progress. Except for murder or manslaughter, as in the case of James Bulger's two child murderers tried at Preston Crown Court, you will be tried in a youth court (the old-style juvenile court) and your parents must be present unless this is 'unreasonable'. It is a sad comment on today's world that, as from early 1995, the 1994 Criminal Justice and Public Order Act will allow ten-year-old children, convicted of serious non-homicidal crimes such as rape or indecent assault, to be locked up in young offender institutions.

When you are twelve You can buy a pet. This provision of the 1951 Pet Animals Act now has a charming old-fashioned ring to it. Sadly more typical of this modern age is the new tough regime of two-year secure

---

[3] The two young defendants were ordered to be detained at Her Majesty's pleasure, the only custodial sentence available for children between ten and fourteen convicted of murder or manslaughter. No other child criminal under fifteen can be 'locked up' but they *can* be placed under the supervision of the probation service or, as a last resort, put in secure accommodation for a limited period of time.

training orders for persistent offenders aged 12–14 introduced by the 1994 Act. The Government hopes to have it operating by the end of 1995.

When you are thirteen You can be employed and paid for your work but there are many restrictions, sometimes shamefully unobserved in practice. You can take on light work such as a paper round but not during school hours nor before 7.00 a.m. or after 7.00 p.m. and for not more than two hours on school days and Sundays and, in any event, for not more than a total of twenty hours a week. Many local authorities also have by-laws allowing those under thirteen to do limited work for their parents, on a farm, or at weekends or during the holidays – and modelling or professional acting, subject to special arrangements to avoid missing school.

When you are fourteen You are now a 'young person' and can be convicted of most crimes without restriction and without the prosecution needing to show that you knew it was wrong. If convicted, you can be fined up to £1,000 (between the ages of ten and fourteen, the limit is £250) but the youth court must order your parents to pay the fine unless 'it would be unreasonable, having regard to the circumstances of the case'. In practice, a court will try to avoid imposing a fine: a wide range of other sentences, all non-custodial, is available. You become responsible for fastening your own seat belt in a car but no longer have to wear a safety helmet when horse riding, although it remains advisable at whatever age. You can own an airgun. You can go into a bar with an adult but cannot buy or consume alcohol. You can be a spectator in a courtroom: until now you could only have been present in court if you were an 'infant in arms' or giving evidence as a witness, although all alleged victims under eighteen of sexual or violent crime now usually give evidence from outside the courtroom via closed-circuit television.

When you are fifteen If convicted of a crime, you are now termed a 'young offender' and can, if the youth court thinks there is no other appropriate way of dealing with you, be sent to a young-offender institution for not less than twenty-one days or, as from early 1995, more than twenty-four months. You can now work up to thirty hours a week.

When you are sixteen   This is another major step forward. You can leave school[4] and work full-time but not at night, except in certain industries such as iron and steelworks, glassworks and paperworks, and, if you work in a factory, you cannot be made to work more than forty-eight hours a week and not on Sundays. Unless you are continuing in full-time education, whether at school or college, child benefit will cease to be payable to your mother. You can drink beer or cider in a pub but only with a meal in a part of the pub that serves meals. You can buy fireworks. You can buy cigarettes and not be at risk of a policeman confiscating your pack if he finds you smoking in the street or other public place (you can smoke legally at any age provided you do not, if under sixteen, buy them yourself or smoke in public) and *thinks* you look under sixteen. You can be ordered to pay your own fine for a criminal offence without your parents necessarily being ordered to pay it for you. You can drive a moped or motorcycle of up to 50 cc. You can join the armed forces with parental consent. You can marry with parental consent but, if it is refused, you will have to get the consent of a magistrates' court (this holds true until you are eighteen). A girl must be sixteen or over to agree to sexual intercourse – unlike boys, who can do it at any age although they cannot consent to homosexual acts until they are eighteen.

When you are seventeen   You can drive a car or any motorcycle. You can go into a betting shop but cannot place a bet. You can have an airgun in a public place. You can be arrested and questioned at a police station, as if you were an adult: until this age the official Code of Practice under the 1984 Police and Criminal Evidence Act would have required the police to inform your parent or other 'appropriate adult' that you had been detained. If that person wanted to be present during the questioning, the police would have had to wait until he or she arrived, except in urgent

---

4   The actual date is not your sixteenth birthday. There are two school-leaving dates in the year: if your birthday falls on or between 1 September and 31 January, you can leave at the end of the spring term; and, if it falls on or between 1 February and 31 August, you can leave at the summer half-term.

cases involving immediate risk of personal harm or serious damage to property. (Police failure to obey the Code could lead to a court throwing out any confession as improperly obtained.)

When you are eighteen You can vote, sue or be sued in your name, marry without parental consent, change your name, apply for a passport in your own right, own land or other property, enter into binding contracts, obtain credit (including hire purchase) and have a cheque card or credit card, serve on a jury, buy drinks in a bar, off-licence or supermarket, donate your blood or any body organ, bet, make a will and join the armed forces without parental consent. If a witness or defendant in *any* court proceedings (many people wrongly think the embargo applies only to cases involving sex), your name and identity can now at last be disclosed in the media, the minimum age having been raised from seventeen by the 1991 Criminal Justice Act.[5]

But that is still not the end of all restrictions. You will have to wait until you are twenty-one to stand as a candidate in a parliamentary or local election, to apply for a liquor licence, to drive a lorry or bus – or to be sentenced to gaol (except that, for all first offenders of whatever age, the court must first rule that no other penalty would be appropriate).

When do you legally reach any particular age? At the first minute after midnight on the start of your birthday.

In later life, one's time is divided between work and non-work but, at this stage, the division is between school and non-school. Let us look at non-school first:

Baby-sitters, child-minders and au pairs

There is no such thing in English law as 'a right not to be left alone', at whatever age. Britain has a growing number of one-parent families

[5] The ban not only applies to the child's own name or identity – but to that of any adult from whom its name or identity could indirectly be revealed. On 31 December 1993, a High Court judge rejected a plea by three newspapers to lift a ban on identifying a 59-year-old woman who had given birth to twins on Christmas Day after being artificially inseminated at a Rome clinic. Mr Justice Ewbank said it was not an issue of public interest, merely curiosity.

and adults under pressure to work. That, coupled with a lowering of moral standards and an appalling lack of childcare facilities – Britain has fewer provisions than any other country in Western Europe – means, sadly, that thousands of children, even including babies, are left on their own. And at risk.

The law is totally inadequate to protect the young and vulnerable. There is no such crime as 'leaving a child on its own'. The 1933 Children and Young Persons Act makes it an offence for a parent – or anyone else over sixteen – who has responsibility for a child under sixteen 'wilfully to neglect, abandon or cause unnecessary suffering or injury' to that child. There is no specific reference to leaving a child on its own or unattended but such an event is undoubtedly covered by this wide wording.

Yet there are no time limits within which a child can be left – nor any specific age at which it can or cannot lawfully be done. In January 1994, *The Times* reported that nearly a million children under ten are regularly left at home alone after school or in the holidays; but prosecutions remain rare. The National Society for the Prevention of Cruelty to Children says that social services are reluctant to prosecute because of the difficulties of proof and because it can cause further distress to the child.

There is not even a legal minimum age for **baby-sitters**. Many decent, concerned parents believe they cannot legally ask anyone under sixteen to baby-sit. That is not so. It all depends on the intelligence and maturity of the particular child. In Scotland, all baby-sitters, without exception, legally have to be at least fourteen; but not South of the Border.

Some parents believe fourteen *is* old enough or, at least, give themselves the benefit of the doubt. But Thomas MacKean, the Southampton Coroner, disagrees. In March 1993 he was presiding over an inquest on a 23-month-old baby boy who, when left alone, had accidentally strangled himself when trying to climb out of his cot. His unmarried mother had gone out 'for a few drinks' on a Friday night leaving him with a fourteen-year-old schoolgirl who had then pocketed her £5 baby-sitting money and gone to a disco, leaving the baby asleep in an empty flat. Said Mr MacKean: 'It is not my function to blame people but the public must feel that mothers who leave their children at night have a duty to ensure the baby-sitter is a responsible person. There is nothing in law which specifies a minimum and maximum age of carers, but clearly a fourteen-year-old girl may not be thought responsible enough . . . it really was unacceptable to have left this baby alone.'

But no law was broken.

Child-minders are in a different legal category.[6] They must be approved by the local Council, who have to maintain a register on which parents can safely rely. The 1989 Children Act says this applies to anyone who is not a parent or foster-parent who looks after a child *under eight* for payment for more than two hours a day. 'Nannies' are not child-minders unless they work for more than two employers. But, if either a child-minder or Council is negligent, the parent can sue for damages: this was laid down in the High Court in January 1994 by Mr Justice Scott Baker.

The child-minder who damaged a baby's brain

When 33-year-old single parent Cora Dowling phoned the Surrey County Council child-minding officer to inquire about placing her six-month-old son Thomas with a local registered child-minder, so that she could go out to work, he did not tell her that three months earlier that same child-minder had been under investigation when a small baby in her care had suffered severe brain injury. But, as Mr Justice Scott Baker laid down: 'He should have told her whatever he knew that a prudent parent would wish to know before placing a tiny baby with a minder.'

As it was, the newly engaged child-minder shook little Thomas so hard that he ended up partly blind and brain damaged. His injuries were so horrific that a priest had to give the last rites.

After a four-year-long legal battle, Mr Justice Scott Baker awarded Ms Dowling damages (the actual amount to be assessed later when Thomas's medical prospects were clearer) against both Surrey County Council and the child-minder who had by then been de-registered.

Most responsible parents – and, indeed, child-minders – would think it wrong to 'shake' a small baby but what about the larger issue of a child-minder's legal right to smack a child?

In December 1994, Virginia Bottomley, as Health Secretary,

---

[6] Technically child-minders, who look after children on domestic premises, are different from day-carers, who do so on non-domestic premises; but the Children Act applies equally to both.

announced new Government guidelines allowing child-minders to smack children in their care – but only rarely and always with parental consent. This replaced earlier guidelines that banned all form of corporal punishment for children and had themselves been brought into question by a High Court ruling by Mr Justice Wilson in March 1994. The judge had ruled in favour of a woman whom Sutton Borough Council refused to register as a child-minder because she would not sign an undertaking not to use corporal punishment. He said that the Council was wrong to adopt a blanket policy of refusing to register child-minders who smacked children and nine months later, despite much criticism from childcare organisations, his view was vindicated by the new official guidelines.

'We've got political correctness on the run,' said Mrs Bottomley. 'The guidelines are a victory for responsible parents who know that children need control as well as care.' But John Bowis, the junior Health Minister, emphasised that child-minders should smack only as a last resort and then only if they had secured the parents' consent. That is the current legal position.

For decades many a middle-class household, with young children, would not have known how to survive without an **au pair girl**. But the rules have recently changed and become more flexible: on 1 January 1994, new Home Office guidance on enforcing the entry and work provisions of the 1971 Immigration Act came into effect. Young men[7] as well as young women can now be au pairs and a clearer distinction is drawn between au pairs from inside and outside the European Community.

All EC nationals have the untrammelled right to live and work in all the member countries, so EC au pairs do not need a work permit. And they can legally take on other domestic jobs besides pure au pair work. They can be a nanny, a mother's help, an au pair plus, a demi pair plus or a demi pair, earning more – or less – than a pure au pair. The specialist licensed employment agencies that have traditionally supplied the domestic market with au pairs from Europe nowadays do as much, if not more, business with these other categories.

[7] At the end of 1992 a young Swede named Johan Engelstedt tried to come into the country as a male au pair and, when he was turned back, there was such amusement in the press that the then Home Secretary, Kenneth Clarke, decided the rules must be revised.

Yet the term 'au pair' still has a precise legal meaning, whether for EC nationals or anyone else. Home Office guidance specifies that they cannot be asked to work for more than five hours a day in return for board and lodging, £35 a week pocket money and the chance to learn English. They are not to be treated as servants or underpaid domestic labour and they cannot be expected to do more than 'light housework and taking care of children'.

Furthermore, they must have one day each week completely free and must be allowed to attend language classes and religious services if they wish. They should have their own room and may be expected to baby-sit for up to two nights a week. They are entitled to at least one week's notice.

Non-EC nationals cannot legally do any of the other domestic jobs without a work permit, which is not easily obtained. But they can legally work as au pairs without one. To qualify for this privileged status they must be unmarried young men and women aged seventeen to twenty-seven inclusive without dependants who are nationals of Andorra, Bosnia-Herzegovina, Croatia, Cyprus, Czech Republic, The Faeroes, Greenland, Hungary, Liechtenstein, Macedonia, Malta, Monaco, San Marino, Slovak Republic, Slovenia, Switzerland or Turkey. They can be here for a maximum of two years and can change host families within that time: they are not tied to their first employer.

But they must have come into the country as an au pair. They cannot try to switch once they first come in as a visitor.

Discipline

It was back in the seventeenth century that the satirist Samuel Butler first coined the phrase 'Spare the rod and spoil the child' and until very recently that was the robust view of Her Majesty's Judges. But no longer. Technically parents still enjoy the right of 'moderate and reasonable chastisement', as laid down in several Victorian judgments, but today's judges are likely to interpret those words in a modern and non-authoritarian sense.

Stern, even though loving, parents seem to be going out of fashion. In June 1990 Princess Diana made front-page headlines, complete with photographs, when she gave the wilful Prince William, then seven years old, a public smacking at his school sports day. She called him to go home at the end of the events but he ignored her and ran off to play with his friends. Clearly angry, she dashed after him, caught him by the arm and gave him a firm smack on the bottom. The future King of England burst into tears but he was pushed into the back of the royal car, given a good telling-off and driven back to Kensington Palace.

But, unless you relish battling with over-zealous officialdom, do not be too quick to follow the royal example. Princess Diana was lucky that no bystander reported her to the local Council's social services department. If so, she might have found her young son put on their children's 'at risk' register. Do not laugh. If a non-royal mother had been seen to act in that way, it might have happened – and the decision could have been upheld in the High Court. I refer you to the 1991 case of *R. v. East Sussex County Council*:

> A young mother in East Sussex smacked her six-year-old son with a wooden spoon because he spat in her face. His teachers noticed bruises and called in local social workers. When questioned, the boy said his mother had hit him for being 'too lippy' and she claimed: 'Every mother corrects her child.' Her son – *and his untouched five-year-old sister* – were put on the 'at risk' register.
>
> She appealed to the High Court to delete her children's names from the register. But Sir Stephen Brown, President of the High Court's Family Division, ruled that the social workers had not acted unreasonably.
>
> 'It may seem to some that this was simply an exasperated parent spanking a child,' he said. 'However, what came to the attention of the authority were the marks of injury. Fortunately they were not very serious but what they did suggest was that there was a basis for concern as to the treatment this boy might receive in the future.' So this cheeky little boy was protected *in advance* from any stern future disciplinary action – which many people might think was one thing he needed.

In the words of the latest (1993) edition of *Street on Torts*, a leading legal textbook: 'Changes in social *mores* and in the status of children have diminished parental rights of discipline. A growing body of opinion supports outlawing any right of physical punishment.' Except, as we have just seen on page 53, in the isolated case of child-minders.

Accidents and Children

These are of two kinds: (a) Those that children cause and (b) those that happen to them.

(a) *Accidents caused by children* The law does not expect a parent to keep their child under lock and key all day. But if you do not properly control your child, you can be held liable to compensate anyone who has been injured or whose property has been damaged by him. This is not so much because the child has misbehaved but because you have been negligent in preventing him from doing so.

Not every risk of injury or damage can be avoided, even by the most careful parent. Their only legal duty therefore is to take 'reasonable care' in all the circumstances, which will include the child's age, his intelligence and his past behaviour.

So if, for example, a ten-year-old boy is playing football in a quiet residential street and accidentally kicks the ball into a nearby window, his parents would probably not be liable. But if they were to allow that same ten-year-old boy access to a sharp kitchen knife and he accidentally stabbed a young friend while playing Cowboys and Indians, they probably would be liable.

The question always is, as Lord Goddard, the late Lord Chief Justice, once said: 'Is it the child's negligence alone or that of his parents?'

(b) *Accidents that happen to children* We will come to accidents at school in a moment but, even out of school, children present a particular problem to the law. They are, after all, particularly vulnerable.

Even giving your small child a birthday party can cause legal problems. In the High Court in May 1989 a north London mother, who had given a toddlers' birthday party for her young child, was ordered to pay £20,000 agreed damages to a girl who, as a one-year-old baby, had been a guest at the party. She had been badly scalded when a pot of hot tea fell from a table while the children were playing.

How did the pot of tea fall? The mother denied that she had been negligent. She said that she had done her best when coping as a harassed hostess with a clutch of small children in party mood and denied that she had left the pot too near the edge of the table. But she still had to go along with the agreed settlement, albeit without any formal admission of liability. She was covered by her household insurance and the company paid out. As an insurance specialist commented afterwards, 'It appears likely that, if she had not got cover, she would have had to pay out of her own pocket.'

The moral is clear: 'Accidents will occur in the best-regulated families,' as Mr Micawber said, and a prudent householder will make sure that his household contents policy contains a personal liability section (at very little extra cost) for injury to visitors. And especially for child visitors.

In more general terms, the 1957 Occupiers' Liability Act says that occupiers of all types of premises, from private houses to cinemas and from schools to supermarkets, owe their visitors a duty to take reasonable care 'to see that the visitor will be reasonably safe in using the premises for the purpose for which he is invited or permitted by the occupier to be there.'

But children are allowed to have less sense than adults. The Act expressly says: 'An occupier must be prepared for children to be less careful than adults.' While adults should take care to avoid obvious dangers (and have any damages reduced because of their own 'contributory negligence' in not taking proper care for their own safety), children are not expected to have the same degree of reasonable caution.

So, when a four-year-old child fell through a gap in railings adjoining a public staircase on a south London council estate and the gap was not wide enough for an adult to fall through but was wide enough for this child, the Council was held liable. They should have realised that unaccompanied children were likely to use that staircase running between two floors of flats.

That case was decided in the mid-1960s; but the principle is of general application and dates back to long before the 1957 Act. On this point, Scottish law is the same as English law and as far back as 1921 Glasgow Corporation was held liable to the father of a seven-year-old child who had died from eating poisonous 'deadly nightshade' berries from a shrub in a public park controlled by the Corporation. The berries were attractive and accessible to children and, although the Corporation knew that children were frequent visitors, they still had done nothing to fence off the shrub or provide some other effective protection.

But what about parents' own responsibility? Should householders or other occupiers of land foot the bill for an accident if the true culprits were the child's own parents in allowing him to be out on his own?

The late Lord Devlin gave the authoritative answer in December 1954 when he was a High Court judge. A five-year-old boy, out picking blackberries with his seven-year-old sister on a piece of open land soon to become part of a Kent council estate where he lived, broke his leg when he fell into an open sewer trench which his sister had safely negotiated. In clearing the Council of blame, Mr Justice Devlin laid down that landowners and others are entitled to expect that 'prudent parents' would not allow their small children to go out unaccompanied in areas where there was likely to be 'an obvious danger', such as an open trench. 'The responsibility for the safety of little children must rest primarily on the parents,' he said.

That remains the law. In 1983, for instance, the Appeal Court had to consider a case where a seven-year-old girl slid down a Welsh mountainside on a picnic blanket. The mountain had a steep slope which became very steep at the bottom – from which she fell thirty to forty feet on to the road below and fractured her skull. Was the Rhondda Borough Council legally responsible? The answer was no. The appeal judges ruled that the Council neither had to fence off the slope nor to warn of the sharp drop – even though they knew unaccompanied children were prone to play in the area. A 'prudent parent' would have warned his children of such an obvious danger. As Lord Justice Dunn remarked, an occupier is not bound to fence every tree simply because a child might climb it and fall out of it.

But children have not changed over the years. As Lord Justice Hamilton said back in 1913, 'In the case of an infant, there are moral as well as physical traps. There may accordingly be a duty towards infants not merely not to dig pitfalls for them, but not to lead them into temptation.'

So where the danger is not obvious but latent or concealed, like broken glass at the bottom of a childrens' paddling pool, or is made particularly tempting for a child by what the law calls an 'allurement', like a defective escalator in a department store, the occupier will be liable – despite the fact that it is irresponsible of parents in the area to allow small children to wander around unaccompanied.

What if the children are trespassers? There can nowadays be liability, although the law is still unclear as to the actual extent. Trespassers used to trespass at their own risk: except when malicious or deliberate injury was involved, they could not complain if they were hurt. But in 1972, in a case where a six-year-old boy got on to an electrified railway track through an unrepaired gap in a fence, senior appeal judges in the House of Lords literally invented what they called 'a common duty of humanity', which remained remarkably vague in its application.

Then, in 1984, a new Occupiers' Liability Act tried to improve on this situation, with not all that much success. For it says that, if an occupier has reasonable grounds to believe that a danger exists on his premises, and the consequent risk is one against which he may reasonably be expected to offer 'some protection', then he will owe a duty to trespassers and other uninvited entrants, of whatever age, who he might reasonably believe would try to enter.

Please do not ask me precisely what is the meaning of this turgid double-talk (which, believe it or not, I have tried to simplify). The only reliable word to latch on to in all this verbiage is 'reasonable'. So, for instance, burglars can expect little or no protection. But, if children are known to be likely to trespass, occupiers must give them some protection – however mischievous the children may be.

What is that protection? The Act is not specific but does say that occupiers can escape liability by putting up warning notices. However, the test of reasonableness still applies. 'DANGER. KEEP OUT. CONCEALED TRENCHES' would probably be a defence to a claim by an injured eleven-year-old, who can reasonably be expected to read and write – but to a claim by a six-year-old? I simply do not know. The answer will partly depend on the intelligence of that particular six-year-old. He may be so bright that he loses his case!

FOUR

The Happiest Days of Your Life

The world is divided into those who say this about their schooldays and those who do not. For some, as they look back, school is a delight to be recalled misty-eyed and with a smile. For others, it is one long nightmare. Personally I think that something must be wrong with your life if you can only pinpoint as the happiest part of it the period you spent before you fully began to live.

But the law does not concern itself with such philosophical niceties. It answers practical questions. So let us examine those aspects of our schooldays where the law has most impact, and we will start at the beginning:

Choosing the school

There is an obvious difference between fee-paying independent schools – which I shall call by their old-fashioned, and still generally known, name, 'public schools' – and state schools.

The restriction on parents' choice of a public school is primarily a financial one: what can they afford? As a rough guide, one should expect to pay £4,000 a year for day schools and at least twice as much for boarding. There are over 2,200 public schools in Britain, educating about 550,000 children or 7 per cent of the school population. The Independent Schools Information Service (ISIS), with its national headquarters in London, keeps a list of most of these schools but, unlike those in the state system, public schools do not by law have to provide information about themselves.

Education at a public school entails a legal contract between school and parent. And, to make sure your choice is properly exercised and that you are assured of your legal rights (and those of your child), you should examine the prospectus carefully, just as you would the basis of any other written contract, and satisfy yourself that you know exactly what you are letting yourself – and your child – in for.

You should check particularly whether important information has been omitted or updated, such as what happened to last year's school leavers; and watch out for euphemisms: 'catering for all abilities' may, in truth, mean 'desperate to recruit'. One should also read carefully what is written about extras: before setting the seal on your choice you should check whether fees include such items as lunches, instrumental tuition, elocution lessons, specialist sports coaching or even books and stationery.

With state schools, education is of course free (a specific legal requirement laid down by Section 61 of the 1944 Education Act) but parents' choice of any particular school is very much restricted by other provisions of the 1944 Act and by the many later Education Acts (there are more recent Acts of Parliament dealing with education than with any other single subject, so great has been official twisting-and-turning on policy).

The Government's 'Parents' Charter' contains a section boldly headed 'The Right to Choose' and states that parents can choose the school they would like their child to attend. This is misleading and, indeed, the Charter goes on to make clear that parents have merely the right to express a preference for a particular school – which is not at all the same thing.

Admittedly the 1944 Education Act requires local education authorities (LEAs), which control and organise all state schools, to 'have regard to the general principle that, so far as is compatible with the provision of efficient instruction and training and the avoidance of unreasonable public expenditure, pupils are to be educated in accordance with the wishes of their parents'. But this has always been more a pious expression of hope than a legal guarantee.

Nowadays the 1980 Education Act spells out categorically that a LEA need not accept any parents' stated preference. Section 6 says it can be ignored if it would 'prejudice the provision of efficient education or the efficient use of resources' (e.g. no spaces are available or children who live nearer to the school are preferred); or if it would be incompatible with the school's normal admission policy (e.g. a church school that only takes children from a particular parish) or if the child has been refused because of 'ability or aptitude' (e.g. he has failed an 11-plus exam, if there is one).

There is a right of appeal against refusal, usually within fourteen days, to an LEA appeals committee. A simple letter will usually be enough to start off the process but you should always state your reasons; for example, that your child lives in the school's catchment area or that his brothers or sisters go to the same school. You will be able to amplify those reasons in person at a private hearing and, if that fails, you can appeal direct to the Secretary of State for Education that the decision was 'unreasonable' – but few, if any, of these further appeals ever succeed.

School transport

With public schools, this is solely parents' responsibility. It is entirely up to you how you get your children to and from school in time. With day schools, the 'mothers' rota' is an accepted part of urban life, although traffic wardens sometimes harass women who get to school too early in the afternoon and sit in their cars causing a minor traffic jam while they wait patiently to collect their charges. An obstruction is an obstruction, even in a worthy cause, and wardens are technically within their rights in asking you to move on.

With state schools, local education authorities are under a statutory obligation to provide free transport for children to and from school, if they live more than 'walking distance' away. This is defined by Section 39 of the 1944 Act as two miles for a child under eight and three miles for a child over that age 'measured by the nearest available route'.

What does that mean? How available is 'available'? The courts have restricted the duty to supply free transport by ruling that a route is 'the nearest available' if it is 'the nearest along which a child can walk to school with reasonable safety when accompanied by an adult'. Such a route does not fail to qualify as the 'nearest available' because of dangers which may arise if the child is unaccompanied.

So, when the shortest public route between a twelve-year-old Essex girl's home and her school was 2.94 miles but it lay partly along an isolated, unmade and unlit track which, particularly in winter, would be both difficult and dangerous for a young girl to walk on her own, the House of Lords ruled in October 1986 that Essex County Council was *not* in breach of its statutory duty in failing to supply free transport. The route would have been perfectly safe if she had been accompanied by an adult and it was up to a responsible parent to see that she was accompanied rather than expect her bus fare to be paid out of public funds.

A local education authority may provide free transport in such cases, but it is a matter for its own discretion. It is under no legal compulsion to do so. Except with children who live more than 'walking distance' away, parents have the ultimate responsibility for ensuring that their children attend school – not the school authorities.

School holidays

Schools, both public and state, are perfectly at liberty to fix their own holiday dates – but have parents the right to take their child away on a family holiday during term time? This often causes problems, especially when one or other parent is constrained through work or some such pressing reason to take the children away on holiday at some time other than late July, August or early September, the traditional holiday season.

Schools can sometimes be 'difficult' about this, and the law is firmly on their side. Section 39 of the 1944 Education Act says that schools, whether private or state, only have to give leave of absence by reason of the child's sickness, his religion (e.g. the Day of Atonement for a Jewish child or Ramadan for a Moslem), absence of free transport when the local education authority is under a legal duty to supply it – and 'unavoidable cause'. This last category is the heading under which you should try to persuade the head teacher to let your child miss school for a family holiday: 'We are really sorry about this but my husband has just been promoted at work and this is the only possible time he can take us all away with him.'

Technically, this should not suffice because Lord Goddard ruled in the High Court back in 1949 in *Jenkins* v. *Howells* that 'unavoidable cause' must mean 'unavoidable' for the child, and not the parent. But most head teachers are unlikely to know of this case and anyway, except in a senior exam term, properly approached, they will usually do their best to be helpful.

Size of classes

There is no legal guarantee, with either a public school or state school, as to how many other pupils will be in your child's class. The only exception is where a public school gives a specific assurance in its prospectus, or otherwise, as to the size of its classes.

Sex education

Public schools can provide this, as they please, and normally the prospectus will say whether or not this is the case.

The 1993 Education Act has made sex education, conducted 'in such manner as to encourage pupils to have due regard to moral considerations and the value of family life', compulsory in state schools. Previously the 1986 Education (No. 2) Act merely required the schools to take 'reasonably practicable steps to secure it was given', and in practice most did. Now *all* state schools have to supply it.

But can you legally refuse to allow your child to take the classes? The 1986 Act said 'No'. But this offended many parents and the 1993 Education Act now gives all parents a statutory right to require their child to be excused from sex education 'insofar as it is comprised in the National Curriculum'. Since there is precious little sex involved in the National Curriculum's ten 'foundation subjects' of English, maths, science, technology (and design), history, geography, a modern foreign language, music, art and physical education, this gives parents plenty of scope to exercise their right of refusal.

Religious education and collective worship

Although most public schools provide both RE and a daily act of collective worship, they are under no legal obligation to do so. And whether you wish to exclude your child from both or either is a matter for you to sort out with the head teacher.

With state schools, it is different. The 1988 Education Reform Act says they must provide both and must 'reflect the fact that religious traditions in Britain are in the main Christian whilst taking account of the other principal religions'. There is still no unanimity among school authorities over what exactly this means or what is the correct balance to be adopted between Christianity and the other main British religions: Judaism, Buddhism, Hinduism, Islam and Sikhism. Official guidelines published in January 1994 suggested that pupils should study three major non-Christian religions by the age of eleven and all five by sixteen. Many parents will probably agree with the *Daily Telegraph*'s comment at the time: 'A grotesque formula for religious indigestion'.

When in February 1993 two Christian mothers complained to the High Court that 'multi-faith' morning assemblies at a primary school in Manchester did not comply with the 1988 Act's requirements, Mr Justice McCullough ruled against them. But one thing is clear: the Act says parents of all religious beliefs, and those of none, can withdraw their child from either RE or daily worship or both. This is about the only untrammelled legal right that parents enjoy in modern state education law.

School uniforms

Who should decide whether children have to wear a school uniform or not – the child, the parents or the school? Although some parents may feel the decision should lie with them, it is, for both public and state schools, the head teacher who the law says has the final word.

As long ago as 1954, Lord Goddard laid down the law in these uncompromising terms:

> A headmistress has the right and power to prescribe the discipline for the school and in saying that a girl must come to school wearing a particular costume, she is only acting in a matter which must be within the competence of the headmistress of any school, whether it is one of the great public schools or a modern state school.

This ruling that the head teacher's views must prevail applies to boys as well as girls, and there are only two exceptions. The first is medical: if, for example, a child is allergic to one of the fabrics used in a school uniform, he can get a doctor's certificate exempting him from wearing it. And the second is non-discriminational: as in the case some years ago of two Moslem sisters in Altrincham, Lancashire, who, after a somewhat acrimonious dispute, were eventually permitted to wear to school the headscarves dictated by their religion.

In the 1954 case a west Derbyshire mother claimed that she was 'the best judge of what her daughter should wear' and insisted on sending her to school in long trousers, although she knew the headmistress would send her back home. The head-on conflict ended with the mother being fined in the local magistrates' court for failing to send her daughter to school, although every morning she had diligently sent her on her way – wearing the forbidden trousers. The mother appealed to the High Court only for Lord Goddard to uphold the fine and make his historic decision.

Since then, the ruling has been extended to other breaches of school rules. So, in the eyes of the law, when parents have sent boys to school with long hair or girls with hair streaked with bright colours, knowing that they would be sent home, this has amounted to failing to send the child to school and the parents have been fined.

For what is a clear breach of Section 39 of the 1944 Education Act, the current maximum fine is £1,000.

Discipline

We have already seen that this is an area where Lord Goddard has ruled that the law concedes to head teachers an undoubted 'right and power' in both public and state schools.

This takes a number of forms. First, **corporal punishment**. The 1986 Education (No. 2) Act outlawed this completely in all state schools and subsequent regulations have also banned it for the 27,000 academically bright children from low-income families who attend some 295 public schools under the Assisted Places Scheme with their boarding fees paid out of public funds. Pupils in those same schools whose fees are paid for privately can still technically be caned; but no school will operate one disciplinary code for children whose fees are paid privately and another code for those whose fees are paid by the State, so in practice no one in these schools is caned. With this exception, all pupils in public schools whose fees are paid privately can still as a matter of law be caned or otherwise physically chastised in accordance with long-standing judge-made law that, for instance, once said a blow which broke a boy's jaw in two places was 'reasonable' because of the need to protect society from 'an excess of sentimentality or sloppy thinking'.

The 1993 Education Act preserved public schools' rights to impose corporal punishment but, taking the wording from the European Convention on Human Rights, said, for the first time, that it must not be 'inhuman or degrading'. What does that mean? I am not at all sure. The Act specifies: 'Regard shall be had to all the circumstances of the case, including the reason for giving it, how soon after the event it is given, its nature, the manner and circumstances in which it is given, the persons involved and its mental and physical effects.'

In a circular to public schools at the time of the 1993 Act, the Department for Education did not give any further explanation but merely commented: 'Schools should bear these considerations in mind.' Not overwhelmingly helpful, one might have thought.

But very few public schools now permit corporal punishment anyway, whether by staff or senior prefects. If a parent does not want his child to be beaten or caned at a public school, he should specifically ask whether they allow it before agreeing to send his child there. If he is given an untruthful answer, and the child is in fact beaten, he would nowadays almost certainly be within his rights in withdrawing the child forthwith, although I can point to no decided case positively affirming this.

I know of no girls' public school which still permits corporal punishment.

Detention A grey area in modern law. The teacher of an individual pupil who has been naughty or guilty of a breach of school rules can still probably 'keep him in after school' for a reasonable period of time, whether in the independent or State sector. But detaining a whole class for the alleged misdemeanour of one or more pupils who will not own up is probably now of dubious legality. This stems by analogy from a High Court decision by Lord Lane, then Lord Chief Justice, in *R. v. Rahman* in 1985 when he ruled that detention by a parent of his own fourteen-year-old child could be unlawful when 'for such a period or in such circumstances as to take it out of the realms of reasonable parental discipline'.

As Lord Mackay, the Lord Chancellor, has said, 'A major philosophical change in recent years has been the way in which both society and the law have looked at the child. The child is now seen more as a person and less as an object of concern. The more a child is seen as a person, the more it makes sense to talk of rights.'

This thinking permeates the interpretation of the whole of modern law dealing with children and young people.

Expulsion

This is the ultimate sanction against serious or persistent offenders. Public schools are traditionally loath to expel, not only for economic reasons but because it is regarded as so draconian a measure as to be employed in only the clearest cases. But the schoolchildren of today are different from those of yesterday.

Many, but not all, public schools are increasingly vigilant about drugs, and possession, at least of hard drugs, almost always leads to expulsion. But, like many parents, schools are more liberal nowadays towards modest drinking and some boarding schools even have their own sixth-form bars. Bullying (if sufficiently serious and capable of being proved) is, however, now increasingly an expellable offence in many public schools.

But the law makes a fundamental difference between expulsion from a public school and a state school. With a public school, neither the parents nor the child has any form of legal redress. There is no appeal procedure and no recourse can be made to the courts.

The alleged bully who could not clear her name

A sixteen-year-old girl and her parents appealed to the High Court after she had been expelled from school for allegedly being a bully and the ringleader of a gang which terrorised other girls. The headmaster admitted they had not been told of the allegations until after she was expelled but explained that he feared the pupils she was said to have bullied might have suffered reprisals.

Mr Justice Brooke appealed for private school heads and governors to ensure pupils received 'fair play' when accused of offences which could lead to expulsion but ruled that he had no jurisdiction. The only legal option open to aggrieved parents was to sue the school for breach of contract. Only state-school pupils could seek judicial review in the High Court to protect their rights to natural justice. He expressed concern at this 'anomaly'.

Expelled state-school pupils are in a much more favourable legal position. They enjoy a statutory right of appeal within the State education system which, according to at least one teachers' leader, Mr David Hart of the National Association of Head Teachers, is so prejudiced in pupils' favour that classroom discipline has become eroded as schools have been forced to readmit an increasing number of pupils expelled for serious offences.

Recent examples of schools ordered to take back seemingly undesirable pupils include four fifteen-year-old boys excluded for pushing drugs on the premises, a teenager who had assaulted a teacher, two fourteen-year-old boys who had sexually assaulted a girl pupil, and two fifteen-year-old boys allegedly caught smoking marijuana.

The moral is that, if your child is expelled from a state school, you stand a pretty good chance of getting him readmitted. The 1986 Education (No. 2) Act says that a headteacher must tell you and your child of your right of appeal to the governors and/or the LEA. If the LEA upholds the expulsion, it will have to find your child an alternative place within the embattled state system so there is considerable pressure to order his reinstatement in the same school hoping that he has learned his lesson. But if you are still not satisfied, you have a final right of appeal to a local appeal committee staffed by the local worthies who will have nothing to do with the school and – allegedly – little sympathy for, or understanding of, its problems.

Accidents at school

The occasional grazed knee, scraped elbow and bruises are all part of growing up; but a school cannot use youthful high spirits as an excuse to avoid its legal responsibilities. As long ago as 1893 Lord Esher, a distinguished Victorian judge, laid down a school's duty: 'A schoolmaster is bound to take such care of his boys as a careful father would take of his own son.'

But the world has moved on since then. Lord Esher was talking of a small private school where a young boy won damages after his chemistry master had left a bottle of phosphorus lying about.

Today, even public schools have larger classes than they used to, while state schools struggle against budget restraints and are often chronically overclassed or understaffed.

Yet, the law, in theory, remains the same for both. As Lord Justice O'Connor said in the Appeal Court in June 1989, 'The law imposes duties on all schools simply because they are schools. These duties are of general application whether the school be provided by the State or privately, and regardless of whether it be fee-paying or free.'

With a public school, the pupil sues the proprietor or governing body; with a state school, he sues the local education authority. That is supposed to be the only difference. In practice, it does not work out quite like that. In all cases of alleged negligence, whether in relation to children or adults, the judges must look at all the facts. They must, therefore, always have regard to reality. A teacher looking after, say, only eighteen pupils in a class will be expected to supervise them more effectively than someone with double that number to cope with.

In fact, nowadays when judges apply the 'careful parent test', as it is called, to an accident in a state school, they usually add the qualifying words 'parent *of a large family*'. This term was first coined by Mr Justice Hinchcliffe in March 1969. He was giving judgment against the Hertfordshire County Council regarding an eight-year-old boy who hurt himself badly when crashing into the sharp-flinted wall of a crowded playground while running a race with other young children. They were all habitually left to their own devices, without any supervision, for ten minutes on arriving at their primary school in the morning.

Ruled the judge, a robust Yorkshireman: 'If one lets loose young

71

children in a playground of this sort with inherently dangerous walls around it, one is simply asking for trouble.'

In all types of school, the judges try to impose a reasonably high standard of teachers' care. Cases have been won by a fourteen-year-old west London schoolboy blinded in one eye when a classroom prank misfired during a chemistry lesson and by a seven-year-old primary-school pupil injured when his teacher gave him sharp scissors to work with instead of the blunt-edged variety; but lost by a twelve-year-old boy whose leg was broken in a playground accident when the only teacher on duty had been called away to deal with another incident.

The judges try to draw the line between what Lord Goddard once said, 'If every master is to take precautions to see that there is never ragging or horseplay among his pupils, his school would be too awful a place to contemplate,' and the view expressed by Mr Justice Veale in a case when a state school tried to argue that a twelve-year-old girl's damages should be cut because of her own 'contributory negligence' in putting her hand out to stop a door with too thin glass swinging back on her instead of trying to catch the handle: 'If the defendants allege this as negligence on the part of a child of twelve,' he said, 'how very much more negligent it was on their part!'

Of course, accidents are particularly prone to happen on a school sports field and here the judges, perhaps with memories of their own schooldays, have tended to be reluctant to find liability proved against a school. But recently a new element has crept into their judgments: the possibility of insurance. In the 1989 Appeal Court case of *Van Oppen* v. *Clerk to the Bedford Charity Trustees*, a sixteen-year-old boy had been seriously injured playing an inter-house rugby match at Bedford School nine years earlier. He made a flying tackle to try to bring down an opponent but ended up crashing into him. His spine was fractured and he had to spend six months in hospital, paralysed in all four limbs. The school, which at that time (back in 1980) considered it had no legal responsiblity to insure their pupils against sporting accidents, denied liability.

But the boy, supported by his parents, took the school governors to court claiming they were to blame for failing to coach him properly – and for not insuring him against sporting injury. The Appeal Court supported the trial judge's rejection of his claim on both counts: the coaching had been impeccable and, as these matters were understood in 1980, the school could not be faulted for failing to insure him.

But all three appeal judges made clear that opinions had changed within the teaching profession since 1980, at least in the private sector, and it had become good practice for a public school to take out personal accident insurance so that its pupils were covered for accidental injury sustained in *any* properly authorised school activity, including outings, adventure camps and organised foreign trips, not only sporting events or authorised games.

If a similar accident were to happen now to a public-school boy on the rugby field or while playing any other authorised game, and the school had not taken out personal accident insurance to protect him, the school would be liable.

But remember that this decision does not apply to state schools, where pupils are still usually only insured against injury at sports meetings, school outings and expeditions – not while playing normal games, however dangerous.

FIVE

Marriage

For many people contemplating marriage in modern Britain today, one of the first questions must be: why bother? Long since gone are the days when marriage was nearly always the consequence for any heterosexual couple in love and wanting to live together and have children.

As the late Sir George Baker once said, when he was England's senior divorce judge, 'There is an increasing tendency, I have found in cases in Chambers, to regard, and indeed to speak of, the celebration of marriage as "the paperwork". The phrase used is, "We were living together but we never got round to the paperwork".'

But that was in the mid-Seventies. Nowadays, marriage is even more an institution under attack. The official General Household Survey, released in January 1994, showed that the number of couples cohabiting had doubled within the past eleven years and that more than a quarter of all homes are now one-person households. Even Buckingham Palace, with three broken marriages among the Queen's four children, has bowed to the pressure: for the first time in history, those invited to the Summer Garden Party in July 1993 were allowed to bring 'companions' instead of the traditional husband or wife, and so established a bastion of the legal profession as the South Eastern Circuit Bar Mess said in its programme for social trips abroad in 1994 that the jamborees were for barrister members of the Circuit 'and their partners'.

As part of this (largely piecemeal and unplanned) development, the legal differences between being married and living together have shrunk considerably. The fundamental difference remains that a husband and wife are under a legal duty to maintain each other during and sometimes even after the marriage but that is never true of cohabitees (the ugly

74

word increasingly being used for those who live together without being married).

But otherwise a wedding ring now brings few extra legal benefits – except with property rights, which we shall look at in a minute. Both a married and unmarried mother can go to the Child Support Agency for help in making the father of her child pay maintenance for the child. Both husband and wife automatically have an equal say in their child's upbringing but an unmarried father will only get it if the mother agrees or a court grants him shared parental responsibility under the 1989 Children Act. A married woman can obtain a state pension in her own right or, in certain circumstances, on the strength of her husband's contributions, whereas a cohabitee can only rely on her own contributions. If either a husband or a male cohabitee uses domestic violence towards his partner, she can go to court and get an order banning him from his own home – except that a wife has the full range of High Court, county court or magistrates' court whereas a cohabitee can only go to a county court (the law may change on this during 1995).

If a man makes inadequate provision for his wife or unmarried partner in his will or he makes no will at all, either can go to court for 'reasonable provision' out of his estate, but a cohabitee only has this right if 'wholly or partially maintained' by her lover at the time of his death. In practice, this qualification, first introduced in 1975, makes very little difference today as both wives and cohabitees tend to be at least 'partially maintained' by the man in their life, and vice versa. That is what sharing is all about.

But an ex-wife, who has not remarried, can ask for 'reasonable provision' from the estate, which an ex-cohabitee, with no new live-in relationship, can never do.

If a husband or wife is killed through someone else's negligence – for example, in a road accident – the widowed spouse can claim damages for his/her own and their children's financial loss plus £7,500 'bereavement damages' for his/her own emotional loss. In 1976, the Fatal Accidents Act extended the definition of 'husband' or 'wife' to include 'any person living with the deceased as husband or wife for at least the past two years'. But only a husband or wife can claim 'bereavement damages'. However long or loving the relationship, a live-in partner of either sex does not qualify.

Yet the acid test for the legal difference between marriage and cohabi-

75

tation comes with the division of property rights when the marriage or relationship ends, and particularly for the woman. Even today a wife is in a stronger position than a female cohabitee – but, with good legal advice, the latter can safeguard herself.

We start with the basic proposition that, when a marriage breaks up, a wife can claim *up to a half* of all the family assets, including the house, even if they are in the husband's sole name, and irrespective of who caused the break-up. But, when a relationship of unmarried partners breaks up, the woman (or man, but it is nearly always the woman who finds herself in this position) can only claim what is legally hers: she has no automatic right to any share of her ex-lover's assets. If she has been so foolish as to allow the house to remain in his sole name, and it is surprising how many women still do, she can usually claim only something less than a full half share in the legal ownership, and then only if she helped pay for the property in the first place (e.g. by contributing to the original down-payment or sharing in the mortgage repayments) or if she has since increased its value (e.g. by physically helping to modernise it, as one cement-mixing Amazon did in a classic case in 1972) or if she has contributed 'in kind' to the family well-being (i.e. by being an old-fashioned housewife and seeing her role as staying at home and looking after her husband and children).

But, in this last instance, a wedding ring is all-important. Her non-financial or non-physical contribution does not count otherwise:

The case of the unmarried housewife

A woman kept home for her businessman lover in Southgate, north London, for twenty years and bore him two sons. He would not marry her because he was married to a Roman Catholic who would not divorce him; but she had changed her name by deed poll and they openly lived together as a married couple. She was an old-fashioned housewife in everything but name, looking after the house, cooking and bringing up the family.

Sadly, the relationship deteriorated and eventually she left, but, when she claimed a share in the house (which was in his sole name), the Appeal Court ruled she was entitled to nothing. Said Lord Justice May: 'When one compares this result with what it would have been if she had been married to the defendant, I think that she can justifiably say that fate has not been kind to her. In my opinion, however, the remedy for any iniquity she may have sustained is a matter for Parliament and not for this court.'

That was back in July 1983 but Parliament still has not taken up the invitation to intervene, although the position has slightly improved by virtue of later cases that have made some minor improvements to the law.

The fact remains that, in these days of ever-increasing economic parity between the sexes, whether you are a man or a woman you should seek skilled legal advice before going to live in your lover's home on any long-term basis. Indeed, this is even more advisable if you decide to buy a place together: whether in both names or only one. This does not mean going to the first high-street solicitor you can find but asking around friends or relations until you find a solicitor with particular experience in this field. If not, I suggest you send a stamped addressed envelope asking for a list of local members to the Solicitors Family Law Association (SFLA) at PO Box 302, Keston, Kent BR2 6EZ (Tel: 01689–850227).

In the meantime, I can give these pointers:

(1) If you reach the stage when you and your lover really think your relationship is going to last, that is wonderful but, in sheer prudence, you should not allow your home to remain indefinitely in your lover's sole name. It is just too dangerous legally. You are a hostage to fortune in your lover's house and he or she can, after giving you reasonable notice, have you evicted as a trespasser – which is what you will have become.

(2) If you are buying a new place jointly or, subject to financial adjustment between the two of you, transferring your lover's home from sole ownership into joint ownership, you should consider very carefully which form of joint ownership you want. There are two kinds. **Joint tenancy** is where both of you own the whole property and do not merely own a share. This is usually to be preferred for married couples and for those contemplating a permanent unmarried relationship: the advantage is that, when one dies, the other automatically becomes the sole owner of the property without need of a will. The disadvantage is that, in their joint lifetime, both parties have to agree on a sale and, if they have not sorted out in advance what is going to happen (e.g. that the person remaining in the property shall have a reasonable time,

say six months, to raise the money to buy out the other before selling to an outsider), one will have to take the other to court and ask a judge to order what he thinks is fair in all the circumstances – which causes delay and expense.

Tenancy in common is where you each own a separate share in the property, although not necessarily equally. This is preferred when two people share ownership on what is probably going to be a temporary basis, as when two working girls club together to buy a flat. If one were tragically to die early, the other does not automatically become sole owner and the dead person's share forms part of his/her estate to be disposed of according to the terms of his/her will or, if there is none, it will go to the next-of-kin.

(3) There is a way round these difficulties. It may not be very romantic but, as the law now stands, a couple contemplating a long-term relationship should, at a very early stage, discuss between themselves and agree on what is going to happen if they eventually break up and part.

The case of the couple who said nothing

A woman went to live with her lover in his rented council flat. After a while they jointly bought his flat from the Council as tenants in common, although, in their happy state, nothing was said as to the shares in which they owned the place. Did they own it fifty-fifty or what? The subject was ignored. In fact, the man provided 75 per cent of the down payment and the woman 25 per cent and they agreed to pay off the mortgage equally.

After some years the relationship broke down and the woman left. The flat was to be sold but they could not agree on how to share the net proceeds of sale, after deduction of mortgage.

The man went to court for a decision. The judge ruled it should be fifty-fifty on the basis that, although neither had said anything about it to the other, each had in their own mind an 'uncommunicated belief or intention' that they were to share ownership equally.

The man appealed and, in March 1992, the Appeal Court said the division should be seventy-five and twenty-five, as with their original down payments. Lord Justice Dillon said that, when a couple buy jointly, they hold the property, in the absence of evidence of 'a common intention' to the contrary, in the same proportion as they made the original down payment. He ruled – perhaps surprisingly – that agreeing to pay the mortgage equally was *not* evidence of 'a common intention' to own the property equally; and he poured scorn on the idea that there might be 'a common intention' to share equally that neither had communicated to the other.

He said the court would refuse to 'do palm-tree justice' to try and provide a fair decision, and gave a swingeing rebuke to solicitors for not thinking about the future when unmarried cohabitees buy property and, in particular, for not advising couples about the need to make provision for what should happen if the relationship broke down and they separated.

(4) So, in plain self-interest, two lovers starting to live together on a long-term basis should nowadays enter into a formal signed **cohabitation contract** with each other. The words 'contract' and 'lover' may not seem to have much in common; but that is the cynical reality of life today.

I would be doing more harm than good by providing specimen cohabitation contracts (or 'living-together agreements' or 'declarations of trust', as they are also called) in this book. Each such document should be tailor-made to the requirements of each couple who have to think through every single one of its detailed terms.

This really is one instance where you need a skilled lawyer's individual help. But it should not cost a fortune. In the last five years or so, such contracts have become much more common. If you are buying a home together you almost certainly will be using a solicitor anyway, so why not ask him to draft this extra document at the same time? *If you write out for him beforehand a rough plan of what you both want*, even if he then spends time asking you to consider certain eventualities you might not yourselves have contemplated, it should not cost much more than about £100 plus VAT for him to put your draft into legal language. And it will be money well spent.

Common-law marriage

How does this concept fit into the scheme of things, and what exactly does it mean anyway?

Very little. It is a myth based on a total misconception of the true significance of this ancient legal term. Sir Robert Megarry, when Vice-

Chancellor of the High Court's Chancery Division, described the phrase as 'a polite cloak for fornication or adultery of the less ephemeral type', and Judge Michael Corley once described its use in a case at Southend County Court as 'slovenly, silly and suitable only for Americans and criminals'.

For most couples who live together in what they call a common-law marriage do so because they have decided not to get married or at least not for the time being. But the whole essence of a real common-law marriage is that the couple are free to marry each other and would dearly love to do so – but cannot!

The concept dates from centuries past when, under the old Common Law of England, a couple became legally married merely by saying to each other in front of witnesses: 'I take you as my husband' and 'I take you as my wife'. They were then married in the eyes of the law.

But the 1753 Marriage Act ended all that when it introduced the calling of banns and the modern church wedding. Since then common-law marriages have had no legal validity whatsoever *except when a couple wish to marry but cannot because of prevailing local or temporary conditions.*

Examples have been cases in the early British colonies where no law had yet been established or in prisoner-of-war camps and foreign internment camps in World War Two. Couples declared they were married in front of witnesses, and so they were. Only divorce can end such a marriage, as actually happened to some real common-law marriages that took place in World War Two internment camps.

If a woman lives with a man these days and shares his life on a permanent or semi-permanent basis, the law, as we have seen, gives her rights that are in many ways not much less than those enjoyed by a full wife. Nigel Dempster, the *Daily Mail* gossip columnist, has coined the more honest phrase 'live-in girlfriend' or 'live-in boyfriend'. But, whichever label is used, the one thing that such a person is not is a common-law wife or husband.

'Real' marriage

All right, let's assume you are one of the couples who still form the majority and want to get married. What does that entail?

For a start, there is no legal obligation to get engaged, although many people still do. Yet it no longer creates a binding contract to get married, which it used to do. Until 1970 a girl could sue for breach of promise of marriage if her fiancé jilted her – although it never worked the other way round.

But engagement ring and engagement presents still remain in a special legal category. If either party breaks off the engagement (it does not matter which one), the girl is entitled to keep the engagement ring – except when the boy specified when he handed it over that he would want it back if things did not work out. This seldom happens, one would have thought.

It is different with engagement presents. In law, they are not outright but only conditional gifts. They are given on condition that the marriage will take place and, if it does not, they should be returned whence they came – if their donors want them back. They should, at least, be given the option of refusing.

Thomas Hardy, the Victorian novelist, cynically defined marriage as 'a licence to be loved on the premises' but the classic legal definition was coined by Lord Penzance in *Hyde* v. *Hyde* in 1861: 'the voluntary union for life of one man and one woman to the exclusion of all others'. That still remains true but nowadays the essence of a valid marriage has to be looked at more closely. It must be voluntary, between two single people who are both over sixteen, of the opposite sex and not too closely related, and the wedding ceremony must take place with due legal formality.

If any one of these essential elements is lacking, there is no true marriage. The courts will not grant a decree of divorce, which presupposes that there *was* a marriage until the court's judgment ended it. Instead there will be a decree of nullity, which, in effect, declares that there never was a valid marriage anyway.

Let us examine each of these requirements in turn:

1. *Voluntary*

All is fair in love and war. There is a limit as to how far the courts will examine just how 'voluntary' the parties were. I know of no case where a marriage has been annulled because a man told a woman that he was much richer than he really was or a woman tricked a man into marrying her by deliberately making herself pregnant through not taking the pill. 'Shotgun weddings', with the couple getting married because the girl is pregnant and her father is metaphorically holding a shotgun to the boy's head, have always been fully binding in law, although it would be different if the father was *literally* holding a shotgun to the young man's head, as actually happened in an American case back in 1928 when a judge later annulled the marriage because, as he said, 'If there had not been a wedding, there would have been a funeral.'[1]

Technically, duress is a factor that *can* invalidate a marriage but the only cases I know of, in recent years, concern arranged marriages within the Asian community. But even so the judges draw a fine line. As shown by these two contrasting cases:

The Sikh marriage that was legal

A young Sikh girl had never seen her husband before the marriage, and only went through the ceremony out of 'proper respect' for her parents and Sikh traditions. But she was bitterly unhappy and asked for her marriage to be annulled on the grounds of duress. In 1971, the High Court refused her petition because there was no evidence of fear. 'Respect' for her cultural and ethnic background was not enough.

The Hindu marriage that was void

A nineteen-year-old Hindu girl was forced into an arranged marriage because her parents said that otherwise they would throw her out of the house, leaving her homeless and destitute. In 1982, the Appeal Court annulled the marriage on the basis that 'the crucial question in these cases . . . is whether the threats, pressure, or whatever it is, is such as to destroy the reality of the consent and overbear the will of the individual'.

It is still uncertain to what extent the bride or groom must actually be put into a state of fear. In an Irish case in 1989 (which is not binding in Britain but merely of 'persuasive authority'), a pregnant woman was pressurised by her parents into getting married, and her

---

[1] A more tolerant attitude prevails today. In June 1993, the *Daily Telegraph* reprinted this item for sale in a local newspaper: 'Wedding dress. Ivory in colour. Designed to hide pregnancy at approximately seven and a half months.'

employer told her she would lose her job if she did not. There was no question of her being put in fear but the marriage was still annulled: there had been no true consent.

2. Between two single people

Fairly obviously, neither party can be already married[2] and, if divorced, the former marriage must have been fully ended by what is called a decree absolute. The 'decree nisi', which is pronounced at the actual divorce hearing, does not end the marriage. It merely entitles the person obtaining the divorce (the 'petitioner') to apply to the court office for the decree to be made absolute after six weeks and one day. This is only a paper formality that does not involve the judge; but until it takes place neither husband nor wife is free to remarry.

Sometimes problems arise because the 'respondent' (i.e. the other spouse) has already met someone else and wants to remarry as soon as possible and the petitioner is vicious or embittered and is in no hurry to facilitate their plans. So what happens if the petitioner does not obligingly ask for the decree to be made absolute after six weeks and one day?

In dire emergency, where for example a speedy remarriage is necessary for a child to be born legitimate, the respondent can apply – personally or through a lawyer – to the judge at the actual divorce hearing to cut the normal six-week period. Otherwise a respondent can make a paper application to the court office but only after a further three calendar months have elapsed: in those circumstances, the total time between decree nisi and absolute can be as long as six weeks and one day *plus* three further months.

It is generally believed that bigamy, where someone goes through a ceremony of marriage while still married to someone else, does not happen nowadays. That is simply not true. Bigamy cases still occur but the Crown Prosecution Service tends to prosecute only where the bigamous person has acted maliciously or fraudulently:

---

[2] A polygamous marriage, where a man is allowed more than one wife at the same time, cannot take place legally in Britain but a polygamous marriage validly entered into abroad can be recognised in this country.

The bigamous oil rigger

A 29-year-old Newcastle oil rigger was jailed for four months in February 1993 at Durham Crown Court after pleading guilty to leading a double life for almost a year, dividing his time between his legal wife and a young office clerk whom he had married illegally. Each woman was in complete ignorance of the other, although they lived just fifteen miles apart in houses shared with the same man. They believed his regular absences were due to his working abroad.

The truth only came out when the bigamous marriage soured after the office clerk became pregnant. He told her to get rid of the child – and he soon stopped coming 'home'. Desperate to trace him, she drove to Wallsend, where she had last dropped him off. A car pulled up – containing her 'husband' and his real wife.

Sometimes genuine misunderstandings can occur when a married couple have been separated for many years and have lost all contact with each other. You do not even know whether your partner is alive or dead. What then? After seven years you can go to court and obtain a declaration of presumption of death and, after only five years, you can obtain a divorce on the grounds of at least five years' separation. But not everyone leads such a tidy life. The 1861 Offences Against the Person Act (and that date is not a misprint) says that it is a defence to a charge of bigamy if the missing spouse 'shall have been continually absent for the space of seven years and shall not have been known to be living within that time'.

There has been no modern interpretation of this mid-Victorian wording but it *could* mean that you do not actually have to take positive steps to trace your missing partner during those crucial seven years. It might suffice if you merely did not know he/she was alive, although you could have done more to try to find out.

3. *Over sixteen*

It may surprise some people to know that before the law was changed in 1929 the minimum age for marriage for boys was fourteen and for girls a staggeringly low twelve.

But, although children of sixteen can now get married legally, until they both are eighteen years of age they will need their parents' consent and, whether the parents are still married to each other or divorced, *both* parents must give their consent. If the parents are not married to each other and never have been, only the mother need consent – except where the father has 'parental responsibility' under the 1989 Children Act, when again they must both give consent.

And if they refuse? The sixteen- or seventeen-year-old denied consent can go along to the local magistrates' court and ask the Bench to allow the wedding to take place without it. There will be a private hearing in front of all the parties and, especially where one set of parents are supportive or (more problematically) the girl is pregnant, the odds are that the Bench will agree.

Incidentally, there is no legal upper age limit for marriage as long as the officiating priest or registrar is satisfied that both parties are still *compos mentis*, i.e. appreciate fully what they are doing. In January 1993, an 81-year-old couple, both in their wheelchairs, were married at St Mary's Church, Old Basing, Hampshire, having met at a local old people's home.

4. *Of the opposite sex*

Gay 'marriages' between two people of the same sex are not legally recognised in this country, although they are accorded some legal effect in Denmark and Holland.

In England, two men cannot go through a legal ceremony of marriage, even though one is dressed as a woman, looks like a woman and considers himself to be a woman. But it does not work the other way round. Two people can legally get married who both look like women, talk like women and behave like women even though one of them was in fact born a man.

This follows from the fact that the yardstick of sex, in English law, is the sex with which you were born. A man may have had his sexual orientation changed by surgery. He may now consider himself to be in every way a woman but legally he remains a man. As Mr Justice Ormrod, a doctor as well as Divorce Court judge, ruled in February 1970 when annulling the marriage seven years earlier of April Ashley, the first British recipient of a sex-change operation, having been born George Jamieson:

Having regard to the essentially heterosexual character of the relationship which is called marriage, the criteria (for deciding the sex of the parties) must, in my judgment, be biological, for even the most extreme degree of transsexualism in a male or the most severe hormonal imbalance which can exist in a person with male chromosomes, male gonads and male genitalia cannot reproduce a person who is naturally capable of performing the essential role of a woman in marriage.

That was well put. But the bizarre consequence of this sensible ruling is that in August 1993 two people, each with a woman's name, were given permission to marry at Fareham register office, Hampshire, because one of them had been born a man and, although having had a sex-change operation fifteen years earlier, still was legally a man and, therefore, of the opposite sex to her partner – who presumably is now legally her 'wife'.

5. Not too closely related

In the eyes of the law, one can be too closely related to someone to marry him or her. The subject is similar to, but not the same as, incest, which (only since an Act of 1908) is the crime of having sexual intercourse with a member of your immediate family (parent, grand-parent, child, brother or sister, half-brother or half-sister). The range of close relations whom you cannot marry is much wider and more specific. The general belief still persists that first cousins in Britain cannot legally marry each other but in fact, ever since the reign of Henry VIII, that has not been the case.

The present law is extremely complex and is mainly governed by the 1949 Marriage Act which refers to the 'prohibited degrees of affinity'. Some are obvious: parent, child, brother or sister, grandparent, grand-child, parent-in-law, daughter-in-law, son-in-law, step-parent, stepchild, uncle-in-law and aunt-in-law. The rest are perhaps not so obvious: the wife or husband of a grandparent who has married more than once, the wife or husband of a grandparent-in-law, a stepchild's wife or hus-band, the wife or husband of a grandchild.

The general rule was that these restrictions applied even after the relationship technically no longer existed. For example, a woman whose husband had died could not marry her son-in-law, even if he had divorced her daughter especially to do so. He was stuck for ever with being within the 'prohibited degrees'. In the rather lovely old language of the law books, 'a husband is of affinity to his wife's kindred and a wife is of affinity to her husband's kindred'. My wife's stepmother, however young and attractive she may be, is legally considered my stepmother too and therefore I can never marry her.

Over the years, Parliament has made a few specific exceptions to this otherwise rigid rule. A man can now marry his dead (or divorced) wife's sister, aunt or niece; and he can also marry the ex-wife of his brother, uncle or nephew. The most recent change in the law was the 1986 Marriage (Prohibited Degrees of Relationship) Act which enables a man to marry his stepdaughter, or a woman her stepson, as long as the couples are over twenty-one and did not live together as a family when the younger person was a child. A man can also now marry his ex-wife's grandmother or his grandson's ex-wife. He can even marry his ex-mother-in-law or ex-daughter-in-law, if both former partners are dead.

6. *Wedding took place with due legal formality*

The subject is very complicated: indeed, the Law Commission has said that it is 'not understood by members of the public or even by all those who have to administer it'. But, with a cold compress wrapped around my head, here is a summary:

Although others can legally perform a marriage ceremony, only two categories of people can give legal approval for that ceremony to take place: a clergyman of the Church of England for the church weddings of Anglicans and a State superintendent registrar for everyone else, including Roman Catholics, Quakers, Jews, other non-Christians and those, irrespective of their religion, who simply want to have a civil wedding in a state register office.

There are thus two stages: the preliminaries and the actual ceremony.

Preliminaries   (a) **Anglican marriages in church**   The traditional procedure is '**calling the banns**': the couple's names are read out, in the parish church of the district where they live, for at least three consecutive Sundays so that anyone who knows of a legal obstacle to their marriage can come forward. If no one materialises, they can marry at any time in the next three months. Then there is **common licence**: if a couple do not wish banns to be published, they can apply for a common licence from the bishop in whose diocese either of them has lived for at least the past fifteen days. That too will allow them to be married at any time in the next three months. Finally, there is the **special licence**, issued only by the Archbishop of Canterbury, which requires no residential qualification and authorises a marriage at any time and in any place. It costs £75, more than double the cost of a common licence, and is restricted to special cases where someone has not lived in the parish for the past fifteen days (e.g. where someone wants to marry in the church of the parish where she was brought up but from which she has long moved away, or where a barrister who does not actually live in the Temple wants to be married in the Temple church) or cases of exceptional urgency. It will require character references, letters of approval from parents and from the vicar of the church where the couple want to marry.

(b) **All other marriages (including Roman Catholic marriages)** A **registrar's certificate** is issued after notice of the couple's intention to marry has been displayed at the local register office for three weeks. It authorises a marriage at any time in the next three months. A **registrar's licence** – sometimes wrongly called a special licence – costs more (£62 as against £19) but authorises a marriage after one clear working day. And there are special preliminaries to facilitate the marriage of the terminally ill, the housebound, prisoners and people in mental hospitals.

The ceremony   There are four permitted types of ceremony. (i) **Marriage according to the rites of the Church of England.** This must be cele-brated by an Anglican clergyman in the presence of two or more witnesses. By Church law, it is usually unavailable to anyone whose previous marriage has ended in divorce and whose ex-spouse is still alive, although a remarriage in a register office may be, and often is, then 'blessed' in church.[3] The clergyman will use the rite laid down in

---

[3] In recent years the General Synod of the Church has allowed local clergy to remarry in church someone who has been divorced, as distinct from a mere blessing, if the diocesan bishop allows it. In December 1994, the General Synod voted to reconsider the whole question of divorcees remarrying in church.

the Book of Common Prayer or authorised alternative form of service. (ii) **Register Office wedding**. The bride and groom each has to make two fundamental declarations. First: 'I do solemnly declare that I know of no lawful impediment why I [ful name] may not be joined in matrimony to [full name].' And then: 'I call upon these persons here present to witness [there must be at least two witnesses and "with open doors"] that I, [full name], do take thee, [full name], to be my lawful wedded wife [or husband].' As soon as they both have made that second declaration, they are legally man and wife. The presiding registrar does not proclaim them man and wife and placing a wedding ring on the bride's finger forms no part of the legal ceremony of marriage. (iii) **Marriages in a registered place of religious worship**. Roman Catholics, Nonconformists and, in modern multi-racial Britain, Moslems, Sikhs, Hindus and Buddhists can marry in their own church, chapel, mosque, temple or other place of religious worship so long as it is registered by the Registrar General. The form of the ceremony, and the words used, are entirely a matter for the parties and their own religious principles, except that at some stage the bride and groom must make the same two fundamental declarations as in a register-office wedding. They must do so in either English or Welsh but ironically there is no specific legal requirement to understand what they are saying. And (iv) **Jewish and Quaker weddings**. These are in a special legal category. So long as religious laws are complied with, they do not have to take place in a registered building and the only requirements of English law are that a registrar's certificate or licence has been obtained beforehand and that afterwards the marriage is registered at the local register office.

What happens if something goes wrong?

It was never the law that the parents of the bride paid for the wedding and that the parents of the groom were merely responsible for the flowers. That was, at best, a social convention that now is increasingly less observed. But *someone* has to pay for the ceremony and the reception: what rights do they have if the food is substandard, the band does not turn up or the DJ operating the mobile disco is drunk?

Increasingly nowadays, with the high cost of formal weddings (according to a recent survey, the average white wedding in London costs nearly £11,000), the couple or their parents take out wedding insurance to cover cancellation or mishap. If not, normal legal liability remains if something goes wrong, as for any other breach of contract – except that the damages may be greater because a wedding is involved. Damages for breach of contract are usually only awarded for identifiable financial loss. The law does not normally allow compensation for injury to feelings, annoyance or social embarrassment. But weddings, like holidays (as we shall see in a later chapter), are an exception to this general rule. And this does not only apply to large-scale 'society' weddings or lavish middle-class functions with a marquee in the garden, as shown by a case at Blackwood County Court in October 1993:

The wedding reception that was a disaster

A mother in Gwent, North Wales, booked a room at a local club for her daughter's wedding reception. It was not to be a very grand affair. She paid a fee of £205, which was to cover £35 for the hire of a room and a disco and buffet food at £2 a head for eighty-five people. Guests were to buy their own drinks at the club's bar. The county court judge ruled that it was implied in the contract that there would be a reasonable sufficiency of food provided for the guests and that proper facilities, in particular toilet facilities, would be available.

In fact, the food was enough for only thirty people so that some guests had nothing to eat at all while others left the reception to go and buy food at a local fish-and-chip shop. The bride and groom were so embarrassed that they left their own wedding reception in their wedding clothes to go and buy more food for their guests. And the toilets were 'messy', with wet floors.

The judge awarded the bride's mother £485 damages, £85 being to reflect the lack of food and £400 for her inconvenience and distress. She had been unwell for a week afterwards because of what had happened.

One final question: Does a woman have to change her surname?

No. It is only a social convention that a woman takes her husband's surname on marriage. There is absolutely no legal obligation. So the authorities have no choice but to respect your wishes. In particular, your passport will not need to be changed and, if you are still of the same mind when it comes up for renewal, the new passport will be issued in the same name.

As for the Inland Revenue and the DSS, all you need do is write to the relevant office saying you are getting married but wish still to keep your existing surname. There should be no problem.

STOP PRESS

In an extension of what I have earlier written about **Register Office weddings**, the 1994 Marriage Act, which received the Royal Assent in November 1994 and will come into effect at some time in 1995, has made two important changes in the law. For the first time, it allows civil marriages to take place in *any* register office of the couple's choice (not only their local one) and, even more revolutionary, in other buildings, such as stately homes, civic buildings or hotels – specifically approved for that purpose by the local council.

Regulations are still awaited setting out the criteria and procedures to be followed in selecting this new brand of 'approved buildings'. As Tom Sackville, the Parliamentary Secretary for Health, has said, 'The Government recognises that the dignity of marriage must not be diminished. That is why we fully support the need to regulate the type of premises used.'

Yet the Government can claim little credit for this innovative and beneficial little Act. It began as a Private Member's Bill introduced by Gyles Brandreth, the writer MP and former television personality, who was concerned that, although half of all weddings now take place in register offices, their procedures had altered little since they began in 1837. In future, civil ceremonies can be much more fun.

SIX

Divorce – (1) The Mechanics

The statistics are appalling. Britain has the highest divorce rate in Europe. More than 160,000 British couples divorce each year, compared with under 30,000 thirty years ago. More than 2 million children are being brought up in one-parent families. Almost one in ten new marriages do not even get as far as the seven-year itch: they break up within two years, compared with one in a hundred thirty years ago.

Marital unhappiness has been with us for centuries. In the sixteenth century John Donne could lament his elopement with a bitter poignancy: 'John Donne, Anne Donne, Undone.' Matters had not improved by the late eighteenth century when Samuel Taylor Coleridge described unhappiness as: 'Those habitual ills / That wear out life, when two unequal minds / Meet in one house and two discordant wills.'

But now couples are no longer content to accept their misery. They are battering down the doors of their self-built prisons on a scale never known before. They go out into the world seeking new happiness, although whether they always find it is perhaps open to question. According to a survey by the European Commission published in December 1993, just over 10 per cent of British women aged twenty to thirty-nine lived alone with their children. The average across the whole European Union was 6.5 per cent.

Divorce has become an essential part of our way of life. Estimates vary that between one in three and one in *two* marriages today are doomed to end in divorce: either figure speaks for itself in terms of domestic unhappiness – or lack of resolve to make a marriage work.

Two recent news items seem to support this latter view: (1) In February 1994, the former Test cricketer Graeme Fowler chose to tell his wife that he was divorcing her by sending her a fax while she was visiting her parents in Australia. He was only thirty-seven but she was already his second wife and he had set up home with another woman who was bearing his child. (2) In June 1993, the *Daily Express* reported that wedding photographers were demanding 'divorce deposits' because couples were splitting up before the pictures of their Big Day were ready. Some firms had been caught with bills of up to £1,000 after orders were cancelled. One photographer in Coventry was reported as saying, 'I've done several weddings where couples have gone away on honeymoon, rowed and parted.' I had been told much the same in Beverly Hills ten years earlier when researching a magazine series on 'Divorce/Los Angeles Style'. I never thought it would happen in Britain.

Nowadays less than 2 per cent of all modern divorces are defended. Nearly all divorces are uncontested or, after protracted negotiation, end up that way: dealt with in private far from prying eyes or ears, usually quite literally through the post with no one going to court. For most, it is mailbox justice. A man or woman who has committed adultery with a married person is still sometimes concerned about having to be named in their divorce. They no longer need be worried: ever since October 1991 the courts accept a spouse's written admission that they have committed adultery 'with a woman (or man) whose name or identity I am not prepared to disclose'.[1]

A divorce is not as in the old days before the 1969 Divorce Reform Act modernised the law and swept away the grim charade of couples revealing to the world the most intimate details of their private life in front of elderly judges and crowded public galleries, with the details of the more 'juicy' cases trotted out for general delight later in the newspapers.

The tone for the New Age was set by Lord Denning, when Master of the Rolls and senior Appeal Court judge, in February 1973, when hearing a dispute between a dentist and his wife from Streatham: 'Divorce today carries no stigma but only sympathy. It is a misfortune which befalls both parties. No longer is one guilty and the other innocent.'

---

[1] The district judge in your local divorce county court who must approve most divorce petitions before they go to the full judge for a decree knows that the case is undefended and that your spouse probably wants a divorce at least as much as you do. Unless the allegations are too blatantly frivolous, he (or she) is often likely to let things go through 'on the nod', although no one will officially admit this.

The rules are surprisingly simple. No divorce is possible within the first year of a marriage but thereafter there is only one ground for divorce: that the marriage has broken down irretrievably. The 1973 Matrimonial Causes Act (which replaced the 1969 Divorce Reform Act) says that this single ground for divorce can be established by proving one of five possible 'facts': i.e. adultery, unreasonable behaviour (which can mean almost anything you want it to mean, from 'he was always coming home late' or 'her love-making was passionless and made me feel used' to more traditional allegations of physical violence or abuse), two years' desertion, two years' separation and consent, and five years' separation without consent.

Of course, there are nuances. Divorce remains a major step. No spouse is expected to take lightly the final decision to part. The 1973 Act allows the parties to continue living together (and having sex together) to try to work out their differences for a trial period of up to six months before parting irrevocably. And, even if the real reason for continuing to have sex is simply that they enjoy it, irrespective of any possible reconciliation, these six months do not have to form one long continual period:

How the six-month trial period works

Adultery: for instance, a wife discovers in January 1994 that her husband has been committing adultery. She tries to forgive him but she cannot. One month later, in February, she asks him to move out on a 'trial separation', and he goes. But in July 1994 he returns at her request (or as the result of his own pleading) to see if they can save the marriage. She then has five more months, until December 1994, to decide whether to divorce him on the basis of his 'old' adultery, although of course this would not affect a divorce on the basis of any 'new' adultery.

Unreasonable behaviour: the six-month period, whether broken up or not, is counted from the last act of unreasonable behaviour. But even if the parties live together for more than six months, a judge could still grant a divorce, although he would be more likely to believe that the alleged misbehaviour was not really all that bad – and, therefore, not 'unreasonable'. He could therefore refuse a decree.

Two years' desertion; Two years' separation and consent; Five years'

94

separation without consent: the six months, whether broken up or continuous, will not prevent a decree but will have to be added to the necessary minimum period of desertion or separation *as from the day the couple first parted*. For example, take two years' separation and consent: a husband and wife part in June 1993. They come back together three months later, in September 1993, then part for good after two months, in November 1993. Their two-year separation has, in fact, been broken by a total of five months' living together so neither can ask for a consent divorce until October 1995: i.e. two years plus five months and one day from the original parting.

There are other niceties. For example, adultery on its own is technically not sufficient. You must also say that you find it 'intolerable' to go on living with your spouse; but this is only a form of words. You do not have to say that you find it intolerable *because of the adultery*: it can be for whatever reason.

Similarly, two or even five years' separation does not necessarily mean that you must have lived under separate roofs during all that time. The courts accept that there can be financial or economic reasons why people have to go on living in the same house, or even the same flat, without actually living *together*. It suffices if there have been 'two separate households under one roof': i.e. you may have shared the same kitchen and bathroom but not the same bedroom or living-room. And you should most definitely not have cooked for one another or have spent evenings together happily watching television; but, in all conscience, who really is to know if occasionally you have done?

With the 'fact' of five years' separation without consent, the 1969 Act tried to throw a life belt to people who were, for the first time in our history, being divorced against their will and with nothing alleged against them. So the Act said that a judge could refuse a decree if he thought it would cause 'grave financial or other hardship and that, in all the circumstances, it would be wrong to dissolve the marriage'. Like so many Parliamentary compromises, this has proved of only limited effect: for instance, the courts soon ruled that a devout Roman Catholic wife's feeling of shame and distress at being divorced in violation of what she considered to be the law of God did not amount to sufficient hardship.

In practice, this so-called 'Casanova's Charter', as its opponents dubbed it when it was first introduced, has only enabled judges to apply a slight brake on the inevitable result: ensuring that a husband gives his wife a larger annuity or extra finance for a little more security in an insecure world. She may have been a splendid wife all the years they were together but she will still end up divorced and often embittered.

Alternatives to divorce

Before we carry on with this chapter, we now have to make a detour from the main highway and, for the sake of completeness, look at the three alternatives to divorce. They are nothing like so frequently resorted to but they are still of considerable importance:

1. *Legal separation*

This is often not so much an alternative as a temporary stage on the way to divorce, as is almost certain to be the case with the Duke of York, the Queen's second son, and probably even with her first-born, the Prince of Wales. In fact, it does not entail going to court. Couples who no longer want to live together agree between themselves on most, if not all, of the practical issues that normally arise when a marriage sours: what is to happen to the children, the family home and the furniture, where they are both going to live, whether one will pay maintenance to the other and, if so, for how long and how much, etc.

Couples can simply exchange letters setting this all out but it is safer to ask a solicitor to draw up a formal deed which you then both sign. If there are future difficulties, a judge is much more likely not to tamper with the terms of a separation agreement in a deed than one merely contained in letters written without legal advice.

But anyone thinking of a legal separation should heed the wise words of Lesley Garner, writing in the *Daily Telegraph* in December 1992 after the announcement of the legal separation of the Prince and Princess of Wales:

> When ordinary couples opt for separation without divorce it is often a refusal to face up to the full misery of the clean break. Speaking as someone who has been separated for three years and as half of an ex-

couple who still haven't faced up to the brutality of divorce, I know that separation is only a halfway house.

There are plenty of rationalisations for the halfway house. It can seem pointless to go through the limb-severing business of divorce unless a second marriage is in the offing. None the less, separation is an uneasy state which confuses everybody. It is the act of stopping banging your head on a brick wall. Divorce is walking away from the wall. Walking away from the wall is the bigger decision. Until we do it, we put our emotional lives in limbo.

2. *Judicial separation*

This is half a stage on from 'banging your head on a brick wall'. It is a sort of reluctant semi-divorce. You have to go to court but you do not have to wait a year. A judge will grant a decree of judicial separation in much the same way as a decree of divorce – *but it does not end the marriage.* That is why it remains quite popular with people, mainly women, who have a religious objection to divorce. Also it is easier because you do not have to prove that your marriage has irretrievably broken down. It is enough to prove one of the five basic 'facts': adultery, unreasonable behaviour, etc.

There are about 1,600 decrees a year, and here is a good example from November 1990:

The vet who lost his case

A 49-year-old veterinary surgeon who complained that his 50-year-old wife criticised him in front of others for being oversexed was refused a divorce for 'unreasonable behaviour'. But Judge Watts granted the wife a decree of judicial separation on the grounds of the vet's adultery. He said the couple remained 'in a state of holy deadlock'.

In fact, the deadlock does not have to be for all time. Judicial separation does not prevent either party later getting a divorce, if grounds exist. This veterinary surgeon, for instance, should be able eventually to divorce his wife, even against her wishes, after they have been separated for five years.

3. Nullity

A decree of nullity ends a marriage not because the marriage has broken down irretrievably, as with divorce. It is because of a fundamental flaw in the marriage itself. Once a marriage has been annulled, it is as if it had never existed, not, as with divorce, it existed but has now been brought to an end. Despite an update by Parliament in 1971 and 1973, this branch of the law remains shrouded in the concepts and phraseology of old ecclesiastical law in which it has its origins.

The law distinguishes between two types of annulled marriages: void and voidable. There is little practical distinction between the two. But a void marriage never was a valid marriage and technically did not need a decree to bring it to an end, whereas a voidable marriage was a perfectly valid marriage until it was annulled. The children, if any, of both kinds of marriage are legitimate except that, with a void marriage, at least one parent must reasonably have believed that the marriage was valid when the child was conceived – which, of course, will usually be the case.

Void marriages we have already looked at in the previous chapter when considering the essentials of a valid marriage; let us now briefly look at the five kinds of situation that make a marriage voidable:

(i) *Incapacity to consummate*   A marriage is consummated when what an early-Victorian ecclesiastical judge once called 'ordinary and complete' sexual intercourse has taken place. There must be both erection and penetration for a reasonable length of time. There does not have to be ejaculation. As Professor Steven Cretney has wryly commented, 'It is not necessary for either party to have an orgasm,' and the House of Lords has ruled (in *Baxter* v. *Baxter* in 1948) that a marriage is consummated whether or not a condom is used.

When one of the parties is incapable of consummating a marriage because of his or her incapacity to do so, *either* can ask for a nullity decree. Impotence can, of course, be either physical or psychological and, if physical, the court has the power to order a medical examination and may draw adverse inferences from a refusal to be examined. Whether physical or psychological, the law does not expect the other partner to go about sex like a bull in a field. There must be tenderness and understanding – and time. I once managed to persuade Mr Justice Barnard that a wife was entitled to leave after only one week of her husband's inadequate love-making. The case, under its strange anonymous title, B. (otherwise S.) v. B., established something of a legal precedent and is reported in (1958) 2 All England Law Reports at page 76; but other less robust judges might disagree.

It is sex between the parties after marriage that counts, not premarital sex. In another case of mine, a man and woman had lived happily together for several years without being married, enjoying full and frequent sex. Then they got married – and at once she refused him sex, and continued steadfastly to do so. The truth was that she could not help herself. As a young teenager, she had been raped by her father and, once her lover was in a close formal family relationship with her, she could not bear him to touch her sexually. It was all very sad. She did not contest his nullity petition.

(ii) *Wilful refusal to consummate* With a more liberal generation of judges on the Bench, this is now the basis of most nullity decrees, although of course it is usually word against word since there is no question of physical abnormality. Even so, decrees are granted when, on an analysis of the whole history of the marriage, there is a 'settled and definite decision' by one spouse to refuse sexual intercourse to the other that has been 'come to without just excuse'.

Not surprisingly, it is only the aggrieved spouse who can ask for the decree. But I emphasise that you can only go for nullity on this ground and for incapacity (which, unlike divorce, you can always do within the first year of marriage) if you have never had sex with your spouse after marriage *at all*.[2] If you have had sex, even though only once, but then you are refused further sex and that destroys the marriage, you will have to go for divorce (on the grounds of unreasonable behaviour) – and wait a full year from your wedding day.

[2] Some solicitors, particularly of the older generation, can be remarkably shy about getting the correct details from their client. Some years ago, I had a case where a solicitor brought a woman down to Chambers for me to obtain the background needed to draft a divorce petition on the grounds of her husband's unreasonable behaviour. By the time she left I had ascertained that they had never had sexual intercourse together. Eventually she obtained a nullity decree on the grounds of his wilful refusal to consummate.

(iii) *Lack of consent at the time of the marriage*   We have already looked at this when talking about 'shotgun weddings', duress and arranged marriages in the previous chapter. It is irrelevant whether or not the marriage has been consummated.

(iv) *Venereal disease*, (v) *Pregnancy by another man* and (vi) *Mental illness*
In practice, these cases are very rare but if, at the time of the marriage, your spouse was suffering from venereal disease in a communicable form (it is unclear whether Aids is a venereal disease for this purpose) or, unknown to you, was pregnant by someone else or was suffering from mental disorder within the meaning of the 1983 Mental Health Act, you can ask for a nullity decree – provided you do so within three years. Again, it is irrelevant whether or not the marriage has been consummated.

To all these different kinds of voidable marriage petitions there is one possible overall defence. It used to be called 'approbation': you could not seek nullity if by your conduct you had 'approbated' the marriage. Now Section 13 of the 1973 Matrimonial Causes Act more specifically says that a court shall not grant a decree when 'the petitioner ... with knowledge that it was open to him to have the marriage avoided, so conducted himself in relation to the respondent as to lead the respondent reasonably to believe that he would not seek to do so ... and it would be unjust to the respondent to grant the decree'.

An obvious example of where such a defence would succeed would be where an elderly widower weds a woman, of whatever age, on the understanding that they are not to have sex together and that their marriage is 'for companionship only', and then he later changes his mind and asks for sex – which she refuses. If he then petitions for nullity on the grounds of her 'wilful refusal to consummate', she can almost certainly get his petition dismissed (if she wants to) on the basis that it would be 'unjust' to grant him a decree.

We have sufficiently examined the practical alternatives; now let us return to the main subject of divorce.

How to get a divorce

Anyone can go to court and get their own decree. You will not have to engage in courtroom advocacy, which, for the non-professional (except when arguing a civil case in the small claims court), can be dangerous territory. So any reasonably intelligent person can manage Do-It-Yourself. It is almost too easy. All you need do is go along to your local county court office (or telephone them) on any weekday between 10 a.m. and 4 p.m. and ask for the name and address of your nearest *divorce* county court. It will be either the same court or not very far away.

You then collect from that court's office a Petition form and, if you have children under sixteen or between sixteen and eighteen but still at school or training for a career, a Proposed Arrangements for Children form (Form D8A), and fill them out. None of this is more complicated than filling in a passport application. But, if you have any problems, the court office staff are always very helpful and they can supply a free thirty-page explanatory booklet. This should be sufficient to get you through. If not, your local Citizens Advice Bureau will generally assist and several useful DIY divorce books are on the market, of which perhaps the best are the *Which? Guide to Divorce* (1992) at £10.99 and the *Eagle Self-Help Divorce Pack* (1993) at £9.99.

When you have completed the forms, send or take them to the court office (together with your marriage certificate or a copy) and £40 court fees. The office will then post these forms to (the legal phrase is 'serve them upon') your spouse and the person you have named as your spouse's partner in adultery (i.e. the co-respondent).[3] They should then post to the court their reply in Form D10, the 'acknowledgement of service', saying whether they are defending the divorce and whether your spouse agrees to the proposed arrangements for the children. If the divorce is to be defended, the case will then be transferred to the Family Division of the High Court: this does not necessarily mean that

---

[3] You may have lost all contact with your spouse and have no current address. What happens then? The answer is time-consuming but effective: you first write to the last known address asking for your letter to be sent on. If that fails and you also draw a blank with the DSS national computer or your spouse's trade union, trade association or last known employer, the court office will help you swear an affidavit detailing your efforts and you will almost certainly be allowed to 'dispense with service of the petition'. Your divorce will go through without your spouse even knowing about it.

you will have to go to the Law Courts in London since some High Court judges are always out on circuit sitting at large provincial cities. But, whether in London or the provinces, you really will now have to get yourself a solicitor, even if you had not engaged one before.

You will, however, need a good one, experienced in family cases and with the right attitude to you and your personal problems. I will come back to this in the next chapter.

You will also need this right kind of solicitor if your spouse replies in Form D10 saying that the arrangements for the children will be contested. The case will stay in the divorce county court and your divorce will continue to go through as undefended but it will not be finalised, and you are not free to remarry, until the divorce judge has made a ruling on the future of the children. Incidentally, property disputes do not hold up the granting of an undefended divorce. Couples are often divorced and even remarried before their differences over the family assets have been resolved. We shall look at this whole question of 'ancillary relief', dealing with disputes over property, money and children, in the next chapter.

In most cases, though, Form D10 confirms that the divorce is undefended and the proposed arrangements for the children are agreed. Your petition will then go smoothly on.

There will be some more paperwork, including a sworn affidavit in which you state your version of the particular 'fact' on which you are relying: adultery, unreasonable behaviour or whatever. The No. 2 judge at the divorce county court, 'the District Judge', will read the papers in the case and decide whether everything is in order and you are entitled to your divorce. He almost certainly will say 'Yes', and you will receive another form (D84A), stating the date and time at which the full judge will grant your decree in open court.

You need neither to attend nor be represented. The names and court numbers of cases will be read out in batches and the judge will simply say: 'Decree nisi granted.'

Even so, your marriage is not yet ended and you are still not free to remarry. Decree nisi comes from the Latin word *nisi*, 'unless'. It means that you will get your divorce soon *unless* someone comes forward to prove there has somehow been a fraud on the court. In the old days, this served some valid purpose: divorces were sometimes obtained by fraud and deceit, usually by the parties themselves trying to lie their way around the strictness of the pre-1969 law. Nowadays such 'collusion', as it used to be called, is hardly necessary; and, even when it exists, it seldom gets brought to the attention of the court. Ideas have changed. Yet a decree nisi is still – unnecessarily, in my view – the general rule.

What will happen next is that you will have to apply to the court office for the decree nisi to be converted into a decree absolute. You do this on yet another form (D36) and with your cheque for a £15 court fee. This is only a paper formality that does not involve the judge; and you will have to wait six weeks and one day.

Sometimes problems arise because your spouse has already met someone else and wants to remarry as soon as possible. You may be in no hurry to help. So what happens if you do not obligingly ask for the decree to be made absolute after six weeks and one day?

In an emergency, your spouse can apply, usually in person, to the judge when he grants the decree nisi to cut the normal period. But usually the application will only succeed if he or she wants to remarry urgently before a child is born. Otherwise they will have to wait a full three months before asking for a decree absolute: posting their own Form D36 and £15 cheque. In that case, the total time between decree nisi and absolute can be as long as six weeks and one day *plus* three further months. So, if you are the petitioner and you want to be bitchy, whatever your sex, there is plenty of scope, even at this late stage.

How long will an undefended divorce case take? On average, the normal uncomplicated case will take from start to finish about four to five months.

One final word about solicitors

If you prefer to go to a solicitor, even on an undefended divorce where you and your spouse have agreed all outstanding issues between you in a civilised fashion, that is of course your privilege. It would also be understandable. Many people might find it disagreeable, to use no stronger word, to do their own dirty work in ending a marriage that doubtless began with so much joy and hope. Depending on the part of the country where you live, the cost would probably be about £300 to £450 plus VAT, including court fees. Provided you choose what I have already called 'the right kind of solicitor' (and we shall soon explore how to find him or her), many people might think that was well worth the price.

As for legal aid, it simply is not available for undefended divorces except for the Green Form Scheme. This is very limited in effect. Taking its name from the colour of the application form, it is available only to the poorest: those with disposable income not exceeding £70 a week and less than £1,000 capital. It entitles them to three free hours of a solicitor's time, which can sometimes be extended. In that time he can help with drafting a divorce petition, giving general advice and perhaps writing a few letters – but not much else.

Full legal aid, including representation in court, is available, subject to the usual property and income limits of £7,080 capital and £136 a week disposable income, in defended divorces and – much more important – in disputes about 'ancillary relief': i.e. children, property and maintenance. But unlike legal aid generally, this can benefit some middle-class wives (at least, those who are not working) because their disposable income is likely to be less than £136 a week and the value of family assets, including the home over which they are usually fighting, is ignored. They are often legally, as well as factually, poor enough to qualify.

The Law Commission has called upon divorcing couples to resolve matters in dispute between themselves, if at all possible, rather than seek 'an unattainable catharsis in a judicial forum'. But that is a counsel of perfection. As we shall now see, an additional sadness of divorce is the problems that arise when the parties cannot settle their differences, and months, sometimes even years, of new unhappiness and stress open up before them.

SEVEN

Divorce – (2) The Problems

When a marriage breaks down, people feel lost, despondent, angry. The trauma is deep and can be frightening. Falling out of love with someone, shattering the mould of your everyday existence, is heart-breaking enough in itself but, when you add the uncertainty of the future, the worry about how you are going to make ends meet, the potential loneliness and the almost inevitable drop in living standards that will follow (at least, for a while), the broken heart can easily harden to steel.

Finding the right solicitor

Despite the expense, this is when a lawyer is needed, and what I have already called 'the right kind of lawyer'. An able divorce solicitor or barrister (who will generally also be needed in the more difficult cases) must have at least as much understanding of the human spirit as of law books and statutes. But all too often lawyers, instead of making life easier, seem to make it worse. Some become too involved in their cases and too partisan, so that their judgment is warped and instead of pouring oil on troubled waters they set a match to it: I know of one case where a woman solicitor acting for a wife found a perfectly normal but tough letter written by a rather aggressive male solicitor on the other side so 'repugnant' that she had to let several days pass before she could bring herself to pass it on to her client and, in the end, wrote back a letter that was so angry and insulting that it torpedoed what would have been an eminently reasonable settlement of the dispute.

Other lawyers are inexperienced in the specialist world of family law or bumbling incompetents or money-grabbing and lacking in basic humanity. I genuinely believe that many solicitors and barristers, however decent and honourable, charge far too much for what they do: that is the going rate – and they go along with it. This not only increases the cost, it also prolongs the agony. When every hour with your solicitor can cost you anything between £100 to £150 plus VAT, or probably even more with a top London firm, it is easy to become obsessed with getting your money's worth. Couples see the pound coins clocking up and become trapped in endless – and expensive – rounds of arguing over who gets the mortgage, the Mercedes, the second home in Cornwall or Spain.

In *Evans* v. *Evans*, in January 1990, the legal proceedings were so drawn out and acrimonious that the costs incurred by the husband and wife amounted to £35,000 and £25,000 respectively. The wife had wanted to remain in the matrimonial home but the house had to be sold to pay the legal bills. Mrs Justice Booth commented forcefully: 'If they are united in nothing else, this husband and wife must be united in bitterly regretting the dissipation of their assets which has so unfortunately occurred.' With the concurrence of the senior divorce judge, the President of the High Court's Family Division, she laid down guidelines for all divorce lawyers. Eight are matters of detail but three deserve to be reprinted here for you to remind your own lawyer:

(1) 'All professional witnesses should be careful to avoid a partisan approach and should maintain proper professional standards.'

(2) 'Solicitors and counsel should keep their clients informed of the costs at all stages of the proceedings.'

(3) 'The desirability of reaching a settlement should be borne in mind throughout the proceedings.'

To refresh your solicitor's memory, you can photocopy for yourself the whole of these guidelines and hand them over to him or her. You will find them at pages 148 and 149 of Mrs Justice Booth's judgment in Volume 2 of the (1990) *All England Law Reports*. These law reports are available at most major public reference libraries.

The question still remains: how are you to find the right kind of solicitor with the right kind of experience? That is more important than choosing the right kind of barrister for you have first to choose your solicitor who then selects the barrister, and he is likely to be on the same wavelength. Unless you have a personal recommendation to a suitable solicitor, I suggest you send a stamped addressed envelope for a list of local members to the Solicitors Family Law Association (SFLA) at PO Box 302, Keston, Kent BR2 6EZ (Tel: 01689–850227). This association, formed in December 1982, is a group of some 3,500 divorce solicitors 'who promote a constructive and conciliatory approach rather than an aggressive or angry one' (their own words). They are dedicated to conciliation and restraint. Many other solicitors share this view but, if you want to be certain of getting someone committed to this attitude, you should consult the SFLA.

Incidentally, please do not confuse conciliation with reconciliation, which you may well feel is neither practical nor what you want. Reconciliation means a couple doing all they can to try to get back together as husband and wife. Conciliation is the process of helping a couple to sort out their problems and create their own tailor-made solutions in a civilised manner.

Here are two sad examples of the non-conciliatory approach from an article in the *The Times*:

> John Rogers [this is not his real name], an estate agent from Oxfordshire, rues the day he went to a solicitor who was not a matrimonial specialist. 'I asked him whether I should attend a hearing as it seemed to be about my two children,' he says. 'He told me it was not and that I had no need to attend. Now I am allowed to see the children only one day a fortnight.'
>
> An experienced south London matrimonial solicitor is quoted: 'Many solicitors feel family law is simple. It is just like claiming from an insurance company. They send off a totally insensitive letter, which ruins everybody's lives, instead of lowering the temperature so that the parties can stay on speaking terms for the benefit of the children.'

Ever since an Appeal Court decision in 1975 in *Calderbank* v. *Calderbank*, a solicitor with the right kind of approach can pressure the other side into accepting a reasonable offer of settlement by writing in the latter stages of protracted negotiation what is called 'a Calderbank letter'. Taking its name from a letter written by a solicitor in that case, it restates the client's final offer and gives this warning: if the other spouse rejects the offer and the judge ultimately makes an award *around the amount offered*, he will be shown the letter and asked to order the rejecting spouse to pay the costs of both parties as from the date of the letter. If this ploy works, it can very much blunt the financial edge of any apparent victory. The judges are usually happy to co-operate and, since the costs incurred after the rejection of the letter are usually the greatest (since they include the actual court hearing probably lasting for several days), a shrewdly timed Calderbank letter can concentrate an opposing solicitor's mind marvellously.

A Calderbank letter that worked

In 1990, a wealthy businessman was in dispute with his wife over money. Negotiations were dragging on between the solicitors on both sides. Finally, a week before the hearing, the husband's solicitor wrote the wife's solicitor a Calderbank letter offering her £400,000. The solicitor, having (presumably) checked with his client, wrote back rejecting the letter – but did not make any counter-offer. The case went on.

After several days in court, the judge awarded the wife £435,000, only 8.75 per cent more than the figure she had earlier refused. He was then shown the Calderbank letter – and ordered her to pay the costs of both sides from the date of her refusal, which probably cost her the better part of another £35,000!

What about legal aid?

As we saw in the last chapter, many middle-class wives who do not go out to work are eligible for legal aid to fight their claims for 'ancillary relief' (concerning the home, money or children) because their husband's income and the value of the family assets in dispute are ignored.

This is obviously good so far as it goes but there are two main drawbacks:

(1) It is difficult to find a competent solicitor, experienced in this field, who is prepared to take on the case at the measly rates paid by the Legal Aid Board. As a London suburban solicitor has said, 'For private work I charge £110 an hour but for legal aid work I get £60. My partners want me to stop but I am committed to it, not least because my mother sorted out her divorce only because of legal aid. Maybe outside the South-East there are firms that find the legal-aid rate profitable' (it has since gone up marginally) 'but fewer and fewer in

this area will touch it. Many of my clients travel for more than an hour to see me because so few firms will do this work. In almost every family dispute, especially during the recession, at least one party qualifies for legal aid.'

A by-product is that, even when a competent solicitor with the right attitude takes on legal-aid work, he is under constant temptation to cut corners and employ inexperienced or even unqualified staff to handle sensitive matters. Solicitors should not have to be philanthropists. They are professional people doing a professional job.

(2) There is a financial trap which many women often discover only late in the day. It is this: if a wife has legal aid, anything over the first £2,500 of the 'property preserved or recovered' (i.e. anything over the first £2,500 in value of her share in the family home or the first £2,500 of any lump sum settlement) is subject to a statutory charge – a sort of mortgage – in favour of the Legal Aid Board. When she wins her case, the judge may make no order as to costs, in which case the parties are thrown back on their own resources, or, as more often happens, he will order the defeated husband to pay his successful wife's costs.

But this does not necessarily mean the Board will get back all the money they have spent on her representation. This can be either because the husband himself has legal aid and that means the Board will be reimbursing itself, which is a nonsense, or because he simply does not have the means to pay his own legal-aid contribution *plus* his wife's costs. In these circumstances, the Board can enforce its charge on 'the property preserved or recovered' by the wife to claw back what it is out of pocket in its fees to her lawyers: i.e. her home. The Board (or the taxpayer) does not suffer; she does.

And remember that this is when she wins her case! If she loses, there will not be any statutory charge because there is nothing to which the charge can attach. She will often have to pay something towards her husband's costs but that will only be what the judge considers 'reasonable'. This usually amounts to the same again as her legal-aid contribution to her own costs: a comparatively small sum.

The bizarre (and unfair) result is that, if the Board enforces its statutory charge on her winnings, it can cost her more to win than to lose. Nothing is for nothing with divorce legal aid.

But to revert to the statutory charge: if, as often happens, the judge orders that the home has to be sold and the wife is to receive the net proceeds of sale, the Board will often demand immediate repayment of its costs from these proceeds of sale – before she gets anything herself. If the house is not to be sold, usually because it is being transferred into her name as a home for herself and her children, the Board may magnanimously allow the charge to remain unenforced until the property is eventually sold: with interest ticking happily away in the meantime. Sometimes the Board will even agree to the charge being transferred to a new property if needed as a home for the wife and children. It is all a matter for the Board's discretion.

These principles were laid down by the House of Lords in May 1980 in *Hanlon* v. *Hanlon*, where a nurse from Waltham Cross, Hertfordshire, divorced her policeman husband after seventeen years of marriage. She had won a protracted courtroom battle to have her home, valued at £10,000, transferred into her name – only to find that the house had to be sold under the statutory charge to pay her unrecovered legal-aid costs of £8,000. All five senior appeal judges were reluctant to come to this decision and called for Parliament to change the law. Lord Edmund-Davies, who had earlier achieved nationwide fame with his meting out of thirty-year prison sentences in the Great Train Robbery Trial, specifically said: 'We live in a busy world and the demands made on the legislature are endless but the present state of affairs could, if permitted to continue indefinitely, substantially erode our present pride in the legal-aid system of this country.'

That pride continues to be eroded. Parliament has done nothing to reform the law, despite a new Legal Aid Act in 1988.

So much for solicitors. The delicate and difficult legal problems involving children on divorce require a chapter on their own. But let us now look, in some detail, at the law on property and money disputes:

Ancillary relief: i.e. property and money on divorce

1. *The overall picture*

Basically, unless the parties can sensibly reach agreement between themselves (helped, let's hope, by their lawyers), everything is up for grabs. The slate of the family assets, property as well as income, is wiped clean and, unless you reallocate your resources yourselves, a judge will do it for you. He will do so carefully and conscientiously, bearing in mind various factors set out for his guidance in Section 25 of the 1973 Matrimonial Causes Act (as amended by the 1984 Matrimonial and Family Proceedings Act), but the result will still be the same: the old set-up will have gone for ever and in its place will be a new reality. The eggs will have been cracked and made into two different omelettes.

These are the factors that Section 25 says a judge must consider:

• the income, earning capacity, property and financial resources of the parties both now and 'in the foreseeable future';
• their present and future needs, obligations and responsibilities;
• their standard of living prior to the breakdown of the marriage;
• their ages and for how long they have been married;
• any physical or mental disability;
• any contributions they may have made to the family;
• their conduct during the marriage 'if such that it would be inequitable to disregard it';
• the value of any benefit (for example, a pension) which either party may lose because of the divorce.

These are all unexceptionable and, one would have thought, reasonably fair. They are also self-explanatory except perhaps for two items:

(i) *'Conduct' that cannot equitably be disregarded*   What exactly does this mean? Precious little, in fact, The old idea that a 'bad' wife should be entitled to a smaller division of the family assets or a 'good' husband to a larger share went out of the window with the old pre-1969 law. As Lord Denning said in a precedent-setting Appeal Court judgment in *Wachtel* v. *Wachtel* in February 1973:

> It has been suggested that there should be a 'discount' or 'reduction' in what a wife is to receive because of her supposed misconduct, guilt or blame (whatever word is used). We cannot accept this argument. In the vast majority of cases, it is repugnant to the principles underlying the new legislation. There will be many cases in which a wife (although once considered guilty or blameworthy) will have cared for the home and looked after the family for many years. Is she to be deprived of benefit because she may share responsibility for the breakdown with her husband?

There will no doubt be a residue of cases where the conduct of one of the parties is both obvious and gross, so much so that to order one party to support another is repugnant to anyone's sense of justice. In such a case the court remains free to decline or to reduce financial support.

But, short of cases falling into this category, the court should not reduce its order merely because of what was formerly regarded as guilt or blame. To do so would be to impose a fine for supposed misbehaviour in the course of an unhappy married life.

Nicely put. But many divorcing couples still do not realise this. They think that, because one party has committed adultery or failed their marital obligations in some other important or hurtful way, that can be used against them to cut their share in the family home or reduce their maintenance. In the overwhelming majority of cases today (there are no official figures but I would say in at least 98 per cent), 'conduct' is not a factor in sorting out the finances.

(ii) *Taking into account the value of a pension* Once a woman is divorced, she loses entitlement to a share of her husband's pension on retirement or death. If she has no private pension of her own, as often happens, she only has the basic State pension to fall back on. And, if she has made reduced National Insurance contributions, she will only get a reduced pension at that.[1]

In most marriages, even when both parties are in full-time employment, the husband usually earns more than the wife (and, if not, all these rules work the other way round: the law is unisex). The husband therefore is usually the only one able to look forward to a substantial private pension, with the wife's rights built into that – so long as she continues to be his wife. A judge is supposed to take into account the value of that lost entitlement when sorting out the finances on divorce; but there is a fundamental flaw in the law as it now stands.

Generally speaking, a judge cannot actually get into the pension

---

[1] As so often with National Insurance, the matter is somewhat complicated but the explanation given in the official NI Leaflet 95, available at all local social security offices, is quite helpful. And all contributors, whatever their marital status, can easily get their own individual forecast of their State pension by filling in Form BR 19 and sending it off to DSS headquarters in Newcastle-upon-Tyne.

fund itself. He can only order the future recipient of the pension – who, as I say, is usually the husband – to borrow a large sum of money or otherwise juggle his finances so that the wife does not lose out too much by ceasing to be his 'wife'.

In practice, if he cannot do this and no money can be made available to compensate for her lost share in the pension, she gets nothing. This is, of course, grossly unfair to many women.

It looks as if there may at last be a remedy: in September 1993, the official Goode Committee, in an exhaustive report on the whole pensions industry in the wake of the Robert Maxwell disaster, proposed a change in the law so that, on divorce, a husband's pension rights are valued as if he was then leaving the pension scheme. The rights are then split and the judge orders the pension fund – not the husband himself, as now – to make to the wife a payout which can then be put towards a new pension for her.

This proposal, or a variant, may well become law – at some time in 1995. Meanwhile, in May 1994, the Appeal Court brought new, more immediate hope to some wives by ruling that, despite all previous understanding of the law, a husband's pension scheme *could* be varied to benefit a divorced wife in cases where it could be treated as a 'post-nuptial settlement' and where varying the scheme would not affect third parties' rights. But because the ruling was only by a majority of two to one, the Appeal Court gave leave for the case to go to the House of Lords. We probably will not know the final outcome until the summer of 1995.

The provisions of Section 25 of the 1973 Act do not stand alone. There are two further matters we must look at:

The 'one-third rule'   For some unknown reason, the judges always say this is not a 'rule' – but it is, in the sense that they all use it as what Lord Denning called in *Wachtel* v. *Wachtel*, the case of the Streatham dentist, 'a starting point'. As he said:

'There may be cases where more than one-third is right. There are likely to be many others where it is the only practicable solution. But it is only a starting point. It will serve in cases where the marriage has lasted for many years and the wife has been in the home bringing up the children. It may not be applicable when the marriage has lasted

113

only a short time or where there are no children and she can go out to work.'

Yet, in practice, despite all this talk of 'starting point' in Lord Denning's judgment and in those of several other senior judges, at ground roots level in most cases a wife is usually entitled to a one-third share in the house or other family assets, a third of the joint earnings by way of weekly or monthly maintenance – *before* maintenance for the children is even considered. Nowadays, as we shall see in a moment, the Child Support Agency, functioning since April 1993, has revolutionised child maintenance so that there is less to go round for the couple themselves, though its effect on the 'one-third rule' is still not clear.

But, without the Child Support Agency complicating the issue, *Wachtel* v. *Wachtel* back in 1973 still supplies the best practical example of how the 'one-third rule' works:

Both the dentist and his wife were forty-seven and their marriage had lasted eighteen years. He earned £6,000 a year and she earned £750 a year, and their house was worth net about £20,000. So she got £6,000 as her share of the house, £1,500 a year as maintenance, and £300 a year as a 'reasonable' sum for their daughter. How was her £1,500 a year arrived at? Joint earnings of £6,000 + £750 = £6,750; one-third of that is £2,250; deduct her own £750 – and you are left with £1,500 to make up her income to the 'one-third of joint earnings' figure.

The concept of 'clean break' The expression was coined by Lord Scarman in 1979. He said that divorcing couples should be encouraged 'to put the past behind them and to begin a new life which is not overshadowed by the relationship which has broken down'. Five years later the 1984 Matrimonial and Family Proceedings Act gave a statutory basis to this noble idea. Indeed, it said that in every case a judge must consider whether it is possible: 'It shall be the duty of the court to consider whether so to exercise its powers that the financial obligations of each party towards the other will be terminated as soon as the court considers just and reasonable.'

A marvellous idea but how is it to be done? The theory is that, if there is sufficient capital available, the more wealthy of the two –

usually the husband – is ordered to make over the family home to his wife and pay her a substantial lump sum immediately and/or maintenance for only a limited period but sufficient to enable her to adjust 'without undue hardship' to life without any more regular payments coming in from her ex-husband. It would then be up to her to make her own financial arrangements in the future for herself and her young children.

This is superb – if the husband can afford it. But the courts have to be reasonable. You cannot get blood from a stone. As Mr Justice Waite said in 1988, there is no point in hounding 'a genuine struggler'. Men readers may be interested in the name of that case: *Ashley* v. *Blackman*, reported at (1988) 3 *Weekly Law Reports*, page 222.

The same principle works the other way round: if a marriage has lasted a long time and a wife is no longer young and has not worked for years or has limited future earning capacity, few judges are going to force her into a financial straitjacket as a sacrifice on the altar of 'clean break'. And here a good case for women readers to know is *Boylan* v. *Boylan*, reported at (1988) 18 *Family Law*, page 62:

The wife who got more than the husband offered

The marriage of a successful partner in a decorating business who had made his wife a director of the company finally ended in divorce. A consent order was made giving her the home and its contents together with maintenance of £1,800 a year. He later sold his share of the business for £1.2 million. All court orders for ancillary relief, whether orders made by consent, or after a courtroom battle, can always be varied if circumstances change, so she applied for an increase in her maintenance. He replied offering a 'clean break' on the basis that, in the changed circumstances, he should no longer pay her maintenance at all but give her a once-and-for-all lump sum payment of £40,000. She refused to accept this.

So what happened? Mrs Justice Booth said that, on the basis of this ex-husband's new finances, his ex-wife would be entitled to vastly increased maintenance of £16,000 a year. The court would not allow her to lose that entitlement unless the ex-husband paid her a lump sum sufficient to guarantee her an income at that new level. The sum of £40,000 was inadequate for that purpose. So there would be no 'clean break' and the ex-husband would henceforth have to pay her £16,000 a year.

One final point: clean breaks are limited to maintenance for a marriage partner only. As Lord Justice Ormrod said in *Pearce* v. *Pearce* in the Appeal Court in 1980, 'People who have children cannot succeed in making a clean break when their marriages are dissolved. Whether they like it or whether they do not, they continue to be fathers and mothers to the children. The relationship, such as it is, continues and so clean breaks are not possible in all cases, or indeed in many cases.' This has great relevance to present-day maintenance awards by the Child Support Agency, as we shall see later in this chapter.

2. Property on divorce

Many couples still believe that, if their home is in joint names, at least that will be safe from the potential carnage on divorce. The home may have to be sold but the proceeds of sale will at least be shared equally between them, after the mortgage and other expenses have been paid off.

But, in the words of the song, 'it ain't necessarily so'. It is an old principle of the law that 'equality is equity' and many property disputes end up in a fifty-fifty division, but there is absolutely no hard-and-fast rule. As Professor Stephen Cretney has written, 'The court now asks the question "To whom shall this be given?" rather than "To whom does this belong?" ' The 1973 Matrimonial Causes Act gives the courts extensive powers, on divorce, to make a property transfer order or a property adjustment order carving up the couple's legal interest in their family assets.

The family home may be in a man's sole name but he may be ordered to transfer it into both names. The home may be in joint names, with each party thinking they share it equally, but the court may make an order giving an ex-wife only a one-third share. An ex-wife may be given a half-share plus maintenance – and then sometimes the value of that maintenance may be offset against the half-share so that in practice she ends up receiving nearer one-third than one-half. It all depends on the facts of each case and how a judge applies the Section 25 guidelines we have already looked at to those specific facts.

As Lord Denning has said: 'The court takes the rights and obligations of the parties all together and puts the pieces into a mixed bag. Such pieces are the right to occupy the matrimonial home or have a share in it, the obligation to maintain the wife and children, and so forth. The court then takes out the pieces and hands them to the two parties – some to one party and some to the other – so that each can provide for the future with the pieces allotted to him or her. The court hands them out without paying any too nice regard to their legal or equitable rights but simply according to what is the fairest provision for the future, for mother and father and the children.'

There are three specific problems that can arise with regard to the family home:

(i) Before you get to the actual divorce stage one party can change the locks and try to force the other out of the house. This is a dangerous ploy and can easily backfire. Regardless of which spouse owns or rents the property, the 1983 Matrimonial Homes Act says that both parties have rights of occupation so long as the marriage lasts, right up to decree absolute. And, if one party evicts the other, the evicted party can go to court – if necessary, on a legal-aid emergency certificate – and the judge will order him/her to be allowed back into his/her home.

Furthermore, if the reason why one party, usually the wife, has left is because her husband has beaten her or the children or threatened physical violence to them, not only will he be ordered to let her back into the house but he will be ordered out of it! This is known as an ouster or exclusion order. A wife's income or property is disregarded and she will qualify for legal aid – if she is lucky enough to find a competent solicitor prepared to take her on at legal-aid rates.

(ii) If the home is in one party's sole name, he or she may sometimes try to sell it behind the other's back. This used to happen quite often but now there is a foolproof way to prevent it. At the slightest sign of marital discord, or in this cynical world as a sensible precaution long before it, the non-owning spouse, who is usually the wife, should ask a solicitor to register a Class F charge under the 1983 Matrimonial Homes Act at the Land Registry against the property. He will probably charge not less than £100 plus VAT but it will be money well spent. Nobody will be able to buy the property without respecting her rights of occupation and, if they want vacant possession, they will have to ask the husband to persuade her to move out or themselves give her a financial inducement to do so. In practical terms, it makes the property unsellable until and unless her interests have been protected.

The only circumstances in which a Class F charge is not effective is

117

when a building society (or other lender) wants to foreclose on a mortgage and repossess the property because of non-payment of instalments. Then she can be made to leave.

(iii) What will happen if, as in many lower- and middle-income divorces, there simply is not enough money available to provide a new home for the husband and a suitable home for the wife *and children*? Something has to give. If only limited resources are available, the judges accept that one party cannot exist on his or her full rights: at least not until after the children have completed their education and begun to build their own lives.

In February 1973, in the early days of the new divorce law, Lord Justice Davies conceived the idea of a 'Mesher Order', taking its name from *Mesher* v. *Mesher*, the name of the case. This says that the matrimonial home must be transferred into the couple's joint names (irrespective of who owned it before) *but* when the youngest child reaches seventeen or ceases full-time education, whichever occurs first, the property must be sold and the net proceeds divided (usually equally) between ex-husband and ex-wife.

Then there was something of a judicial rethink and it was realised that this can sometimes give children too decisive a role in the life of their mother. Is she to be forced to give up her home merely because her children have grown to a certain age?

Nowadays the Mesher Order is often replaced by the Martin Order, which takes its name from the case (*Martin* v. *Martin*) in which the Appeal Court first approved it. This specifies that an ex-wife is allowed to remain in the former matrimonial home not until the children have reached a certain age but until her death or remarriage or until she cohabits with another man for at least six months. Then at last the house is finally sold and the net proceeds of sale divided: not necessarily on a fifty-fifty basis. Quite often, depending on all the circumstances, an ex-husband may get only a 25 per cent share.

In this way, an ex-wife remains for all practical purposes the owner of the place (often having to take over the mortgage), while her ex-husband keeps a financial interest in the proceeds of an eventual sale, so that he is not entirely out of pocket on the deal.

With the best will in the world, property arrangements on divorce often boil down to horse-trading: with varying degrees of politeness.

3. Maintenance on divorce

This, so far as a wife is concerned, has already been covered in the preceding paragraphs about the Section 25 guidelines and 'the one-third rule'. But two other major questions remain:

(i) When does a maintenance order end? Unless it is a 'clean break' situation, when the judge will say that the order is to last only for a comparatively short time (usually no more than three years) to enable an ex-wife to adjust to her new financial reality, it continues for joint lives or until remarriage: i.e. until one of them dies or she remarries. Cohabitation with another man does not revoke the order. If an ex-husband can prove that he should pay less because his ex-wife's new man is wholly or partly supporting her, a judge can reduce the amount of the order but that is all. Cohabitation, unlike remarriage, has no automatic effect. A woman may be living with a man and still be receiving maintenance from her ex-husband.

(ii) What about a 'nominal order'? One often reads in the press that a judge has made a nominal order of 5p a year in favour of an ex-wife. It sounds strange: what is the point of it?

In fact, it is a vital 'last backstop' for her protection – or for that of a husband, if roles are reversed and it is she who has been ordered to maintain *him*. So long as a maintenance order is in existence, for however small a figure (it cannot be for less than 5p a year), the person in whose favour it was made can, if circumstances change and he or she has not remarried, come back to court and ask for maintenance to be reconsidered: however many years later that may be.

A good example is *Hepburn* v. *Hepburn*:

The wife who got a nominal order

After divorce there was a consent order giving an ex-wife maintenance of £6,500 a year. Some while later she began cohabiting with another man and lent him substantial sums of money. They seemed very happy together. Both she and her ex-husband then applied to vary the consent order: she to increase it and he to end it. A judge threw out both applications – but gave her a nominal order of 5p a year. The ex-husband appealed on the basis that it was time for a 'clean break' because it looked as if his ex-wife's cohabition with the other man was likely to last indefinitely.

But he lost. The Appeal Court ruled that the judge's approach had been correct in not equating cohabitation with marriage. A court should not put pressure on a former wife to regularise her position with her cohabitee so that he would assume a husband's obligations.

So much for the wife. What about maintenance for a child? There has been a revolution in the law, summed up in the three words Child Support Agency. That, plus the new look given to the law of custody by the 1989 Children Act, requires a chapter of its own.

But before we get that far, we need to look at the proposed changes in divorce law that are currently being considered by the Lord Chancellor in consultation with a wide range of professional and social organisations.

The proposed new divorce laws

The whole thrust of divorce law today is away from confrontation and towards greater use of conciliation. And so it came as no surprise when, in December 1993, Lord Mackay, the Lord Chancellor, unveiled proposals to move much further down this path. In a Government Green Paper, he proposed a radical reform of divorce law. Similar proposals had been suggested by the Law Commission three years earlier but speed and law reform seldom go hand in hand.

Under Lord Mackay's plan, irretrievable breakdown of marriage would remain the sole ground of divorce – but there would be no need to prove any of the old five 'facts' (adultery, desertion, unreasonable behaviour, etc.) required by existing law.

Instead all couples would have to wait twelve months for 'consideration and reflection' and, if they then still wanted to proceed, a court would almost certainly have to grant a decree. Those vital twelve months would begin with a mandatory hour-long interview at one of a network of centres where couples would be given information about legal procedures, marriage guidance and mediation. The intention would be to help identify marriages that were capable of being saved by making marriage-guidance facilities available where appropriate and to encourage couples who insisted on divorce to mediate rather than litigate their differences.

Lord Mackay declared that he was aiming to 'minimise bitterness and conflict between the parties and reduced the trauma for children'. That is a laudable ambition and many people will hope that eventually the proposals become law. But I would not count on it, and certainly not on it happening fast. There have already been protests that the proposals are at odds with the Government's stated commitment to 'family values' and the necessary period of consultation with all the interested bodies will be long and anxious before the Government is finally able to draft a Bill. That will then require many more months of no doubt heated debate in Parliament before finally, if at all, a new Act goes on the Statute Book.

For some considerable time to come, we are going to have to cope with divorce law as it still is today.

EIGHT

Children After Divorce and Relationship Breakdown

Children suffer whenever a marriage or relationship breaks down: it is inevitable. All that the law can realistically hope to do is provide a machinery whereby, if the parents cannot agree on the best solution in the circumstances, the wisdom and experience of a Bench of magistrates or (more often) that of a judge is available to minimise the damage.

That is why the 1989 Children Act, which came into effect on 14 October 1991, is so important. For the first time it created the concept of 'parental responsibility', defined as: 'all the rights, duties, powers and responsibilities and authority which by law a parent has in relation to the child and his property'. As we have seen in an earlier chapter, unmarried mothers and married parents enjoy parental responsibility automatically from their child's birth, while unmarried fathers may obtain it with the mother's consent or by an order of the court. In the old days, the court itself could take over responsibility for a child's upbringing when it was made 'a ward of court'. That procedure is still available but 'wardship proceedings', as they are called, are now much less common. The whole ethos of the Children Act is to encourage other close family members to take over responsibility for children rather than entrusting that to the courts themselves.[1] A court can, for instance, award parental responsibility to grandparents where a child is suffering through its own parents' neglect of their duties.

---

[1] This, of course, is apart from very extensive court powers to put children who are at risk from lack of parental control into the care of a local authority, but that is outside the scope of this book.

This power even extends to an unmarried father at loggerheads with the new husband of his ex-girlfriend, as in the 1993 case of:

The unmarried father v. his child's stepfather

The parents of a two-year-old child parted without ever having married each other. The mother eventually married someone else – and then refused to allow regular contact to continue between the father and his son because of her new husband's attitude. Although a consent order was made saying that the father was to see the boy every fortnight, the child's stepfather wrote to the father that the marriage was at risk because he was not happy with this continuing contact. The father then applied for parental responsibility and for contact, but a judge refused both applications.

The Appeal Court then made a judgment of Solomon. It ruled that the judge's refusal of contact was justifiable because the stepfather's continuing attitude would place the marriage – and the welfare of the child – at risk. But it awarded the father parental responsibility because he was 'entirely qualified' and the wife's marriage might break down anyway and it wanted the father's legal position to be preserved so that, if that happened, he could step in to safeguard his son's best interests.

Stepfathers and stepmothers are in a special legal category. They do not automatically assume shared parental responsibility when marrying the mother or father of a child. But they can specifically apply to the court for parental responsibility if they want to, although it will probably be refused if likely to create difficulties with the other parent which could rebound on the child.

Parental responsibility is a vague but essentially flexible notion. It endures until the child is eighteen and continues despite divorce or remarriage. But there is nothing to sign, no piece of paper stating what exactly your rights and duties are. Parents with shared responsibility do not have to consult with each other, although it would obviously be sensible to do so. Schools sometimes express nostalgia for the certainties of the old custody order when, for example, a father breezes in without notice to take a child out of school for the afternoon, airily citing his joint parental responsibility. But the flexibility also has its advantages, as when a mother does not have to obtain the father's consent before allowing their child to have an emergency operation.

But the value of the Children Act goes much further than the new notion of parental responsibility, however important that may be. Section 1 of the Act not only restated the widely approved basis of the old law: 'When a court determines any question with respect to a child, the child's welfare shall be the court's paramount consideration.' It went on to display a totally new attitude to the intervention of the courts.

For it proclaimed this fundamental new principle: 'A court shall not make an order unless it considers that doing so would be better for the child than making no order at all.'

It is not that the courts are now hearing fewer applications with regard to children: far from it. In February 1994, Mr Justice Wall adjourned the normal private hearing of a case in chambers into open court so that he could deliver a public rebuke to lawyers in general for giving unrealistic estimates of the time required to hear their cases with the result that many ran over time and inordinate delay was caused to others.

The courts are used at least as much nowadays as in previous years but, unknown to the general public and not commented upon in the press because all hearings are in private, their role has subtly changed: from *always* ending in a court order setting out parameters for the future to increasingly providing a catalyst for parents so that they can better sort out their problems for themselves. 'What on earth is the judge doing? He has deliberately put off a decision until late July,' a retired solicitor who was also an irate (and extremely involved) grandfather complained to me in March 1994, when a Family Division district judge in the High Court had deferred making a ruling for another four months on the solicitor's ex-daughter-in-law's application for contact with her five-year-old daughter, then living with her father who had gone back home to his parents after the divorce. I had gently to explain that nowadays, except in cases when they believe that a child is really at risk, judges tend to give parents as much chance as possible to find their own solution. I have to admit that he was not very impressed.

What he failed to appreciate is the new thrust to the law of children brought about by the Act and the considerable change in judicial thinking slowly building up in the last few years before it came into effect. As the Cambridge lecturer Andrew Bainham has written in his book *Children – The Modern Law*: 'Children law is still in its infancy but is fast coming of age.' I remember, in the Fifties, a judge (the late

Mr Justice Wallington) said that he would not give custody to a mother who had committed adultery because a woman who had shown that she was a bad wife could not be trusted to be a good mother. He was a prejudiced old commercial lawyer marooned by the nature of judicial appointments back in those days in the divorce court.

But it could not happen nowadays. From top to bottom, all courts that today hear child disputes are staffed by experts with specialist knowledge or experience. Family Division judges in the High Court, who were all family law practitioners when at the Bar, hear the most difficult or most sensitive cases; nominated family judges hear the every-day run of cases at county-court level sitting in local 'family hearing centres', and specially trained magistrates hear the lowest rung of cases at specialist magistrates' courts dubbed 'family proceedings courts'. Do not worry about which court to go to: apply at your 'ordinary' local county court or magistrates' court, and they will point you in the right direction.

People, even experienced journalists who should know better, still talk about 'custody', 'care and control' and 'access'. In fact, those terms ceased to exist on 14 October 1991, discarded because they seemed to imply that a child was some sort of possession or, at best, a kind of second-class citizen. Section 8 of the Children Act now provides this range of orders (when a court can be persuaded to make one!):

A *residence order* This is perhaps the nearest to the old custody or care-and-control order. It spells out where the child is to live. In most cases, it will be with one parent, usually the mother; and is only made after a court welfare officer has visited both prospective homes and talked to both parents and the child as well as, if necessary, grandparents and school teachers. This officer is crucially important, for the judge will usually – but not always – follow his or her recommendation and, if not, must give reasons.

Even so, do not misunderstand me: it is the judge's decision, which he will only come to after a long and anxious hearing in chambers with both parents (sometimes other interested parties as well) and the child giving evidence. The Children Act specifies that 'the ascertainable wishes and feelings of the child (in the light of the child's age and understanding)' must be taken into account. Normally only children of at least nine will be asked to attend chambers and they will not be questioned in front of everyone else: the judge will interview them in private.[2] A residence order, like all Section 8 orders, continues until the child is sixteen unless the court is satisfied that the circumstances of the cases are 'exceptional'; but in practice no court will make an order against the wishes of a child who is over about fourteen years of age.

Several of the old restrictive ideas have gone. It used to be presumed that it would always be best for a small child to stay with its mother, but in June 1990 (when the Children Act was already on the Statute Book but not yet in force) Lord Justice Butler-Sloss said in the Appeal Court: 'It may have been thought previously that young children and girls approaching puberty should be with their mothers and that older boys should be with their fathers. But that is not applicable any longer.

'Where there is a dispute, it is for the magistrates or the judge to decide which parent is better for the child: it cannot be "best" because the parents are not together. While it is natural for young children to be with their mothers, where there is a dispute it is but one consideration, not a presumption.' (For those interested, the name of the case is In re H (a Minor), reported in (1991) Family Court Reporter, page 155.)

Similarly, it used to be said that only in the most exceptional case would a 'joint care and control order', as it was called, be made allowing children to live part of the time with their divorced mother and the other part of the time with their father. As late as 1986 the Appeal Court ruled that such an order should not be made. But in A v. A (Children: Shared Residence Order) in February 1994 the Appeal Court ruled that, where there was 'positive benefit to the child' and the family atmosphere was harmonious with, as Lord Justice Butler-Sloss put it, 'no possibility of confusion in the child's mind as to where he would be at any particular time', such an order should be made. So two children in Newcastle-upon-Tyne were allowed to live with their mother most of the time but to stay with their father on alternate weekends from 10.00 a.m. on Saturday until 6.00 p.m. on Sunday and

---

[2] I once asked Mrs Justice Lane, at my client's request, not to ask a ten-year-old girl the specific question with whom did she want to live, her mother or her father, and received the magisterial (and justifiable) reply: 'Mr Bresler, do please credit me with *some* intelligence.'

half all school holidays including school half terms. This established an important precedent for the future.

Where parents are failing in their responsibilities to their children, grandparents may obtain a residence order even though a judge is not prepared to go so far as to give them a parental responsibility order. This is really a distinction without a difference as someone with a residence order has in practice much of the rights (and duties) of someone with a parental responsibility order. The same is true for step-parents who not infrequently are awarded shared residence with the child's parent, even though not qualifying for full-scale parental responsibility.

The new law is all about reality and helping the child to the uttermost, not labels.

A *contact order*   This really replaces the old 'access order' but is much more child-centred. It provides for the child to visit or stay with a named adult, whereas the old orders were the other way round: they allowed the named adult to 'have access to' the child. 'Access' only allowed visits or staying with someone. 'Contact' embraces all forms of contact: chats over the telephone, letters, school outings – whatever.

A *specific issue order*   This is entirely new, and is exactly what it says it is: a way for someone who has parental responsibility to come to court and get the answer to a specific issue – for example, which school the child should go to.

A *prohibited steps order*   This also is new and has the effect of restraining someone with parental responsibility from doing what he would otherwise be able to do. This is most often used to stop a child's surname being changed or to prevent the child from being taken abroad for any long period of time.

Pre-Children Act, the position was clear: a child's surname could not be changed without both parents' consent or the consent of the court, which was rarely given. As yet, no decision reached in chambers (therefore private and unreported) has filtered up to the Appeal Court where it can be reported in the law books and we all know for sure what the new law is. But, on general principles, the answer would seem to be that anyone with parental responsibility (usually, of course, a mother on remarriage) can change the child's surname without asking anyone's permission, but, if objection is taken *promptly* by the other parent, a prohibited steps order would be made. If there was a long delay and the child had become adjusted to the new surname, it would probably be refused.

As for taking a child abroad, if there is a residence order it will automatically allow the child to be taken abroad (for example, on holiday) for up to a month but, for longer than that, all parties with parental responsibility must technically give their consent: if refused, the opposing party may well apply for a prohibited steps order. Whether it would be granted would, of course, depend on all the circumstances. However, if there is no residence order, anyone with parental responsibility can usually take the child abroad for as long as they like without anyone else's permission.

If someone with parental responsibility wants to start a new life abroad and emigrate with the child (usually a mother who has remarried and wants to go and live with her new husband in his native country), anyone else with parental responsibility can oppose it by asking for a prohibited steps order. There have been no new cases reported in the Appeal Court but, on the basis of pre-Children Act decisions, the law is reasonably clear: courts will usually allow children to start a new life afresh with one parent, even though it will cause much heartache to the other parent and grandparents, if there is a real possibility that refusal would spark friction and bitterness within the new marriage which would, in itself, be detrimental to the happiness and welfare of the children.

On this basis, in 1986 the Appeal Court allowed two girls, aged eleven and ten, to be taken by a mother to live in New Zealand with their stepfather and two young half-brothers, despite their close continuing relationship with their father and his parents. Yet all these cases turn on their own facts: in 1989 the Appeal Court refused to allow a mother, living with her two young sons in a council house in Leeds, to start a new life with them in her parents' home in Australia because it would mean tearing them away from their father and their roots on the farm in Lincolnshire where they had grown up.

There is one factor we have missed out in all this: money. Who is going to support the child and how much is maintenance likely to be? This requires consideration of that other major new piece of legislation affecting children in the Nineties:

The 1991 Children Support Act

This created the **Child Support Agency** which started functioning on 5 April 1993 and has acquired the unenviable reputation of being the most unpopular Government measure apart from the poll tax and VAT on fuel.

Like the poll tax, it was the brainchild of Margaret Thatcher when Prime Minister, appalled by the increasing number of single-parent families and the financial burden they imposed on the State. (Of the 1.3 million single parents in Britain in 1991, nearly a million were on means-tested benefits, costing the taxpayer some £5 billion a year.) So, in a speech in January 1990, she bemoaned the fact that: 'Nearly four out of five lone mothers claiming Income Support receive no maintenance from the father.' A Government White Paper called 'Children Come First' (it should really have been entitled 'The Treasury Comes First') followed nine months later and then the Act itself setting up the Child Support Agency. Its proclaimed task was to take over from the courts their somewhat slapdash method of assessing children's maintenance on the basis of what was 'reasonable' and substituting a rigid system of assessing maintenance on the basis of a fixed formula and then collecting it from what was called 'the absent parent'. Nine times out of ten, this was expected to be the father; and that is how it has worked out.

The Agency was not to take over existing maintenance orders until April 1996; but all existing Income Support cases (whether or not the parents were married) and all new cases, Income Support or otherwise, were to be dealt with by the system – except where the parties were civilised enough or sensible enough to agree maintenance between themselves. Argue over maintenance for the children and you found yourself enmeshed in the system: that was the message. Recourse to the courts was no longer available, with or without legal aid. In future, maintenance assessment for children was to be largely a paperwork job, devoid of humanity or compassion.

It was mainly, at least in the first instance, designed as a cost-cutting exercise with an announced target of saving the taxpayer £530 million in the first year alone through clawing back money for the Treasury from 'absent parents' who were paying nothing at all or a mere pittance for their children's maintenance.[3] What was *not* announced at the time and only leaked out in January 1994, nine months after the Agency opened its doors, was that its 4,939 staff at six regional centres around the country were enjoying performance-related bonuses.

This was justice with a profit motive and it was not even doing those on Income Support a great deal of practical good. In December 1993, Alistair Birt, the Social Security Minister, had to admit in Parliament that, of the £530 million then expected to be clawed back from the absent parents of children whose mothers were on Income Support, only £50 million would actually go to the mothers: £480 million would go to the Treasury. And, as several stories in the press confirmed, if the amount clawed back 'floated' a mother off Income Support, all too often she was likely to lose out on other fringe benefits from the State, including housing benefit, council-tax benefit and free school meals, prescriptions and dental care.

It did not make a great deal of sense.

But what soon emerged was that, although the Agency's original aim was to target 'absent parents' whose children were on Income Support, many proved difficult to find (often the mother had no idea where the father was) and, even if they were found, no money could be clawed back from them, except perhaps a token £2-a-week, because they were unemployed or earning low wages or themselves on Income Support. The plain truth was that the State was trying to extract money from some of the poorest in society and, to say the least, it was not an overwhelming success.

So the Agency changed direction. Instead of going for the increasingly elusive target of the feckless or missing poor, it went for the easy 'soft touch' of middle-income husbands who were not feckless or missing but were *easily traceable*. In mid-September 1993, an internal memor-

---

[3] In fact, it did not reach this target. In May 1994, the Agency announced that, despite all its efforts, it had only managed to save the taxpayers £335 million.

andum leaked to the press revealed that Agency workers had been told to give top priority to 'good quality cases ... where the absent parent is already paying ... and is able to pay'.

Another memorandum, quoted in a *Times* leader, was even more explicit: 'The name of the game is maximising the maintenance yield. Don't waste a lot of time on non-profitable stuff.'

As part of the extensive publicity surrounding the opening of the Agency, it was claimed that average maintenance would only go up from £25 a week under the old court system to just over £48 a week per child. With the new easy target of middle-income husbands in their sights, that estimate soon proved laughably – or tragically – inaccurate. Middle-class husbands who were already paying towards the upkeep of their children were reassessed by the Agency and ordered to pay hugely increased amounts, often twice as much and sometimes three or four times higher than sums previously fixed by the courts. Second marriages were put under stress and some actually broke under the strain; at least one husband killed himself, others left the country and increased bankruptcies were forecast.

For her part, Ros Hepplewhite, then the Agency's chief executive, remained unrepentant. 'Many people were paying at quite unrealistic levels which in no way reflected what it costs to keep a family,' she said. 'Some absent parents are able to afford their current life style because to some extent their first family is being supported by other taxpayers.'

But how was this New Look possible? How could court orders be overruled in this seemingly cavalier way? What about the specific provision in the Child Support Act, and Regulations made under it, that existing cases were not to be touched until April 1996? And what about the 'clean break' concept we looked at in the last chapter and under which many existing court orders were made?

Let us get the 'clean break' query out of the way at once. Despite all the hot air in the press in the autumn of 1993 and beyond, it is invalid. Newspapers and magazines carried many distressing stories about husbands complaining that the court had imposed 'clean break' orders on them or that they had agreed 'clean break' consent orders that were now being broken. But that cannot be right. They had either been badly advised at the time of the orders or they had misunderstood that advice. As we have already seen, on page 116, most 'clean break' orders or settlements were never meant to extend to the children. As Lord Justice Ormrod said in 1980, 'Whether they like it or whether they do not, people continue to be fathers and mothers to their children', and their needs change as they get older.

What is perhaps more difficult to understand is how the Agency came to be dealing with these cases at all, and there the answer is simple. Human greed. Mothers, realising that they stood to collect more money from their ex-husbands by getting themselves into the new system, went to court to have their existing orders revoked and then they were 'new cases' so far as the Agency was concerned. How did so many mothers come to this realisation? They either had astute solicitors or perhaps helpful Agency staff suggested it to them.

In October 1993, Judge David Bryant, in a case at Teeside County Court, dubbed the practice 'inappropriate' and overruled the earlier revocation of a divorced woman's 1986 order. She had written to the Agency and received a reply from 'customer services' advising her that, if she revoked the order, she could apply for assessment. So she got her order revoked at Darlington County Court and the Agency promptly increased her ex-husband's maintenance for two of their three children from £123 a month to £473 a month. He was by then a health service executive earning £26,000 a year and living with a girlfriend and their own two children. He claimed the increase threatened the financial stability of his new home, and Judge Bryant agreed. 'It seems to me that an assessment from the Agency is not necessarily in the best interests of the children,' he said. 'It might produce a higher figure but it may be that other matters outweigh the purely financial.'

Many people might take the same attitude but, since only a ruling at county court level, it is not legally binding and to date (in December 1994) I can find no record of any other judge following Judge Bryant's example.

The rights of 'clean break' husbands have been further undermined by a High Court decision of Mrs Justice Booth in December 1993 when she refused to unscramble the four-year-old 'clean break' consent order of a divorced £9,390-a-year wood machinist. He had handed over to his ex-wife his share in their house in Carlisle, Cumbria, on the agreed basis that there would be nominal maintenance of only 5p a year for their son, then aged five, and that she would have full responsibility for maintaining him. Nevertheless the Agency had said he must pay maintenance of £29 a week, although he now lived with a new partner with whom he had two children. Mrs Justice Booth accepted that her ruling could be seen as 'harsh' and that the couple would never have reached their agreement if they had thought the husband would be required to pay maintenance – certainly not of the magnitude calculated by the new formula.

But she repeated what all family lawyers should know anyway (but do not always seem to have told their clients): that a couple are free to achieve a clean break between themselves but they cannot do so in respect of any child.

So what is wrong with the Agency's maintenance formula?

It is too rigid and too tightly drafted. Devised by the Treasury when John Major was Chancellor and Norman Lamont his Chief Secretary, it is written into the legislation and cuts out many factors that the courts used to take into account under the old, more flexible rules evolved by the judges.

It gives a father only his housing costs, plus £44 a week essential living expenses and half his pension contributions, before working out how much he should pay. If he has a new family, he is allowed at most £15.05 a week for a child of primary-school age. After that, 50p of every pound he earns is taken to meet the same basic charge for his children by a previous relationship, plus £44 a week to the mother plus £9.45 weekly towards family expenses. Once he meets the basic target, he must still carry on giving a quarter of his wages up to a fixed ceiling.

Using the Agency's own figures, a man earning £20,000 a year with rent or mortgage of £60 a week can expect to pay £105.43 a week for two children under eleven or £112.53 for two children aged eleven to fifteen; and a man with an income of £32,000 a year and rent or mortgage of £150 a week can expect to pay £140.62 a week or £147.72 for children of that same age.

It does not take into account school fees, holidays and debts; nor the cost of visiting his children or buying them presents or his help towards the upkeep of any stepchildren or the children of a new marriage or relationship. And, perhaps the meanest anomaly of all, only the mortgage on his own home is taken into account – not any mortgage he may still be paying for his old home so that his children and his ex-wife can go on living there.

Just before Christmas 1993, after months of pressure from campaigning groups and concerned MPs of all political parties, the Government reluctantly announced minor reforms in the formula. They are mainly matters of comparatively unimportant detail combined with a pious resolve to keep the system 'under review'. Since then Ros Hepplewhite has resigned as Chief Executive, the House of Commons Social Security Select Committee has reported scathingly on the functioning of the Agency, and the barrage of negative criticism has not abated.

However, no reforming Bill appeared in the Government's legislative programme for 1995, as outlined in the Queen's Speech, and, despite occasional reports in the press about possible forthcoming major changes in the formula, it looks as if the Agency will remain in substantially the same deeply unsatisfactory state for quite some time to come.

Is there anything you can do about it?

This is the question that you are bound to ask if you are a 'clean break' husband in an old case or facing hard-bargaining with your soon-to-be-ex-wife in a new case. The answer is: 'Not very much.'

There is an appeal procedure built into the system but it is unlikely to get you very far. You must first ask the Agency to review their initial assessment and, if that fails, you have the right of appeal to a local Child Support Tribunal with a legal chairman; but legal aid is not available. In any event, these new tribunals have limited powers: if the Agency has made a wrong assessment by basing its calculations on wrong data, a tribunal can send back the assessment with a recommendation that it be redone – but that is all. As Judge Thorpe, then President of the Independent Tribunal Service of which these tribunals form part, has admitted to the legal correspondent of *The Times*: 'We are essentially stuck with the formula. All we can say is that a certain factor was inconsistently addressed or calculated.'

With child maintenance nowadays, even more than before, the only sensible course, however bitter the breakdown of your marriage may have been, is to try to sort out things direct with the other parent. Mediation and compromise must, if at all possible, be the name of the game – for the benefit of all parties, adults as well as children. Useful people to contact, besides the Solicitors Family Law Association mentioned in the previous chapter, are:

One Parent Families at 255 Kentish Town Road, London NW5 2LX (Tel: 0171–267 1361); Families Need Fathers at 134 Curtain Street, London EC2A 3AR (0171–613 5060); National Association of Family Mediation and Conciliation Services at Shaftesbury Centre, Percy Street, Swindon, Wiltshire SN2 2AZ (01793–514055); Family Mediators Association at The Old House, Rectory Gardens, Henbury, Bristol BS10 7AQ (01272–500140 or 0181–954 6383); and Divorce Conciliation and Advisory Service at 38 Ebury Street, London SW1W 0LU (0171–730 2422). Also the Child Support Agency has its own telephone inquiry line on 01345–133133.

In the words of the old Swedish proverb, 'Children are certain sorrow but only uncertain joy.'

Part Two
YOU AND YOUR JOB

NINE

Basic Employment Law

Employment law has changed out of all recognition in recent years. It is the fastest-growing part of the law with which we will have to deal in this book. A splurge of legislation and case-made law that began in 1963 with the Contracts of Employment Act has continued unabated right up to the present time – and even beyond, with six new Health and Safety at Work Regulations due to come into full effect in 1996. In many respects, it has become almost too complicated for its own good. This is not because it confers too many rights on the nation's workforce, far from it; it is because its complexity means that it is difficult for workers and middle-management executives, whom it is primarily designed to protect, to understand it or even to know fully what their rights are.

Senior management and top executives have always enjoyed a strong bargaining position and are able to negotiate advantageous service agreements with generous built-in 'golden handshake' provisions, backed up if necessary by the financial clout to sue for breach of contract or wrongful dismissal if things go grievously wrong. They are not really in need of further help.

Ironically, the same is often true of the average worker at the opposite end of the income range if he or she is a member of a trade union or is fighting sexual discrimination, in which case the Equal Opportunities Commission is only too happy to provide expert legal assistance. Senior management, the unions, the Commission – and, on the employers' side, large corporations – all have easy access to the new breed of skilled (and often expensive) specialist employment lawyers.

But, as so often in Britain today (unlike other parts of the law, modern employment law is the same throughout the entire United

139

Kingdom), it is the man or woman in the middle, the middle-management executive *and* the middle-class small businessman (for he too has rights!) who are most in the dark and have to rely on their own resources for their protection.

Yet the modern law, for all its complexity, which I shall try to simplify as much as anyone can, is still a great deal better than what went before. Until the mid-Sixties, when employment law reform first came powerfully on to the political agenda, the law of master and servant (as it was then called) had changed little since Victorian times. The employer was – quite literally – the 'master', with the legal right to expect, and demand, that an employee turn up for work on time, put in a full working day, not take time off without proper authorisation and do his job conscientiously and to the best of his ability: if not, he could expect to be sacked without apology or compensation. The employer had virtually unbridled 'power of hiring and firing'.

Many people might think that, in some respects, those were the Good Old Days but, of course, the other side of the coin was not so appealing: an employee was, truly, a 'servant'. He had, in almost all circumstances, to do his master's bidding and accept his working conditions with very little redress to the law. His legal rights, if any, were only those given him by his contract of employment, which he usually had to accept on a take-it-or-leave-it basis and of which he did not even have the legal right to demand a written copy; and his personal safety at work was only protected, apart from specific Acts like the 1937 Factories Act, by the judge-made general principle, grounded in late-Victorian notions of social philanthropy, that, as Lord Herschell laid down in 1891, an employer must 'take reasonable care to provide proper appliances, to maintain them in a proper condition and so to carry on his operations as not to subject those employed by him to unnecessary risk'.

The process of change accelerated when Harold Wilson's first Labour Government came to power in October 1964, but it has been a bipartisan approach with varying degrees of support from successive Labour and Tory Governments. Alongside the traditional courts presided over by a judge in robes and steeped in legality, a whole new nationwide network of local 'industrial tribunals' has been created to which the employee can go to assert most of his or her new-found rights. These are staffed by a legally qualified chairman flanked by two lay members,

one from employers' organisations and the other from employees' organisations. These can overrule the legal chairman, and quite often do so.
However, the law comes more into its own on appeal to the Employment Appeal Tribunal (EAT) in London, where the two lay members
almost never overrule the legal president who, although never robed
and only called 'Sir' and not 'Your Lordship', is always a High Court
judge on secondment.[1]

This was originally supposed to be an area of the law where lawyers
were to be seldom used and intended to have little or no place. 'Industrial tribunals will be like industrial juries,' forecast one early pioneer
of the new system. It has not worked out like that. Legal aid is not
available and, even if you win, the tribunal will hardly ever order the
losing side to pay your costs, which is the general rule in the normal
courts. Nevertheless, many low-income employees usually obtain skilled
representation through their trade union or the government-funded
Equal Opportunities Commission in sex discrimination cases. It is the
middle-income employee or the small businessman who most often has
to try to argue his own case because he simply cannot afford a competent lawyer. For all the tribunals' deliberately low-profile atmosphere,
sitting in plain, almost austere rooms with no legal robes or ceremonial,
the middle-ranking employee – or small employer – arguing his own
case is undoubtedly at a disadvantage. In June 1993, *The Times* reported
that only 22 per cent of applicants are represented by lawyers and,
when they are not, their chances of winning are diminished. With
representation, the success rate is 49 per cent; without it, the success
rate, if opposed by lawyers, is down to 29 per cent.

Enough of preliminaries: what are employees' legal rights today? I do
not write specifically of employers' rights, whether those of large or
small businesses, because one cannot discuss employees' rights without
also touching upon employers' rights: the two are inextricably inter-
woven. Similarly, when writing about employees or the owners of small
businesses, I shall write 'he' for both sexes except when logic dictates
that I specify one sex rather than the other. This is nothing to do with

---

[1] There is a further right of appeal, with the leave of the EAT or the Appeal Court itself,
to the Appeal Court, which is, of course, solidly within the framework of the normal
court structure and from there in rare cases to the House of Lords, the highest court in
the land.

being politically incorrect (my natural impulse) or correct: it is merely a matter of convenience. The subject is complicated enough already without using more words than are absolutely essential.

So where shall we begin?

For a start, there are three different kinds of rights with which we are concerned:

(1) Those which an employee enjoys merely by virtue of being an employee, however short the period of time he may have been working for that particular employer;

(2) Those to which he is entitled only after working continuously for at least six months for the same firm; and

(3) Those to which he is entitled only after working continuously for at least two years for the same firm. (Please note that, with both the six months' and two years' time span, this does not mean that you must have held the same job for that period: merely that you have worked for the same employer during all that time, although you may have gone from one job to another.)

In the rest of this chapter, we shall deal with the first category: i.e. your rights merely by virtue of being an employee. In the next two chapters, we shall examine those for which you need to have worked for the same employer for a particular time.

So what are your rights simply because you are an employee?

(a) *A written statement of the main terms of your contract*

You are entitled to this, even though the contract may have been by word of mouth and nothing was said about putting it in writing at the time. The 1993 Trade Union Reform and Employment Rights Act (which re-enacted and strengthened two earlier Acts) says that, within two months, an employer must give every new employee working for at least eight hours a week 'written particulars' of certain specified details. The most important of these are pay and sick pay, holidays, hours of work, place of work, notice periods, date when the employment began, job title, disciplinary procedures, and, when the employment is not intended to be permanent, for how long it is expected to last.

A specific word is needed on *sick pay* and *notice periods*. Irrespective of what is said in the written particulars, every employee is entitled to *statutory sick pay* (to be phased out in favour of *incapacity benefit*, as from April 1995) when unable to work through illness. The figures are absolutely minimal but still better than nothing. The subject is excessively complicated, although a helpful free leaflet (NI 244) is available at all local Social Security offices.

In essence: to qualify, you must earn at least the lower earnings limit for National Insurance contributions – £58 a week, as from April 1995. It is paid when you are off sick for four or more days in a row – including weekends and bank holidays – and must be paid by your boss for up to twenty-eight weeks at a time, although he gets a refund from the State. After twenty-eight weeks, you normally become eligible for Invalidity Benefit.

Anyone with gross earnings of £58 to £199 a week is entitled to around £47.80 a week. Those earning more than £200 a week gross get around £52.50 a week. But no one should get too excited: neither statutory sick pay nor incapacity benefit is paid for the first three days of illness so you have to be off sick for four days before you even qualify for one day's pay!

Do you need a doctor's certificate before claiming? The position is much the same as with non-statutory sick pay when, as usually happens, the written particulars of your contract specify the circumstances in which your employer will continue to pay your wages while you are off sick. If an employee phones in sick and wants to be excused work for a few days because he is (allegedly) not feeling well, most employers will not ask for a doctor's certificate except when dealing with someone known to make a habit of it; but after a week they may well do so. With statutory sick pay, if the illness is for less than a week, most employers will accept a self-certificate: a form that you fill in yourself confirming that you are ill and specifying what you think is wrong with you: a bad cold, food poisoning or whatever.

Similarly, irrespective of what the written particulars may say about the notice period, the 1978 Employment Protection (Consolidation) Act gives you a statutory right to *minimum notice* when dismissed without any fault on your side. You are entitled to one week's notice if employed for at least a month, two weeks' notice if employed for at least two years and one additional week's notice for each further year of service up to a maximum of twelve weeks.

What about employers, if an employee suddenly walks out on *them* or only gives them a couple of days' notice? Especially with a small firm, that can sometimes cause major inconvenience. But, needless to say, there is no statutory minimum notice period to which an employer is entitled. According to Parliament, what is sauce for the goose is not sauce for the gander. Technically, the more robust rules of judge-made Common Law *do* give employers equal rights with employees to sue if their business is damaged or disrupted by staff walking out without adequate notice, and once many years ago in Marylebone County Court in London, on behalf of a client, I won £50 damages in exactly those circumstances: I am not sure whether my client ever got his money and it certainly cost him far more than that to bring his case but I remember him saying that he was well pleased 'as a matter of principle'. Nowadays, for similar stout-hearted employers, the small claims court would seem an ideal, inexpensive venue for just such an action.)

If you do not receive your written particulars within two months, you should write a polite letter asking for them (and keep a copy of your letter). If you still do not get them, you can apply to an industrial tribunal and your boss will be ordered to supply you with them. If you disagree with any specific term, you can ask a tribunal for a ruling. A good example dating back to 1976 is when written particulars gave a job title as 'Planner and associated duties' and a new employee thought it should have been 'Senior Planning Engineer': the tribunal gave a Solomon-like judgment that it was 'Planning Engineer'.

But do not go over the top on this. There is no point in running the risk of antagonising your boss unnecessarily. You are only entitled to details of the specific terms referred to in the 1993 Act. There may be many other important terms that a tribunal could rule at a later date may have to be implied, but this will not always be to your advantage. This happened in a 1992 case where the Appeal Court ruled that British Telecom had rightly withheld a branch manager's wages for four days when she had taken part in *unofficial* strike action: the appeal judges held that she had acted in breach of a term to be implied in any manager's contract that he would faithfully serve his employer and not wilfully disrupt his business.

There are two popular misconceptions about employment contracts that we ought to get out of the way at this early stage:

(i) *There is no minimum legal wage* There used to be but, outside farming, it no longer exists. Wages Councils used to set the legal minimum wage for many different industries but in 1993 the Government abolished the last survivors that fixed minimum rates for two million low-paid women throughout the country. Nowadays only a Wages Board for the agricultural industry remains. In every other sector of industry and commerce, the naked power of market forces, unrestricted by the law, prevails.

(ii) *There is no maximum working week* It has never existed in Britain. In November 1993, the European Union formally adopted a directive, which member states have three years to implement, imposing a maximum forty-eight-hour working week, four weeks' annual minimum holiday and an eight-hour limit on night work on all countries within the Union. David Hunt, then Employment Secretary, prompty called this an attempt to impose 'arbitrary legal limits on British working hours' and in March 1994 the Government applied to the European Court of Justice in Luxembourg for an order blocking implementation in this country. Cases before the Court usually take several years to crawl towards a final decision. So it is far too early to tell whether, or when, British employers will have to comply with this directive.

(b) *Physical safety in your job*

Modern judges have gone beyond Lord Herschell's already quoted cautious words in 1891 about an employer's legal duty to take reasonable care not to subject his employees to 'unnecessary risk'. Nowadays there is widely accepted case law that anyone injured in an accident at work can sue his employer for damages if the accident occurred through the employer's failure to take reasonable care for his safety and provide him with a safe system of work including safe equipment, plant and premises, adequate supervision and proper training where necessary.

And an employee is bound to get his money, however small the employers' financial resources may be. Few people realise that the 1969 Employees' Liability (Compulsory Insurance) Act says that *every* employer in Britain must insure against his liability for bodily injury or disease sustained by his employees in the course of their employment.

In addition, the 1974 Health & Safety at Work Act imposes a general duty on all employers 'to ensure, so far as is reasonably practicable, the health, safety and welfare at work of all their employees'. For years, this Act and two others (the 1961 Factories Act and the 1963 Offices, Shops and Railway Premises Act) imposed detailed health and safety standards at work. Now, prodded (as so often) by enlightened European Union directives, they have been upgraded and modernised by six new sets of Health and Safety at Work Regulations applying to almost all non-domestic workplaces, including factories, shops, hotels, offices, sports halls and theatres: home workers are exempt. The Regulations came into force on 1 January 1993 for all new workplaces but employers were given three years, until 1 January 1996, to bring existing workplaces into line with the onerous new requirements.

In the words of an editorial in the *Solicitors Journal* in January 1994, 'People spend more of their waking day at work than they do at home. A nine-to-five job in an office means that a minimum of thirty-five hours a week is spent in one location. Not at any other time in the week, except when you are asleep, do you spend so much time in one place.' Supported by an approved Code of Practice and by guidance issued by the Health and Safety Executive, these new laws are meant to ensure greatly enhanced and highly detailed new standards in the nation's workplaces. Anyone, whether employer or employee, wanting specific further information can write to the Health and Safety Executive Information Centre for a set of helpful free leaflets: the address is Broad Lane, Sheffield S3 7HQ, Tel: (01742) 892345, Fax: (01742) 892333.

There are three specific matters you may be particularly interested in:

(i) *Visual Display Units* Some seven million people in Britain work with VDU screens, while the number of machines in operation has more than doubled in the last nine years. Under the new regulations – specifically the Display Screen Equipment Regulations – employers are under a legal duty to protect 'habitual users' of VDUs from the health threat posed by their work. Screens must be glare-free with no flicker and have adjustable brightness and contrast. Firms must provide suitable office furniture, including specially designed chairs and matt-surface desks, and rooms must have adequate lighting and ventilation. Free spectacles must be provided for those specifically needing them for

VDUs (but not merely for normal reading) and 'regular' free eyesight tests, although no precise time scale is laid down. And the daily work routine must be broken up by breaks or changes of activity that do not involve the screen.

(ii) *Repetitive Strain Injury (RSI)*   If an employer is in breach of the Display Screen Equipment Regulations, once they are fully in force, it will be easier for an employee suffering from RSI caused by repetitive VDU keyboard use to claim compensation. But it can already be done. People should not be put off by the wide media publicity given to Judge John Prosser QC's ruling in the High Court in October 1993: 'RSI has no place in the medical dictionary', when throwing out a claim from a former Reuters subeditor that Reuters had caused his RSI through failing to provide advice on correct working posture when using his VDU keyboard or on the necessity to take regular breaks. Both before and after Prosser's decision, there have been several cases where RSI sufferers have recovered substantial compensation from their employers.

Less than two weeks earlier an electronics worker suffering from RSI won £20,000 and in May 1993 the National Communications Union secured an out-of-court settlement from British Telecom for eleven women RSI sufferers shortly before the Appeal Court was due to hear an appeal by BT from a county court judge's adverse ruling. Several unions, including the National Union of Journalists, now have many cases in the pipeline.

It is not only computer-users who are at risk. Less than three months after Prosser's ruling, a record out-of-court settlement of £79,000 was awarded in January 1994 to a former Inland Revenue typist who developed RSI after working for years on an electric typewriter for over seven hours a day with only a thirty-minute break. Mr Clive Brooke, General Secretary of the Inland Revenue Staff Federation, which had supported her claim and was said to be actively pursuing more than 150 other cases against the Inland Revenue, told a reporter: 'Judge Prosser was out of touch with the pain and reality of life with many workers suffering from RSI. There is a growing army of RSI sufferers.'

Nowadays they stand a reasonable chance of obtaining compensation from employers who are at fault.

147

(iii) *Smoking at work*   Some people cannot stand it, others cannot work – or live – without it: what does the law say? Increasingly it is coming down on the side of the non-smokers. In January 1993, a woman worker at Stockport Borough Council accepted an out-of-court settlement of £15,000 after claiming that she had developed chronic bronchitis as a direct result of working in a smoky atmosphere. Though the settlement did not set a legal precedent because it was resolved out of court, it increased the pressure building up on employers to implement and enforce smoking policies. As a matter of principle (there is as yet no decisive ruling by the Employment Appeal Tribunal), the policy can apply to either all or part of the premises, but they must always be 'reasonable' in all the circumstances. A ban should not be imposed overnight and should not favour one section of the company as against others: for example, it is not all right to say 'yes' to directors but 'no' to their secretaries.

(c) *Freedom from discrimination at work*

This is the fastest-growing part of this rapidly expanding section of the law. In 1992, the latest year for which there are official figures, the Equal Opportunities Commission (EOC) based in Manchester, Wales and Glasgow (Tels: 0161–833 9244, 0141–332 8018 and 0141–332 8018 respectively), which takes up cases of sex discrimination across the nation, received 47 per cent more complaints than in the year before. The London-based Commission for Racial Equality (Tel: 0171–828 7022), also Government-funded and with a similar brief to aid victims of racial discrimination, announced in February 1994 that it was to 'deploy staff in new ways and coordinate work more effectively with other agencies' in an attempt to step up the fight against ever-increasing racial discrimination at work.

The 1975 Sex Discrimination Act covers all forms of discrimination on the grounds of sex but claims over discrimination in the workplace are the most likely to succeed. Not only is there no qualifying period of employment before you can claim compensation: you can claim simply because you have *not* been employed. Whereas in all other cases there is no compensation for 'injury to feelings' but merely a hard-nosed assessment of what the employer's unlawful behaviour has cost you in material terms, in discrimination 'injury to feelings' is a factor in every case. And, whereas the limit in all other cases is £17,150 no matter how great your financial loss, there is no limit whatsoever with discrimination.

There used to be a limit of £11,000; but in August 1993 the European Court of Justice at Luxembourg, in a case brought (with EOC help) by a 62-year-old woman dietician in a Southampton hospital forcibly retired three years earlier than her male colleagues, ruled that a financial limit on sex discrimination claims by public employees was contrary to European Community law. Ministers could have responded by merely removing the ceiling for public employees but, as a junior Employment Minister said: 'The Government believes that all types of unlawful discrimination should be liable to the same penalties.' So the law was changed to remove all limits on claims for sex and race discrimination in both the public and private sector. Since then awards of several tens of thousands of pounds have become not infrequent. It can often be a profitable business being discriminated against at work.

'We don't want to see businesses going under because of sex discrimination cases,' an EOC lawyer told the press after an award of over £24,000 in March 1994. 'We want them to be taking it seriously in the first place and making sure that it doesn't happen. But, if they are going to discriminate, they now know that they will lose not just a good worker but they can lose £24,000 as well.'

Another point of view was expressed by a spokesman for the Institute of Directors, who said that such awards could put small firms out of business.

The essential – and laudable – principle of the 1975 Sex Discrimination Act, passed during the third Labour Government of Harold Wilson, is that no employee is to be treated at work in a different way from any other employee on account of his or her sex.

Except when one's sex is 'a genuine occupational qualification for the job' (such as when a man is wanted by a department store to play Father Christmas at Christmas-time), this applies throughout the whole gamut of employment activities. The Act applies to recruitment procedures, pay differentials, promotion or transfer prospects, holidays and time-off allowances: everything. It even applies to social engagements involved with one's work: I can point to no specific tribunal decision to prove my point but it is quite clear, on the basis of case law as it has evolved, that it is unlawful sex discrimination for an employer to perpetuate the practice of not allowing female staff to bring their husbands or boyfriends to the firm's Christmas party – so long as the same restriction is not also put on male staff's wives or girlfriends.[2]

It is also clearly in most cases unlawful sex discrimination to differentiate between married and single staff in terms, for instance, of promotion and transfer prospects, unless the same restrictions apply to staff of both sexes.

Job advertisements must also not be 'discriminatory'. The 1975 Act says: 'Use of a job description with a sexual connotation (such as waiter, salesgirl, postman or stewardess) shall be taken to indicate an intention to discriminate, unless the advertisement contains an indication to the contrary.'

That is why you see so many newspaper advertisements for 'male or female ground hostess', 'male or female chambermaid', 'waiter or waitress', 'male or female night porter', and the like. Ads with job descriptions that are sexless in that they use the bland unisex word 'person' abound: as I write, the London *Evening Standard* has an ad for a 'Person Friday'. Robinson Crusoe would turn in his grave! Employers sometimes have to resort to subterfuges to get what they want: if, for instance, the governors of a boys' school want to advertise for a male sports teacher, they might get away with saying 'rugger essential' because, after all, some girls play rugger – knowing that the applicants are more likely to be male.

Until very recent years, the whole thrust of the EOC's endeavours to encourage compliance with the Act was to protect women from sex discrimination at work. Men hardly came into it. But the recession has changed all that. A 'significant number' of the complaints received by the EOC in 1993 were from men claiming they had been unfairly turned down for jobs in favour of women. One successful claimant, helped by the EOC, told *The Times* in February 1994: 'There's no reason why clerical work should be regarded as women's work. But I think executives like to be surrounded by attractive young girls.'

But it is not only clerical staff. In November 1993, a retired admiral and former Surgeon-General to the Armed Forces withdrew his claim

---

[2] Mind you, staff-only Christmas parties also have their problems. Every spring there is a crop of sex discrimination cases with women complaining about unwanted sexual advances by drunken male bosses.

of sex discrimination against the Health Department and a local health care authority, after a woman, who he claimed had no previous medical experience, was preferred to him as chairman of a local county health-care trust. There was no formal admission of liability but he accepted an undisclosed amount in compensation, and the Health Department said it would review guidelines that called for women to lead such trusts.

Before we leave this chapter, there are two specific aspects of the problem that we should look at:

Equal pay   Despite significant advances, this has proved a bitter dis-appointment for many women. The 1970 Equal Pay Act of Harold Wilson's second Labour Government, coupled with his third Adminis-tration's 1975 Sex Discrimination Act, is supposed to guarantee women equal pay with men for 'like work', work of a broadly similar nature where any differences are not of 'practical importance', work of 'equal value' and work rated as equivalent under a 'job evaluation scheme'. That is the theory but it has proved impossible to achieve in practice on any universal basis.

The subject has become bogged down with entrenched opposition from many employers, including some of the major corporations, and by an appalling legal complexity made worse by protracted delays.

As David Pannick QC, an accepted expert in this field, told the Employment Lawyers' Association in London in November 1993, delays in resolving equal pay claims by women are 'a major scandal' and the procedures for dealing with such claims are 'slow, convoluted and full of opportunities for obstructive employers'. He cited a recent instance where the Employment Appeal Tribunal, in giving judgment on legal issues in a case that was already seven years old, estimated that a final answer was probably unlikely for another five years or more.

If you can persuade the EOC or your trade union to take up your case, you have a chance, provided you are prepared to be patient. If not, you may as well forget it or try to find another job.

Sexual harassment   For many women – and some men – this is a curse of their everyday working lives. It is not even good for employers: in the words of a 1992 study by the European Commission, 'It has a direct impact on the profitability of the enterprise . . . where employees' productivity is reduced by having to work in a climate in which an individual's integrity is not respected.'

In November 1991, the European Commission adopted a Code of Practice on sexual harassment at work which drew extensively on the EOC's experience of dealing with complaints in Britain. As the EOC has said in its latest Annual Report, 'It is largely due to our persistence that sexual harassment is now regarded so seriously by tribunals.' Helpful free booklets entitled *Sexual Harassment in the Workplace*, one for employers and the other for employees, are nowadays readily available at local job centres.

But what exactly *is* sexual harassment? Surprisingly there is no legal definition: neither the Employment Appeal Tribunal nor the Appeal Court has yet given us one. But, for practical purposes, you cannot beat what the European Code says: 'Unwanted conduct of a sexual nature or other conduct based on sex affecting the dignity of women and men at work, including unwelcome physical, verbal and non-verbal conduct'.

In France and Spain it is a criminal offence but not in this country. Even so, an employer who tolerates it, let alone encourages it, can rightly find himself paying out substantial sums by way of compensation. Here are some recent awards or out-of-court settlements: £7,182.50 to a twenty-two-year-old typist from Portland, Dorset, whose employer offered her £10,000 for sexual intercourse; £2,500 to a nineteen-year-old shopgirl in Leeds whose twenty-five-year-old manager pestered her to go out with him, asked her to strip off to attract customers and quizzed her about her underwear; £10,000 to a thirty-four-year-old married manageress of a dry-cleaning chain in Rochester, Kent, whose area manager told her that there was a 'special chemistry' between them and constantly pestered her for sex; and £10,000 to a female firefighter in Dorset who was subjected to childish and barbaric behaviour, such as when she was thrown on to the bonnet of a Land-Rover while a fireman stood between her legs pretending to have sex with her.

You can even claim compensation if sexually harassed at a recruitment interview for a job you did not accept, as in the case of a twenty-year-old student from Shoreham-by-Sea, West Sussex, who won an award of £1,710 in September 1993. She had turned down the offer of a summer job after her prospective employer had said she could have it if she had sexual intercourse with him twice a week.

Many women are loath to complain to senior management because they are scared they will lose their job, as undoubtedly does happen. But you have to stand up for yourself. 'You have to be brave to do this because it's such a sensitive and emotional thing,' said a twenty-five-year-old Rochester salesgirl who won a 'substantial' out-of-court settlement after being sacked for refusing to spend the weekend with her boss. There is also this practical consideration: if sacked because you complain or you leave because you simply cannot stand the pressure and resentment that your complaint has caused, that will only increase your compensation.

For instance, the thirty-four-year-old dry-cleaning manageress from Rochester whose boss spoke of their 'special chemistry' was told, when she complained to head office, that she had been made redundant and her allegations were unsubstantiated. Yet she won her £10,000 award, then only £1,000 under the limit, after only four months in the job.

One final note: in modern Britain, harassment does not come only from the opposite sex. In June 1990, a seventeen-year-old female cook made legal history as the first woman to win an award (£1,000) because of harassment by another woman: her middle-aged married supervisor in an Isle of Wight restaurant. Two years later, in June 1993, came the first man-to-man case when a 21-year-old male security guard was awarded £4,500 compensation after being sexually harassed by his supervisor, a 50-year-old married man, in the ultra-macho setting of a steel plant in Newport, Gwent.

But even today, when so many are ready to put a money value on everything and try to turn every misfortune in life into financial gain, there is a limit. Employers will be pleased to learn that staff still have to use their common sense. In February 1994, an Exeter industrial tribunal threw out as 'trivial' a case brought by a young packaging machinist. She complained that her middle-aged production manager, a married Northerner, had used traditional North Country terms of endearment such as 'darling', 'love' and 'sweetheart', and was constantly touching her arms and shoulders.

The tribunal accepted that such words were 'natural in the North of England', where people also tended to be much more tactile. 'I feel I have been branded a sex pest and I did nothing wrong,' said the production manager afterwards. 'It could happen to any man in a work situation. You are treading on eggshells. The accusations have changed my life. The tribunal was a nightmare. I will be a lot more cagey in future and save the words "sweetheart", "darling" and "love" for my wife.'

Rightly or wrongly, in today's climate that is good practical advice.

TEN

Maternity Rights

Few things in the law are simple but it is little short of a disgrace that the law on something so basic and important for so many working women as their rights when they have a baby should be quite as complicated or intricate as unfortunately they are. And, as if that were not bad enough, women in the UK have the worst maternity pay rights in Europe.

I suppose one should be thankful for small mercies. There were no minimum legal rights at all for pregnant working women until twenty years ago, when, on the same day in 1975, the Sex Discrimination Act and that year's Employment Act came into effect. Until then, unless a woman's contract of employment specifically gave her the right to take paid leave to have a baby and assured her of her job back afterwards, she had absolutely no legal redress if having her baby meant that she lost her job. Motherhood all too often came with a price tag.

Nowadays, often women's employment contracts spell out generous maternity rights but that is still not the norm. At least, the modern law – with four later Acts complicating the initial two (plus a European directive incorporated into British law in March 1994) – does give a certain minimum measure of protection to many (but still not all) working women. The trouble is that even one of our most distinguished judges admits that he does not always understand it!

In April 1982, Mr Justice Browne-Wilkinson, now a Law Lord but then presiding over the Employment Appeal Tribunal in London, said:

> These statutory procedures are of an inordinate complexity. We find
> that especially regrettable bearing in mind that they are regulating the

everyday rights of ordinary employers and employees. We feel no confidence that, even with the assistance of detailed arguments from skilled advocates, we have now correctly understood them: it is difficult to see how an ordinary employer or employee is expected to do so.

Where judges fear to tread, the rest of us can only follow on tiptoe. I regret that this chapter will not be fun reading, but do not blame me: blame the law-makers. Here is, I hope, a useful guide, which takes into account both the inadequately named 1993 Trade Union Reform and Employment Rights Act (whose fundamental changes to employment law are far more important and far-reaching than its effect on trade union law) and the 1992 European Pregnant Workers Directive, which was finally, and somewhat reluctantly, enacted into British law by new Government regulations in the summer of 1994. The law is stated, as of 16 October 1994, when both these major new pieces of legislation came into effect, and applies to every woman whose baby is due on or after that date:

1. Antenatal care

Any pregnant women – full-timer, part-timer, no matter how short a period she has worked for the same firm or how little she earns a week – is entitled to reasonable time off, with pay, to receive antenatal care which a Government spokesman said in the House of Lords during the 1993 Act's passage through Parliament includes relaxation classes and parentcraft class. But, of course, this is not specified in the Act itself! An employer can ask to see both a medical certificate confirming the pregnancy and a woman's appointments card.

2. No dismissal for pregnancy

This is a special form of unfair dismissal, which we shall examine in general in the next chapter; but the 1993 Act has strengthened its application to women sacked because they are 'pregnant or for any other reason connected with pregnancy or maternity leave' (which we shall discuss in a minute). This is now automatically unfair and she is entitled to compensation, irrespective of her length of service or hours

156

of work: unlike the earlier legislation where there was a qualifying period.

Furthermore, under the old law, contained in Section 60 of the 1978 Employment Protection (Consolidation) Act now rewritten by the 1993 Act, a pregnancy dismissal was deemed to be fair where a woman could not adequately do her job because of her pregnancy *and* her boss could offer her no suitable alternative work. Cynically put, she could safely be dismissed. Now she has to be suspended on full pay.

However, one good thing remains from before: the vital principle spelt out by Lord Griffiths, then a senior Law Lord, in the first Section 60 case to reach the House of Lords in 1988. It was in *Brown* v. *Stockton-on-Tees BC*, reported in (1988) 2 *All England Law Reports*, page 129.

His words are worth knowing:

> Section 60 must be seen as part of social legislation passed for the specific protection of women and to put them on an equal footing with men. I have no doubt that it is often a considerable inconvenience for an employer to have to make the necessary arrangements to keep a woman's job open for her whilst she is absent from work in order to have a baby, but this is a price that has to be paid as a part of the social and legal recognition of the equal status of women in the workplace.

So where a care supervisor on a Youth Training Scheme had been made redundant because she was pregnant and would soon be claiming maternity leave, the Lords overruled both the EAT and the Appeal Court and held that her redundancy also amounted to unfair dismissal – for which you get a higher rate of compensation than for redundancy alone.

The 1993 Act goes beyond even Lord Griffiths's trenchant statement and specifically says that a woman's newly enlarged protection against a pregnancy-related dismissal extends from the start of her pregnancy through to the end of her maternity leave, and even possibly four weeks beyond, if she produces a medical certificate that she is still not fit to return to work. Even though she does not ask for it, an employer has to provide a sacked pregnant woman with a written statement giving the reasons for her dismissal, however short a time she has worked for him, and, if not, he is liable to pay her two weeks extra pay. She is also given special protection against being unfairly made redundant while she is away on maternity leave and being victimised by being sacked on her return from it; and there is no exemption for small businesses no matter how hard they may be hit financially.

Because of the 1993 Act's extension of pregancy-dismissal rights to a wider category of working women, fewer will need to be thrown back on the alternative way of obtaining compensation: i.e. on the basis of sex discrimination. Back in 1985 the EAT ruled that, although a woman might not qualify for unfair dismissal under the old rules because (for instance) she had not worked for the same employer for long enough, her sacking could still count as sex discrimination – so long as she could show that a man employed by the same firm and, like her, temporarily unable to work through physical incapacity would not have been dismissed as she was.

In June 1993, for instance, the Equal Opportunities Commission (EOC) helped a project manager with GEC-Plessey, Britain's biggest electronic firm, to win a sex discrimination out-of-court settlement of £7,000 after she was fired when medically unable to return to work on the due date after having had her baby. The basis of the case was that a male employee taking sick leave after a sabbatical would allegedly not have been treated as harshly. An EOC lawyer commented afterwards that pregnancy-related complaints to the EOC had risen in the past five years from 289 to 1,088. 'We hope this settlement sends signals to employers that they must consider carefully how they treat pregnant employees,' she said. The 1993 Act strengthens the impact of this warning.

3. *Maternity leave*

Again, a pregnant working woman's entitlement to this has been substantially rewritten, enlarged – and made even more complicated – by the 1993 Trade Union Reform and Employment Rights Act.

There are now two kinds of maternity leave:

(i) *Fourteen weeks' maternity leave* Every pregnant working woman, irrespective of how long she has worked for the same employer, is entitled to this. If she wants to claim it, she must write to her employer at least twenty-one days before the start of her proposed leave telling him that she is pregnant and giving the expected week of childbirth. There is no mystique about this: an ordinary letter in ordinary language – beginning 'Dear Mr Smith', 'Dear Jim', 'Dear Susan' or whatever – will do, although it would be prudent to keep a copy. She must also give the date on which she would like to start her leave, but technically she only needs to put this in writing if asked to do so. Also, if her employer asks for it, she must supply a copy of her maternity certificate (form MAT B1), which her midwife or GP will give her. She does *not* need to say in her letter that she wants to come back to her existing job when her leave is over: that will be assumed, although, if she knows that she definitely will want to come back, there is no harm in saying so.

If she cannot give twenty-one days' written notice, perhaps because she suddenly has to go into hospital ahead of time, she must write her letter as soon as she reasonably can.

The choice of when she starts her leave is entirely up to her; an employer has no say in the matter. The only restriction is that it cannot start earlier than eleven weeks before the expected week of childbirth. A woman can even work right up to the week of childbirth, if she wants to. The only exception is that if she is off work for a pregnancy-related reason during the last six weeks of her pregnancy, she may find herself forced to start her leave ahead of time even if she was only off work for one day.

When her fourteen weeks are up, she is entitled to come back to work and does not need to claim that right in her original letter saying she wanted to take maternity leave. In fairness to her employer, however, who may have taken on substitute staff during her expected period of absence, if she wants to come back to work earlier she must give him written notice at least seven days beforehand. If not, he can send her away for seven days or until her leave was due to end, whichever date is earlier.

If her baby is born very late and her leave has already run out, she can extend it by two weeks from the actual date of birth; if there are any other complications, she should tell her employer to see if they can work out a satisfactory compromise. Bearing in mind the sex discrimination aspect, he would be a fool not to take a reasonable line. In case of trouble, she should consult her local Citizens Advice Bureau or trade union representative.

(ii) *Forty weeks' maternity leave* This used to be the only kind of maternity leave and, although still available, is of limited application. It applies only to women who have worked for the same employer for two years full-time (sixteen or more hours a week) or five years part-time (eight to sixteen hours a week) and not at all to women who work for less than eight hours a week.

Eligible women need to have a calendar in front of them. They can claim a total of up to eleven weeks' leave before the expected week of birth and up to twenty-nine weeks' leave after the birth; additionally, this latter period can be extended for a further four weeks on production of a doctor's certificate. As with fourteen weeks' maternity leave, it is the woman and not her employer who has the right to say when it shall start; but it cannot be earlier than eleven weeks before the expected week of childbirth. There is also a similar need for her to write to her boss at least twenty-one days before the proposed commencement date claiming her leave and, if asked, giving the starting date, but, unlike with the other written notice, she *must* specify that she will be wanting her job back afterwards. She should do this even if she is not yet sure that she really wants to return: this may be dishonest but it is essential to guarantee her legal right to come back if afterwards she decides to do so.

4. Maternity pay during maternity leave

Until most women actually begin to plan for their pregnancy, or even much later, they probably do not realise that State Maternity Pay is available for only less than half of a forty-week maternity leave – but for four weeks longer than the fourteen-week version. As Christine Gowridge, Director of the charity Maternity Alliance, has said, 'This is bound to confuse everyone. The Government has created a muddle.'

Anyway, during both kinds of maternity leave, a woman's contractual rights all continue, including holiday entitlement, pension rights, company car, etc. – except for her entitlement to wages! Unless her firm has a better scheme than the Government's, as many do, she is only entitled to be paid State Maternity Pay (SMP), and only for a maximum of eighteen weeks. This is ridiculous: she is not covered at all for the remaining twenty-two weeks of a forty-week leave, whereas if her leave is only fourteen weeks she loses the last four weeks of her entitlement. It makes precious little sense, on any basis.

But not every pregnant working woman is entitled even to this. SMP is restricted to women who have worked for the same employer for at least six months before the end of the fifteenth week before the baby is due – which is Civil Service jargon for at least forty-one weeks before the expected week of birth – *and* who earn more than the threshold weekly salary for National Insurance contributions of £58 a week, as from April 1995.[1]

How much is it? Under the new rules, a woman gets 90 per cent of her average pay for the first six weeks but for the remaining twelve weeks she is only entitled to a miserly £52.50 a week; and that is an increase on the previous rates! Some 285,000 working women every year are expected to get a boost from this pathetic increase. Most of the estimated extra cost of £55 million a year will come from the nation's employers, with no contribution from the Government. But 'small employers', defined as employers paying £20,000 or less annually in gross national contributions, will continue, as before, to be reimbursed by the State.

5. Coming back to work afterwards

Life moves on. Nothing stands still. Few employers, large or small, especially nowadays, can preserve their work patterns in embalming liquid. According to the 1978 Act, a woman is entitled, as of right, to return to her old job. But what is that job? The Act merely says that it is sufficient for her to be offered employment on 'terms and conditions not less favourable' than before. If not, she can claim reinstatement or compensation for unfair dismissal.

But often an employment contract only defines an employee's job in wide terms. So, unless the written job description is very specific, a woman will have to accept a similar job as long as the pay, hours, holidays and other terms are the same. If her job description, for example, is 'secretary' but not secretary to a named person or designated executive (e.g. 'sales manager'), she can insist on being taken back as

---

[1] Maternity Alliance calculates that 20 per cent of all pregnant working women are excluded from SMP by this National Insurance threshold requirement. In effect, the lowest paid women, who most need it, are denied the benefit of the scheme.

a secretary on the same 'terms and conditions' as before but not necessarily as secretary to that same person or designated executive.

This can cause problems: for instance, before taking maternity leave
a woman was a Grade 13 bookkeeper looking after the accounts of two
companies. When she came back from leave she was offered a post on
the same Grade but dealing with only one company, while her former
part-time assistant now dealt full-time with the other. An industrial
tribunal rejected her claim that she had, in effect, been unfairly dismissed because she was still a Grade 13 bookkeeper, albeit with reduced
responsibilities. But grading – and even pay – is not everything. When
an established C63 clerk in the Building Section of a local public
transport authority returned to work as supernumerary C63 clerk in the
Traffic Research and Development Section of the same authority,
another industrial tribunal ruled that she *had*, in effect, been unfairly
dismissed. It was not the same kind of job. She no longer had her own
desk, she was no longer getting a full day's work and there was a drop
in job security, supernumeraries being more at risk in the event of
redundancies.

On the other hand, if, while a woman is away having her baby, other
employees with the same job description receive a pay rise or their
terms of employment improve in some other way, she will automatically
be entitled to the same benefits when she returns.

There is, alas, yet one more complication. If it is not 'reasonably
practical' for a woman to return to her exact old job or one with the
same 'terms and conditions', one more Act (the 1980 Employment
Act) says that an employer can offer her a suitable *alternative* job which
she must accept. But this is not meant to be an easy option. When the
manageress of an exclusive shoes outlet in a luxury department store
was offered a job as sales assistant in the sports shoe department in the
same store on her return to work, she received £3,996 compensation.

The only exception is with small firms employing no more than five
people. If it is not 'reasonably practicable' for such a firm to give a
woman her old job back or even a suitable alternative, she will have
no legal remedy.

How is a woman to make sure of such rights as she has? With the
new fourteen-week maternity leave, there is no problem: it is automatic.
But with the old-style forty-week leave, it calls for even more paperwork. Once she has had her baby, she must finally make up her mind

whether she wants to return to work or not. If yes, she must give her employer at least twenty-one days' written notice of her intended return date. If she has not yet done this within seven weeks of the baby being born, he can write asking whether she still intends to return to work; and, if so, she must confirm back to him in writing that she wants to do so.

These 'written notices' are all perfectly ordinary letters just stating the essential facts: for instance, 'I intend coming back to work in my old job as secretary to Mr Smith from maternity leave in four weeks' time, on 4 November 1994' or whatever. But all these dates that I have given are absolutely vital:

The woman who lost her job – by two days

Back in 1980, a woman working for a telecommunications company expected to have her baby on 2 April. She notified the company in proper time and took her forty-week maternity leave. Unknown to the company, her baby was actually born eighteen days late, on 20 April. Twenty-nine weeks from that date expired on 8 November but twenty-nine weeks from her expected birth date expired on 27 October. As the law then stood, an employee had to give seven days' written notice of intention to return, not twenty-one as now.

But she made a mistake and only gave five days' notice on 22 October to return on the 27th. That was two days too few.

The company took advantage of those vital two days and rejected her right to return at all – and the Appeal Court ruled, with considerable reluctance, that they could legally do so. She had given inadequate notice and it was irrelevant that she would have had sufficient time to give the full seven days' notice if she had wanted to return on the last day she was entitled to, 8 November. She had chosen the earlier date and her notice was two days short: that was all there was to it.

The principle of this stern ruling still stands. It is unfortunate that, with all the subsequent tinkering with the law by Parliament in the intervening years, no time has been found to make failure to comply with the notice requirements for maternity leave less devastating in its effect. They are a snare for the unwary.

One final thought: What about paternity leave? Since 1982 the EOC has been calling without success for at least five days' statutory paternity leave for working men when their wife or partner has a baby. Britain remains one of the few European states that has no such State scheme. However, private schemes are on the increase: including such market leaders as Tesco, Gateway, Marks & Spencer, Littlewoods, Nissan and Ford, not to mention Rowntree, United Biscuits, the BBC, and Cable and Wireless. Yet, without any formal scheme, many businesses will allow a man a few days off when his wife or partner has a baby. It all depends on how reasonable everyone is.

ELEVEN

Redundancy and Unfair Dismissal

Losing your job is like a kick in the stomach. The pain is great and the trauma does not easily go away. In recent years too many people in the nation's workforce have been experiencing this particularly unpleasant body blow. It is bad enough for anyone, whatever his or her individual circumstances, but at least those at shop-floor level may be featherbedded to some extent by their trade union and the legal obligation upon employers whenever possible to consult with labour and keep it well informed of large-scale sacking.

But, for the executive at middle-management level and above, losing your job at the stage when it looks as if you were really starting to go places or perhaps had at last arrived can have a particularly cruel edge to it. For a middle manager in middle age, finding an equivalent job may prove virtually impossible or, at least, extremely difficult. His whole life style, and that of his family, may be destroyed overnight.

Some are lucky enough to have contracts that give them reasonable severance pay or even the proverbial 'golden handshake' of a large tax-free (up to the first £30,000) farewell gift.

But, if you are not one of those fortunate, what are your basic legal rights? The answer is, in general, much the same as with most of our modern employment law. Some protection from the chill blasts of economic reality is provided, there is a basic legal framework of remedies – but in many respects the law is unnecessarily complicated (as if grudgingly handed down by a reluctant Parliament successfully lobbied by Big Business interests, irrespective of which political party is actually in power), with the sums allowed by way of compensation sometimes grossly inadequate.

It is truly a legal minefield. The aim of this chapter is to provide a portable mine detector, helping to guide you along a perilous path.

There are two main aspects of the problem: redundancy, which can hit large numbers of people at the same time; and unfair dismissal, which more often occurs on an individual basis.

Redundancy

No sector of the business community is immune. Banks, supermarket chains and computer firms are just three new areas that have recently joined the more traditional victims such as the construction industry, shipbuilding, coalmining and aerospace, where redundancy has long been an occupational hazard.

The 1978 Employment Protection (Consolidation) Act, as at present enforced, says that anyone who has worked continuously for the same employer (although not necessarily in the same job) for more than eight hours a week for at least two years is entitled to a minimum lump-sum payment if he or she is made redundant. The same applies to claims for compensation for unfair dismissal. Until an epoch-making decision of the House of Lords in March 1994, this covered only full-time employees (i.e. those working more than sixteen hours a week): part-timers working only eight to sixteen hours a week had to wait three more years. But, in a case where a Hertfordshire woman had lost her redundancy claim after working as a part-time school cleaner for just under the requisite five years, five Law Lords ruled by a majority of four to one that, since 87 per cent of Britain's five million part-timers are women (i.e. almost a quarter of the total working population), the different time limits amounted to unlawful sex discrimination contrary to European Community Law and should be ignored.

(It was only in December 1994 that the Government implemented the House of Lords decision by laying before Parliament regulations (which came into effect in February 1995) putting part-timers and full-timers on the same basis for employment protection legislation. Yet during all that time the decision had *by itself* altered the law and, in effect, re-written the 1978 Act.

Almost totally unnoticed by the media, legal history of great importance was made: for the first time ever, a House of Lords ruling had something like the effect of a decision by the US Supreme Court in

Washington, DC, striking down parts of an Act as unconstitutional. Until now, their Legal Lordships were not supposed to have that power: they only ruled on whether an Act of Parliament was being correctly interpreted by the parties; they never took it upon themselves to decide that the Act was itself without legal validity. That had to be accepted without question as part of the concept of parliamentary sovereignty. Membership of the Common Market has altered all that. We live in jurisprudentially interesting times.)

Who cannot claim redundancy pay?

Apart from those who have worked for the same firm for at least two years since they were eighteen or who work less than eight hours a week, certain types of employee are specifically exempted from the State scheme:

(a) If you normally work outside Great Britain or are self-employed, a partner in a firm, a share fisherman, a merchant seaman, a Crown or public servant, a policeman, a member of the Armed Forces or a domestic servant working for a close relative (except a spouse);

(b) If you are sixty-five or older – unless there is an earlier 'normal retiring age' in your job, in which case that age applies;

(c) If you are on a fixed-term contract of at least two years and you have specifically waived your right to a redundancy payment in writing. **But** all other people employed on a fixed-term contract are covered if they have, in fact, worked for at least two years before the contract is not renewed. And it does not matter that you thought the contract might not be renewed when you first started the job.

The lecturer who won his case

An ex-teacher was given a one-year contract as a lecturer in a teacher-training college run by Nottinghamshire County Council. He realised that, because of Council policy, there would be a diminishing need for lecturers. In fact, his contract was renewed for a further year but at the end of that time he was told to go. The Appeal Court ruled that he was still entitled to redundancy pay.

(d) If – and this is *very* complicated! – you unreasonably refuse suitable alternative employment offered by your employer to follow on within four weeks of your old job ending or, having accepted a four-week trial period in the new job, you then unreasonably refuse to carry on with it, you will lose your rights to redundancy pay. But your employer or 'an associated employer' (e.g. another company in the same group) must offer you the new job: it is not enough for them to find an outsider prepared to take you on.

Furthermore, the standard of what is 'suitable' alternative employment is set by you, the employee, not by your employer:

The school cleaners case

Gloucester County Council unilaterally reduced its school cleaners' working hours. It offered them alternative employment at higher pay but for fewer hours. Two cleaners thought they could not get through their work to a satisfactory standard in that time and claimed they had been made redundant. An industrial tribunal said they had acted reasonably but, on appeal, the EAT ruled that it was not for the cleaners to set a satisfactory standard but their employers. The Appeal Court then overruled the EAT and upheld the claim.

The offer of the new job must specify the material facts: remuneration, status, job description and the like. It cannot just be airy-fairy. You are entitled to be told exactly what you are being offered.

Yet, even if you are not in an exempt category, merely because you have been made redundant does not necessarily mean you are entitled to redundancy pay. You must also prove that you were *dismissed* because of that redundancy. That may seem simple but it does not always work out like that.

Dismissal Whatever you do, do not 'dismiss' yourself. Hang in there, if at all possible. As far back as 1967, in the early days of the State redundancy scheme begun only two years earlier by the first Wilson Labour Government, Lord Parker, then Lord Chief Justice, ruled that a foreman in a fabric company, who, having been told he would 'shortly' be made redundant, found himself another job and handed in his notice, had effectively dismissed himself and was not entitled to redundancy pay. Lord Parker ruled that for a notice of impending redundancy to rank as 'dismissal' it must give a date of termination of the employment – or at least state facts from which that date can fairly be inferred. Simply to warn that redundancy is on the way is not dismissal.

But, even if an employer specifies a date, that does not mean you can safely leave before that date and still qualify for redundancy pay. When an engineer, faced with a three-month redundancy notice, resigned rather than work out his notice – seldom an easy thing to do – he was ruled to have dismissed himself and not be eligible for redundancy pay.

So the moral is clear: Do not jump the gun. Unless you really can find another job with sufficient salary and perquisites not to worry about redundancy pay, wait until you are unequivocally 'dismissed' and your employment is finally at an end. The 1978 Act says that you *can* give written notice that you are opting to leave early; but the procedure is complicated and your boss can serve a written counter-notice demanding that you work out your time and your redundancy pay may be reduced.

However, this is not to say that you cannot be 'constructively' dismissed. If your position has really been made impossible so that you cannot do your work properly and you are made forcefully aware of the fact that they are trying to 'squeeze you out', you need not wait until you feel your ribs are actually cracking beneath the pressure before you write (keeping a copy of the letter) to your immediate superior setting out the behaviour of which you complain and saying that it has been made impossible to continue with your duties. You should use some such phrase as: 'I consider, in the circumstances, that the firm has constructively dismissed me.' On no account should you write: 'I, therefore, resign.'

'Constructive dismissal' cases are often very difficult to argue on behalf of a claimant in both redundancy and unfair-dismissal situations – but it can be done. As witness the story of a man in his late fifties who had worked for the same firm of taxi operators for well over thirty years, rising to general manager. The firm was then taken over by a larger concern and, as so often happens, his face no longer fitted. He was told almost at once that he would keep his salary but would no longer be general manager or authorised to sign cheques – and would eventually be put in charge of a workshop at new premises.

He was a proud man. Claiming they had forced him out, he asked for redundancy pay – to be met by the answer that he was too sensitive and had sacked himself. But the National Industrial Relations Court, the EAT's precursor back in the mid-Seventies, ruled that, if after a takeover or merger the new regime offered a long-standing or senior employee an alternative post that involved a significant loss of status, that might amount to a repudiation of his contract of employment which he could rightly interpret as 'constructive dismissal'. It does not matter that the salary is unchanged. The law accepts that conscientious staff do not work for bread alone. As Sir Hugh (later Lord) Griffiths said: 'A change of status may be a change of such a nature as to show repudiation of the contract.'

But we still have not tackled the question:

What is the legal definition of redundancy?

Apart from stipulating that there must be a written redundancy notice, the 1978 Act gives no definition of this deceptively simple word. Section 81 of the Act merely trots out this mumbo-jumbo:

> An employee shall be taken to be dismissed by reason of redundancy if the dismissal is attributable wholly or mainly to:
>
> (a) the fact that his employer has ceased, or intends to cease, to carry on the business for which the employee was employed by him or has ceased, or intends to cease, to carry on that business in the place where the employee was so employed, or
>
> (b) the fact that the requirements of that business for employees to carry out work of a particular kind, or for employees to carry out work of a particular kind in the place where he was so employed, have ceased or diminished or are expected to cease or diminish.

The verbiage is appalling but the principle is reasonably clear: you are entitled to redundancy pay if, through no fault of your own, your job ceases to exist or changes so fundamentally that it is no longer your job as you have known it. In practice, this arises in four different types of situation:

(i) *All or part of your employer's business closes down*   It does not matter why: death, financial problems or physical disaster such as a major fire, the result is the same – redundancy. If part of a business – for example, one factory in a group – is shut down, the employees become redundant if suitable alternative employment cannot be found for them elsewhere in the group.

(ii) *The business is moved* If your contract contains a 'job mobility clause' saying that you will work wherever required, as often in the construction industry, you will not be 'redundant' at one workplace if asked to move to another: you agreed in advance to move with the job. But, if there is no job mobility clause, it becomes a question of degree in each case: for instance, two men were based at a fire-alarm firm's area office in Liverpool and were able to return home every night. Then work in the area declined and they were asked to move to Barrow-in-Furness 120 miles away. They refused and the Appeal Court ruled they had been made redundant: there was an implied term in their contract that they would work within daily travelling distance of their homes.

These cases are likely to be fewer in future because the 1993 Trade Union Reform and Employment Rights Act says that written particulars of all new contracts must contain a clause specifying where you are to work, so there will be less room for argument.

(iii) *The business is sold or taken over* Here the Common Market complicates the issue immensely. On top of the 1978 Act, three years later the Government had to enact the 1981 Transfer of Undertakings (Protection of Employment) Regulations because it was based on a European Community directive to which they were committed. As Gwyneth Pitt, Senior Law Lecturer at Leeds University, has commented: 'Unfortunately no one bothered to ensure that the Regulations made sense in the context of existing redundancy law. The result is two overlapping sets of provisions whose operation may be inconsistent.'

You will need to seek skilled help in any particular instance, but, as a general rule, there is a difference between where a business is transferred as a going concern (complete with stock, goodwill, existing contracts and customer contacts) and where only the assets are sold and the business does not continue as a going concern. In the first

171

case, there is no redundancy, as the contracts of the workforce pass to the new owners along with all the other existing contracts, but, if anyone is dismissed *solely* because of the transfer, he or she may be able to claim compensation for unfair dismissal.

Yet if only the assets are sold, regardless of any possible unfair dismissal situation, there usually is a redundancy and the normal rules apply.

(iv) *Your work is reduced* No business can stand still if it hopes to survive in these competitive times. Reorganisation, rationalisation and new working methods can all lead to a reduction in the number of staff required or in the need for the particular work done by any specific employee. This will all too often mean that people will be sacked. As we shall see in a minute, they may well have a good claim for unfair dismissal but have they been made redundant? Not necessarily. Reorganisation and all the rest only create a legal redundancy if the actual amount of work to be done by any particular employee is reduced. Merely changing the hours of work is not sufficient.

The two women police clerks

Back in 1973, two women police clerks in Nottinghamshire worked a five-day week, from 9.30 to 5.30 each day. Then the local police authority asked them to work two daily split shifts, six days a week, in alternate weeks. They claimed redundancy but Lord Denning ruled sternly: 'The change in the hours of work was not due to redundancy but to a reorganisation in the interests of efficiency. The same work was done by the ladies afterwards as before. But they did it at different hours.'

There are four other matters that have to be considered:

(i) *You are laid off or put on short time* This does not often happen at middle-management level but it may still be useful to know that if an employee has been laid off (i.e. told not to come to work and not been paid) or put on short-time working (i.e. been paid for only half a week's work or less) he may, in effect, declare himself redundant in writing to his boss and therefore become entitled to redundancy pay. The law is contained in Section 88 of the 1978 Act but it is, of course, devilishly complicated and you should really seek skilled advice before committing yourself.

(ii) *Time off to look for a job* Once you have been served with a redundancy notice, Section 31 of the 1978 Act says that your employer must give you 'reasonable' time off during paid working hours 'to look for new employment or to make arrangements for training for future employment'. How much time is 'reasonable'? It all depends on the circumstances: your needs have to be balanced against your employer's business demands. Technically, you can complain to an industrial tribunal if you think he is being unreasonable, but the most a tribunal can do is order him to pay you an extra two day's wages!

(iii) *Voluntary redundancy* It has become very common for employers to ask for voluntary redundancies to try to cut down the number of compulsory sackings, and it generally poses no legal difficulties. Even with enhanced severance payments, voluntary redundancy still counts as a dismissal, as the employee is taken to have volunteered to be dismissed – which is still not the same as volunteering to resign. But be careful about early retirement! That does not count as redundancy and you should ensure that the deal includes full recompense for giving up your job, for that is all you are going to get: in 1985, when a lecturer accepted an early retirement scheme from a university forced to make staff cuts, the Appeal Court ruled that he could not later also claim redundancy pay.

(iv) *Redundancy pay* It has two positive advantages: (1) it is usually tax-free and (2) it does not matter if you start another job the very next day, you are still entitled to your full money. *But* it is not calculated on a very generous basis. It depends on how old you are when sacked, your gross wages at that time (calculated on a weekly basis, even if you are paid monthly) and how long you have worked for the firm. Full details are readily available in the free Department of Employment booklet *Redundancy Payments* (PL 808 [REV 1]), one of a range of useful employment law pamphlets obtainable at local job centres and unemployment-benefit offices; but, in principle, if you are between 41 and 65, you should get one-and-a-half weeks' pay for each year of work, one week for each year if 22 to 41 and half a week's money if you are between 18 and 22.

Service below the age of eighteen does not count, although many people start work at sixteen, and, if you are made redundant after sixty-four (whether man or woman), you lose one-twelfth of the payment for every additional month up to your sixty-fifth birthday. So if you are sacked, say, when aged 64 years and 9 months, you will not lose three-quarters of your *total* redundancy pay (that would be ridiculous, even though some books state this!) but, as specifically confirmed to me by the Department of Employment, you will lose three-quarters of the compensation due *for that last year.*

But please note two other important restrictions, for which no one had been able to give me a satisfactory explanation: (i) you cannot claim redundancy pay for more than twenty years, even if you have worked for the same firm for much longer, and (ii) any weekly wage over £205 is disregarded, even if you have earned considerably more. The maximum redundancy pay possible, even if you have worked the full twenty years, is $20 \times 1.5 \times £205 = £6,150$. And that holds true whatever the individual circumstances or however much you have earned over the years.

An example of how the system works

A youth joins an engineering firm straight from school at sixteen. He works his way up the ladder until, twenty-two years later, at the age of thirty-eight, he is earning £500 a week as senior projects manager. He is then sacked as redundant. Although he has worked for the same firm for twenty-two years, he can only claim compensation for eighteen years – i.e. since he was himself eighteen. At thirty-eight, according to the official sliding scale, he should then be entitled to sixteen-and-a-half weeks' wages as redundancy pay. But this will not be calculated at the rate of $16.5 \times £500$, his actual wage, which would total £8,250, but only at the rate of $16.5 \times £205$, which totals less than half that amount: i.e. £3,382.50.

It is usually the employer, not the State, who pays. Most employers used to be able to reclaim half the amount from a state Redundancy Fund, but this rebate system was whittled down to apply only to firms with fewer than ten workers getting back 35 per cent of the money, until that too was abolished, by the Thatcher Government in 1989. Undoubtedly, many firms hand over the money without question and, indeed, it is an offence against the 1978 Act for an employer not to give a written statement showing how the payment is calculated. But, if redundancy pay is not volunteered, you can either write within six months to the firm asking for your money or take them to an industrial tribunal. (You should fill in form IT1, available at any job centre or unemployment-benefit office, and send it to the Secretary to the Tribunals, Central Office of the Industrial Tribunals (England and Wales), Southgate Street, Bury St Edmunds, Suffolk IP33 2AQ (Tel: 01264–762300), if you live in England or Wales, or to the Secretary of Tribunals at St Andrew House, 141 West Nile Street, Glasgow G1 2RY, if you live in Scotland. They will then allocate your case to a local tribunal.)

There is another way. Once you have asked your employer and a reasonable time has gone by without payment (perhaps because he has gone bust), Section 106 of the 1978 Act says you can write direct to the Department of Employment at Caxton House, Tothill Street, London SW1H 9NP. The Department will then pay you out of public funds, taking their chance on getting back the money, or some of it, from your ex-employer – or his remaining assets.

So far we have only been talking about *pure* redundancy and the maximum £6,150 compensation payable for it. But, if you have not merely been dismissed for redundancy but *unfairly* selected for that dismissal, you will qualify for the increased compensation payable in cases of unfair dismissal: i.e. a maximum £11,000 compensatory award as well as a basic £6,150 award. The age limits and other eligibility categories are much the same as for redundancy pay but, unlike redundancy, the compensatory award is not payable if you immediately get another job. Indeed, you are under a legal duty to 'mitigate your loss' by doing your best to get other employement. The award is intended to compensate you only for your actual loss or expense: pay, tax rebate, business 'perks' including free or subsidised meals, private health cover, pension benefits, company car, the cost of seeking alternative employment and so on. The basic award is essentially a mathematical calculation with a maximum of twenty years worked out on a similar basis to redundancy: i.e. at one-and-a-half weeks' gross pay for each year from the age of 41 to 65, one week's pay for each year between 22 and 41 and half a week's pay for each year between 18 and 22 (but not starting at 20, as with redundancy).

In fact, according to official figures released by the Employment Department in January 1994, the average awards made by industrial tribunals for redundancy and unfair dismissal come nowhere near these maximum amounts, but the average compensation for unfair dismissal still works out at much more than for 'pure' redundancy: i.e. £1,923 for unfair dismissal as against only £688 for redundancy. But you will not get two lots of compensation: your redundancy pay will be swallowed up in the unfair-dismissal award. Yet it is usually worthwhile, when filling up form IT1 and making your application to the Secretary to the Tribunals' office at Southgate or Glasgow, to put that you are claiming for 'unfair dismissal or redundancy or both' – leaving the industrial tribunal that eventually hears your case to decide what is the most appropriate award in your particular circumstances.

There is one other important difference between 'pure' redundancy and unfair dismissal, whether for redundancy or for any other cause, and this relates to *time limits*. As we have seen, you have six months in which to make a redundancy claim, but in the case of unfair dismissal you have only half that time. This three-month rule is strictly applied and will be extended only in exceptional cases, when a tribunal considers it was 'not reasonably practicable' for you to have applied earlier. This usually arises through receiving bad or inaccurate advice or because your application has been mislaid in the post. If bad advice is the cause, the legal position depends on who gave you the advice: if it came from your own lawyer or other outside person, such as a Citizens Advice Bureau worker or a trade union official, you will be stuck with it and unable to pursue your claim (although you may be able to sue the person responsible for negligence), but if it came from a clerk or someone else on the tribunal's own staff it will be overlooked and your claim allowed to continue.

As for claims sent by post, in 1985 the High Court ruled that, generally speaking in the law, when documents are sent by first-class post they are expected to arrive by the second working day after posting, but with second-class post it is the fourth working day. However, with unfair dismissal claims you can never be too careful, as this recent EAT decision shows:

The claim that took too long in the post

A woman shop assistant was dismissed on 5 February 1992. Her solicitor sent her claim to the Secretary of Tribunals at the Central Office on 25 March. On 27 July of that year, inquiries revealed that the application had not been received and the solicitor resubmitted it on 4 August. An industrial tribunal later ruled that, because that first application had been lost in the post, it had not been 'reasonably practicable' for the woman to have submitted her claim in time: i.e. by late April, within three months of 5 February. But the employers appealed – and won their case.

The EAT ruled that the tribunal had erred in accepting that there was nowadays a presumption that a posted letter (whether first- or second-class) would be delivered in time, or at all, without expressly considering whether reliance on that presumption was reasonable in the particular circumstances. In the present case, it would have been reasonable for the solicitor, not having heard anything from the authorities for some time, to have checked long before 27 July whether the first application had arrived. (The law report does not state whether the woman then sued her solicitor for negligence, but the ruling stands as a stern warning to us all not to trust blindly to the post.)

Unfair dismissal

There is no easy definition of unfair dismissal. As a past-President of the Employment Appeal Tribunal has said, 'Unfair dismissal is in no sense a commonplace expression capable of being understood by the man in the street ... in fact it is narrowly, and, to some extent, arbitrarily, defined.' An employer who has sacked a grievously incompetent or even dishonest employee may find himself paying unfair-dismissal compensation because he acted too fast or because of a technical failure in his dismissal procedure, while an honest, decent employee may be deprived of remedy because, through no fault of his own, he did not make his claim within three months or because he was too quick to give up his job under adverse pressure.

Justice is by no means guaranteed. As Judge Timothy Lawrence, the President of Industrial Tribunals for England and Wales, admitted to *The Times* in June 1993: 'The system has become increasingly legalistic.' Perhaps that was only to be expected: for the legal infrastructure for dealing with the whole concept of unfair dismissal was brought in hurriedly, by the new Tory Administration of Edward Heath in its 1971 Industrial Relations Act, to try to steal some of the clothes of the previous Labour Government's legal pro-worker policy; and it was then re-enacted by the next Labour Government, in its own 1978 Employment Protection (Consolidation) Act, without any concerted attempt to iron out many of the wrinkles that had by then already appeared. And it has remained substantially the same ever since.

In principle, the idea is that, if you have worked for the same employer for at least two years and can prove to an industrial tribunal that you have been 'dismissed' – and this means the same as we have already seen with redundancy (including the advisability of not resigning but obstinately remaining until you can claim 'constructive dismissal') – the employer must then satisfy an industrial tribunal that you were not dismissed 'unfairly'. If you have been dismissed because of your membership of a trade union or refusal to join a trade union, that counts as *automatically* unfair; but in all other cases an employer must prove that he had a 'fair' reason for dismissing you, which the 1978 Employment Protection (Consolidation) Act defines as a reason relating to one of these five categories:

(i) redundancy;

(ii) your capability;

(iii) your conduct;

(iv) a statutory restriction on your doing your job (e.g. a long-distance lorry driver who is banned from driving for a year); or

(v) 'some other substantial reason'.

But that is not all. An industrial tribunal must also be satisfied that your employer acted 'reasonably' in deciding to sack you *for that reason*. If he gets his reason wrong, he is in trouble. Furthermore, a sacked employee should always put his ex-boss on the spot by availing himself of his right, under Section 53 of the 1978 Act, to ask for a written statement of the reason for his dismissal. For his part, an employer should never treat such a request lightly, although too often this does happen. In fact, he should at once seek skilled legal advice, if he has not already done so, because the reason that he puts in his statement will tie his hands for ever after.

This imperative need for an employer to act 'reasonably', even when he has a fair reason for sacking someone, has proved the bugbear of the system, so far as many employers are concerned. For example, if an employee of mine ever told me to 'Fuck off!' I would sack him on the spot, whatever the circumstances. I just would not tolerate that sort of behaviour from anyone – let alone someone whose wages I paid. But I have to tell you that I am *not* a 'modern' employer. If that person had worked for me for at least two years, a tribunal would probably order me to pay him compensation for unfair dismissal.

Several EAT decisions have laid down that, when an employee uses bad language to his superior, he should not be sacked on the spot. Rather, the employer must be 'reasonable' and ask such questions as: Who was the person insulted? How senior was his status? Had such an incident occurred before? Was the employee given a chance to explain and apologise? Was he given a formal warning that repetition would lead to dismissal?

As Lord Bridge said in the House of Lords in 1988, when giving general guidance to employers: 'In the case of misconduct, the employer will normally not act reasonably unless he investigates the complaint of misconduct fully and fairly and hears whatever the employee wishes to say in his defence or in explanation.'

What, then, does this much overused word 'reasonable', so beloved of lawyers, mean in the context of modern industrial relations? Section 57 (3) of the 1978 Act tries to spell it out but only succeeds in getting lost in its own well-intentioned verbiage. For it says that reasonableness

> shall depend on whether in the circumstances (including the size and administrative resources of the employer's undertaking) he acted reasonably or unreasonably in treating it as a sufficient reason for dismissing the employee; and that question shall be determined in accordance with equity and the substantial merits of the case.

Originally employers had to prove positively that they had satisfied this test, but, in its 1980 Employment Act, the Thatcher Government tried to ease their burden by saying that the onus of proof with regard to reasonableness is neutral. This means that neither side has to prove its case one way or the other. The tribunal is left to form its own conclusions on the evidence – but they still tend to be far more gentle than many an old-fashioned type of employer.

In practice, nowadays the reasonableness test usually means that an employer must not have acted precipitately. He must, where appropriate, have consulted beforehand with his employee before sacking him or effectively have warned him that he must improve his performance and that time is running out or have followed a fair disciplinary procedure. As Mr Justice (now Lord) Browne-Wilkinson said, when EAT President, in 1983:

> In many, though not all, cases there is a band of reasonable responses to the employee's conduct within which one employer might reasonably take one view, another quite reasonably take another. The function of the industrial tribunal, as an industrial jury, is to determine whether, in the particular circumstances of each case, the decision to dismiss fell within the band of reasonable responses which a reasonable employer might have adopted. If the dismissal falls within that band, the dismissal is fair: if it falls outside the band, it is unfair.

Even if an industrial tribunal rules that an employer has 'reasonably' used a 'fair reason' for dismissal, that is still not an end of the matter. The employee will get full compensation only if the tribunal is satisfied that he has not been guilty of what is called in lawyers' jargon 'contributory fault', for Section 74 (6) of the 1978 Act states: 'Where the tribunal finds that the dismissal was to any extent caused or contributed to by any action of the complainant, it shall reduce the amount of the award by such proportion as it considers just and equitable.'

It is legally possible for a 'successful' applicant's award to be cut by 100 per cent because of his contributory fault; but tribunals are rarely so bold. Usually reductions of, at the most, a half or a third are made, as in January 1994 when a waiter at a north London restaurant, who was 'frequently insubordinate' to the restaurant's woman owner and literally threw coins at customers who left inadequate tips, won his case for unfair dismissal because the owner had not followed correct disciplinary procedures. He had his award cut by a third but she still had to pay out £900 to an employee who, as she told the tribunal, 'stole money from customers and was rude and abusive to everyone'.

For the sake of completeness, I should add that compensation is not the only available remedy for unfair dismissal. A tribunal can order that you be given your old job back on the same terms ('reinstatement') or re-employed but in a different job and on different terms ('re-engagement'). But these are only alternatives to compensation: you cannot be given both a cash award *and* reinstatement or re-engagement. In fact, they are very rarely ordered: there is generally too much bad feeling or tension in the workplace to make either a practical possibility.

So how does it all work out in practice? We need to look, in turn, at the five 'fair reasons' for dismissal laid down by the 1978 Act:

(i) *Redundancy* In this context, this word has an extra edge. It is not enough for you merely to be redundant. Your employer must also prove that he was fair in his selection of employees to be sacked. Selection criteria must be vigorously adhered to. A simple policy of 'last in, first out' is not always enough. There must be a comparative, objective analysis of all the relevant information before a decision is made.

But an employer must also, at least in theory, consult with his workforce. Many experts are of the view that lack of consultation is the single greatest source of trouble in this area. Because bigger companies often cannot afford to leak information about redundancies in advance, they sometimes ignore the need for consultation and dismiss without prior warning. Such behaviour will usually only be upheld by an industrial tribunal if it considers that the employer could reasonably have concluded, in the light of the situation as then known, that consultation would have been 'futile', to use Lord Bridge's expression, or 'would serve no useful purpose', as Lord Mackay, the Lord Chancellor, put it in the same 1988 case.

In 1993, the EAT ruled that it was fair when a foreman painter was dismissed as redundant after eighteen years' service even though his employers had not even thought about consultation. The objective reality was that they had waited until the last possible moment before sacking him but, owing to the recession, no further work came in.

(ii) *Your capability* You may be doing your very best but you are still not up to the demands of the job in these highly pressurised times:

what then? If your employer sacks you one year and 364 days after you started with him you will only be entitled to the notice payment provided in your contract of employment, but if you have clocked up the full two years you may well be able to claim compensation for unfair dismissal. This comes fully within the 'reasonableness' yardstick: an employer will generally be expected to do all he can to help employees. They should be given a chance to improve their performance and receive proper encouragement and training from management. They should also usually be sent at least one letter (of which an employer should, of course, keep a copy) clearly warning that they will lose their job if they do not improve their performance.

How long should they be given? It all depends on the individual circumstances. In one case, three months was held to be enough for a sales director who had been employed for two years; in another case, six months was appropriate for a works director who had been six years in the job. But five weeks' notice has been held insufficient for another works director with six years' service.

Particularly difficult, and sad, cases arise when sickness or ill health prevents employees doing their job well – or even at all. Of course, if the individual employment contract or a union house agreement specifies in detail what is to happen if illness strikes, everyone knows where he or she stands. Otherwise, there simply is no hard-and-fast rule as to when management is entitled to say: 'Enough is enough.'

The legal principle evolved by the courts, ever since a pioneering decision of Sir John (later Lord) Donaldson when he was sitting as President of the Industrial Relations Court in 1972, is that an employer can dismiss staff without fear of a claim for unfair dismissal if things have reached the stage where the employment contract has been so 'frustrated' by events that, through no fault of either party, the contractual obligation has become impossible or radically different from that foreseen by the contract.

Each case will turn on its own facts: How much longer is the employee expected to be away from his normal duties? How long has he already been off duty? What do his medical reports say? Can any suitable alternative job be found? and, if so, has it been offered and what was his reaction? and so on. You can really use your own common sense to find the answer.

Unfortunately everyone, including EAT judges and industrial tribunal chairmen, may well have a different idea of what is common sense. For instance, in 1977, Mr Justice Phillips, then EAT President in London and a kindly, wise man whom I remember well, said in a case where there was no prior discussion with an ailing borough surveyor before he was sacked: 'The employee has to be consulted and the matter discussed with him ... One thing is certain. If the employee is not consulted, an injustice may be done.' But three years later the EAT in Edinburgh ruled that, where a barman at a Shetland camp for North Sea oil riggers who had been ill with asthma for six months was told by telephone that both his own doctor and the firm's medical officer agreed that he was medically unfit to continue and this was followed up by a letter sacking him, that was *not* unfair dismissal. The President of the Scottish EAT ruled that, since it had been overwhelmingly proved that the barman had become medically unable to do his job, no consultation was necessary. 'The purpose of consultation is to establish the facts of the case, and, if it is clear that that purpose cannot be achieved, the need for a consultation diminishes or disappears.'

The fact is that neither party can demand anything. It is all a question of balance and of fairness to be worked out on the basis of the specific situation. Indeed, comparatively few disputes ever get as far as an industrial tribunal for the very reason that the general principles of law are so well settled. Sometimes an executive will feel the need to get professional advice and bring a solicitor into the negotiations, but usually the parties work things out satisfactorily for themselves.

(iii) *Your conduct*   This can range from insisting on keeping your office door closed (as in one recent case in east London), persistently coming back late or drunk from lunch, wearing clothes (or a hairstyle) to work that the boss considers inappropriate, and an unhelpful reluctance to work occasional overtime right through to downright dishonesty, bad language, violence or flagrant disobedience to orders. The basic yardstick in all these cases is whether the conduct adversely and unreasonably affects life at work and the efficiency of the work unit.

Fine lines are drawn. In one case, a married chargehand and a young girl worker were often seen fondling each other in their workshop and in the factory canteen. Gossip spread, they were both sacked – and a Bedford industrial tribunal rejected their claim of unfair dismissal. 'We take the view that this is the kind of misconduct for which there can be no explanation,' said the tribunal chairman. An important factor was that 'other girls were being embarrassed by misconduct on company premises'.

But in another 'love at work' case, a couple had done nothing to provoke the gossip – indeed, they had not even been having an affair. A Birmingham works superintendent had formed a one-sided infatuation for a woman clerk but she had done nothing to encourage him and it was his own secretary who had spread untrue stories about him. He lost his job and a local industrial tribunal ruled that he had been unfairly dismissed.

Human relations are very important in a work environment. 'A boss's relationship with his personal secretary must be one of complete confidence,' Mr Justice Bristow once said in the EAT. 'They must respect each other. They must treat each other with consideration. I suspect they must like each other.' So when a middle-aged woman secretary walked out on her boss after he had called her 'a bitch on Monday mornings', Bristow ruled that she had been constructively dismissed because their working relationship had been 'shattered' by that one ill-advised, intemperate remark and upheld her £3,756 award. Similarly when, during what the local industrial-tribunal chairman termed 'a trivial argument' between a turf accountant's woman cashier and her branch manager, he called her a 'bloody fat sod and a stupid stuck-up bitch' – and had once before sworn at her in front of customers – she was also held entitled to walk out and claim constructive dismissal.

Can you be told what to wear at work? Do male bank clerks have to wear ties? Can girl office workers be sent home if they turn up for work in trousers? Can you be told to 'get your hair cut'?

The efficient running of the work unit is still the main yardstick – but now there is another dimension: that of freedom and personal choice. A girl typist in a Midlands co-operative society office was rebuked by her boss for wearing trousers to work. To avoid trouble, she wore a skirt thereafter – until she had to go to a college training scheme in the afternoon and wore trousers to the office in the morning. Result: she was handed a letter saying she was 'redundant'. But she was awarded compensation for unfair dismissal: the chairman of the local industrial tribunal said that her departmental head had 'antiquated ideas on dress'. Similarly, a Suffolk industrial tribunal has ruled that a local engineering firm's sixty-year tradition of 'neatness, tidiness and smartness' was not broken by a fitter's refusal to obey his managing director's ultimatum to shave off his beard or be sacked.

And in July 1992 a computer engineering firm in Slough was ordered to pay £4,351 to an engineer who had lost his £32,000-a-year job because he refused to cut his twelve-inch-long hair. 'I would have tied my hair in a ponytail if it meant keeping my job, but the option was not offered me,' he told a central London tribunal. He fought the case himself and afterwards urged others to follow suit: 'There are a lot of closet long-haired people out there just waiting to pop out,' he told a reporter. 'They should stand up and be counted.'

If you are sure of your ground, that is good advice: industrial tribunals seldom order unsuccessful redundancy or unfair-dismissal applicants to pay their winning ex-employer's legal costs. So, if you genuinely think you have a worthwhile case and have the courage to go it alone, you are at little financial risk – and your ex-employer could well be advised by his solicitor that it is worth his while to offer you a reasonable out-of-court settlement to buy you off. Cynical but true! *Industrial tribunal procedure* (ITL 1) and *Unfairly dismissed?* (PL 712 [REV 8]) are two excellent free Employment Department pamphlets available at job centres and unemployment-benefit offices.

The other side of the coin is that every employer, no matter how small the firm, should, in sheer prudence, have his own set procedures for dealing with these matters: even if it is only something so basic within a very small firm as the boss calling in the person to see him, perhaps offering to let him bring someone with him and then listening patiently to all that he has to say. The Advisory Conciliation and Arbitration Service (ACAS), an independent official body charged with promoting the improvement of industrial relations, revised in 1993 its Code of Practice for Disciplinary Practice and Procedures in Employment.[1] In industrial-relations terms, this is rather like the Highway Code for drivers: it is not illegal to fail to observe the Code but

---

[1] At the same time ACAS also revised its Codes of Practice for Disclosure of Information for Collective Bargaining and Time Off Work for Trade Union Activities, but these are outside the scope of this book.

an employer who does so will find himself in trouble when facing a claim for unfair dismissal.

It is, in fact, one of the fundamental documents of modern employment law and all commentators emphasise its importance. The problem is that they usually do not bother to tell you how to obtain a copy, and it took me several phone calls to ACAS and the Department of Employment before a helpful ACAS official told me that the Code is available for 75p at branches of Her Majesty's Stationery Office (HMSO), whose local address you will find in most phone books. He also said that ACAS has issued an advisory handbook called *Discipline at Work*, which contains the Code as an appendix, and is available at a cost of £1.50, plus £1.00 packing and postage, from ACAS Reader Ltd., PO Box 404, Leicester LE4 9ZZ (Tel: 01533–463346).

The Code is too detailed to go into here, but, whether employer or employee, if this problem really affects you it is worthwhile investing 75p for the Code alone or, even better, £2.50 for the advisory handbook.

(iv) *A statutory restriction on doing your job*   The most obvious example is where a chauffeur or long-distance lorry driver is disqualified from driving for a year or more for a serious motoring offence – or for only six months under the 'totting up' procedure for minor offences. But, even with this seemingly straightforward category, reasonableness is all. An industrial tribunal would want to know the answer to such questions as: How long is the ban? Could a temporary replacement have been found? Could the banned driver have been offered another job in the meantime? and so on.

(v) *'Some other substantial reason'*   This is a catch-all provision. The courts have deliberately left vague this phrase in the 1978 Act. It means almost whatever you – or, rather, an industrial tribunal – want it to mean, but, in practice, it has worked out to favour employers far more than employees. So it has been used to make fair the dismissal of a female employee who had upset her male colleagues by frequently boasting of her sexual exploits with a younger man; an employee in an old people's home whose behaviour, though not deliberately offensive, had upset the elderly residents; and an office worker sacked for refusing

186

to do reasonable voluntary overtime because a tribunal ruled that the needs of the business required that the overtime be worked.

This is also the heading under which sacking because of reorganisation and modernisation has been held fair. As Lord Denning said in 1977, in a case involving a local county secretary employed by the National Farmers' Union, 'It is important that nothing should be done to impair the ability of employers to reorganise their workforce and their terms and conditions of work so as to improve efficiency.' But the overall need for reasonableness remains, and this may sometimes call for prior consultation or the offer of a suitable alternative job – even at a lesser salary. So, for instance, a bed upholsterer working for a firm going through a period of economic difficulty was held not to have been unfairly dismissed when he refused an offer of a new job doing much the same work at a lesser rate and all the other upholsterers (and their union) had accepted a similar proposal.

The actual framework of the law undoubtedly has its shortcomings and the old idea of an industrial tribunal as an 'industrial jury' dispensing informal common-sense justice has long been exposed as a myth. But I would like to end this section of the book with these words from a judgment of Mr Justice Bristow in 1982. It sets the tone of modern employment law at its best, although I am far from saying that it always reaches this standard:

'[The law] is concerned only with the reasonableness of what you do, not how you do it. But very often the way in which you do something affects or may affect the question "Was it reasonable for you to do it at all?" If you dismiss a senior employee or one of long standing at a moment's notice with no consultation whatsoever, you are not simply treating him with discourtesy: you are depriving yourself of the opportunity to explore with him the possibility of finding another slot in which to place him and leaving yourself open to the accusation of having acted unreasonably.'

Part Three
YOUR HOME

TWELVE

Neighbours, Visitors and Pets

Neighbours

The average Englishman or woman is traditionally viewed as being a reasonable sort of person. 'Live and let live' is supposed to be their motto. They are thought to be always ready to see the other person's point of view.

This may generally be perfectly true. But frequently it does not seem to apply when they are living next door to each other. As G. K. Chesterton wrote more than seventy years ago, 'Your next-door neighbour is not a man; he is an environment. He is the barking of a dog; he is the noise of a pianola; he is a dispute about a party wall; he is drains that are worse than yours or roses that are better than yours.'

The Law Reports – and daily newspapers – abound with tales of the most unseemly battles between neighbours. Noise, smoke, smell, fumes, leaking drains, late-night parties, Do-it-Yourself disasters, vibrations from nearby factories and workshops, broken-down fences and hedges, overhanging branches of trees, disputes about dustbins and parking space, marauding pets, windows shattered by cricket balls: all these, and much more, have led to court cases between warring neighbours. And when I say warring, I mean warring.

In one case, a man could not stand the noise when the music teacher next door gave piano lessons. So he banged on trays and whistled and shrieked whenever lessons were being given. Result: a High Court judge granted an injunction ordering him to stop and ruled he must pay damages as well.

In another case, a woman living in a maisonette complained that her life had been made 'absolutely intolerable' by the hammering, stamping and jumping on the floor above. The people upstairs retorted that she banged on her ceiling, interfered with their part of the garden and had once stuffed a deed mouse through their letter box. *Both* were ordered to stop causing what is technically called 'an actionable nuisance' to each other.

The second case is very recent; the first was well over ninety years ago. Human nature has not changed very much.

The Common Law, that part of our law which is made up by the decisions of our judges over the years, has always insisted that reasonableness must be the keynote of the law of neighbours. The Victorian judge Vice-Chancellor Knight Bruce may sound pompous (and prematurely anti-Common Market) to modern ears. But what he said in 1851, in the case of *Walter* v. *Selfe*, is still – perhaps incredibly – the current legal position:

> Ought this inconvenience to be considered in fact as more than fanciful, more than one of mere delicacy or fastidiousness, as an inconvenience materially interfering with the ordinary comfort physically of human existence, not merely according to elegant or dainty modes and habits of living, but according to plain and sober and simple notions among the English people?

In April 1994, the defence lawyer used this very quotation in his final speech to the magistrates at Wetherby, West Yorkshire, to help obtain the acquittal of an aviary owner in a nearby village cleared of causing a nuisance after a neighbouring couple had bitterly complained about the 'incessant' chirruping from his forty budgerigars. The hearing lasted for seven days, was reported in all the daily newspapers and cost Leeds Council, which had taken up the neighbours' case, an estimated £100,000 in legal costs.

The application of Knight Bruce's venerable principle varies from locality to locality. As a later Victorian judge said in 1879 (but still quoted in all the law books): 'What would be a nuisance in Belgrave Square would not necessarily be so in Bermondsey.' Similarly, in 1935 an Appeal Court judge laid down: 'A reasonable person would not expect precisely as much light in Mayfair as he would get in the country and he would not expect precisely so much light in the City of London as he would get in Mayfair.'

It follows that people living in the country can expect different standards from those living in London or other large cities. In July 1992, for instance, Judge Deirdre McKinney overruled at Bournemouth Crown Court an earlier order by magistrates in Wimborne, Dorset, ordering Mr Dereck Orman, a local smallholder, to dispose of a stag turkey called Bernard and four cockerels. His family had kept poultry on the smallholding since the turn of the century without any complaints, but when a couple retired from London to a nearby bungalow they soon found the noise too much. The local magistrates agreed but, on appeal, their counsel successfully quoted to Judge McKinney this extract from a leading article in the *Daily Telegraph*: 'The appropriate noises of nature should be left alone. If Mr Orman had blasted his new neighbours with loud pop music over the garden fence, then it would be easier to feel some sympathy for their case. If people living in the country object to its immemorial sounds, they should retreat to the man-made cacophony of city life.'

Judge McKinney's ruling confirmed that was the attitude of the law. Crowing cockerels, barking dogs, smells from drains, cesspits and pig farms are typical countryside 'problems' which neighbours usually have to put up with. Country-dwellers often keep several cockerels or dogs on the premises and 'country smells' are a fact of rural life.

But there is a limit. In one country case, cockerels who sounded like 'a football crowd cheering a Cup-tie' were ruled to be a nuisance, and when, back in November 1968, three neighbours in deepest Berkshire joined forces to sue over the noise from over ninety dogs in newly opened training kennels for greyhounds, Mr Justice Hinchcliffe came down at 8.00 a.m. from the High Court in London to hear for himself the barking chorus. Later, back in court, he ruled with some feeling: 'When country dwellers are unable to open a window or to enjoy working, resting or pottering about in the garden, when the barking of dogs can be heard above the sound of a washing machine, when rest is interfered with and one has to leave for peace and quiet – then a substantial nuisance has been caused.' He awarded the plaintiffs an injunction and damages.

Yet there is a delicate balance to all this. The mere fact that any particular activity has been going on for years before someone comes to an area does not, *in itself*, prevent a newcomer from complaining of an 'actionable nuisance' if it is objectively unacceptable. That was first decided by the Appeal Court in 1879 and in May 1994 there was an interesting modern example at Slough County Court:

The case of the village cricket club

A couple came to live in a house overlooking a Buckinghamshire village green where cricket had been played at weekends for the past seventy years. Soon cricket balls were being hit into their garden and the couple found it most unpleasant. They asked the village cricket club to put up two huge 25-feet-high nets as protection but the club claimed it did not have the money and the nets would be an eyesore. Negotiations broke down and the couple sued for an injunction preventing the club from continuing to play any more cricket without the two nets.

They lost their case. Judge Nigel Hague said: 'An injunction would deprive many people of the pleasure they obtain from watching cricket and the focus of social life. The mere fact that cricket balls sometimes penetrate and even fly into the grounds of nearby houses does not mean that the playing of cricket is an actionable nuisance.'

It might have been different if someone had actually been hit by a cricket ball or the house itself damaged in some way with windows broken or roof tiles dislodged. As it was, the risk of serious injury or damage was 'minimal' and the interference to the plaintiffs' enjoyment of their property not undue. 'Such interference is a consequence of the character of the neighbourhood. Nearly all of us have to put up with a certain amount of annoyance from our neighbours.'

Let us now have a quick look at some of the most frequent causes of complaint, whether in town or country:

Trees Do the branches of your neighbour's tree(s) overhang your garden? If so, you may lop them off at the boundary without even warning him beforehand – although it would clearly be more polite to do so. As long ago as 1895, in the classic case of *Lemmon* v. *Webb* Lord Macnaughten ruled: 'A man is not bound to permit a neighbour's trees to overhang the surface of his land.'

The same principle applies to tree roots spreading out below your land. If they endanger your foundations, you can cut them back to the boundary – but you must take care not to damage the tree itself. In fact, you should first complain to your neighbour and offer him facilities to do the job himself. If he refuses, you then have a much freer hand to engage contractors yourself and recover the cost from him. Furthermore, once warned his roots are creating a potential danger, this will make it easier to claim compensation for whatever damage they cause. Poplar trees, in particular, figure highly in the reported cases.

But please remember that, if you cut offending branches yourself, you cannot use them for firewood or eat any of the fruit. Both branches and their natural attachments remain your neighbour's property. The strictly legal position is farcical: he cannot insist on coming in to reclaim his property and, if he enters without your consent, he commits trespass for which (technically) you could sue him. But you cannot pick them up or use them yourself! That would be a trespass on your part. Your only legal right is to let them lie there to rot. The law sometimes favours the bloody-minded.

(This same principle applies to balls and other such objects hit accidentally on to your land. Technically, the couple in the Village Green Case need not have handed back the cricket balls hit into their garden, although they usually did. They could have insisted on the balls lying where they fell. When some years ago a golfer in Harwich insisted on going on to private farmland to retrieve a golfball despite the farmer's objections, the police were called and the golfer ended up being bound over by the local magistrates to keep the peace.)[1]

Reverting to trees: their owners must take reasonable care of them and lop or trim them when safety requires it – or risk being sued if the tree falls and does damage. Not everyone can afford this. In one recent case, an elderly widow living on a modest pension could not pay an expert to lop a large old tree, even though her neighbour warned it was unsafe and might fall and hit someone in his garden. She explained her financial position and said she would be happy to allow a contractor to come in and do the job if her neighbour paid the bill. And that is what happened, even though legally it was her responsibility.

But no one can come on your land and cut down your tree without your permission, as happened in discreet, respectable Kensington in August 1979. A woman complained to her neighbour that three plane

[1] There is a recent statutory improvement to the law. The 1992 Neighbouring Land Act says that, if you do not allow a neighbour on to your land *to repair or maintain a structure on his own land,* he may get an order to that effect from the local county court – on condition he makes good any damage.

trees at the back of his garden partly overhung her land and blocked the light to her house (we shall see about 'the right to light' in a minute). While the tree-owner and his wife were away on summer holiday, she instructed a tree surgeon to go into the next-door garden and 'thin' the trees but, because one was diseased, his workmen felled the whole tree. Result: after Mr Justice Woolf had visited the garden (which, as we have seen, often happens in this type of case), he held the woman and her tree surgeon jointly liable to pay £750, the value of the 40-foot felled tree.[2]

What perhaps many people do not realise is that you can be fined for cutting down a tree in your own garden! The 1990 Town and Country Planning Act says that, when you live in a conservation area, you cannot cut down, lop, top or uproot any tree standing on your own land without the local authority's consent – except when the tree is dead, dying or dangerous. The penalty is a fine of up to £5,000, although usually nothing like this amount is handed down.

The same prohibition applies, even outside a conservation area, if a local authority has imposed a tree preservation order on a particular tree because of its 'amenity value'. So it is prudent to check with your local Town Hall before taking drastic action: in 1980 the High Court ruled, on an earlier piece of similar legislation, that ignorance of a tree preservation order is no defence.

Fences Arguing about who should keep a garden fence in good repair is another frequent cause of contention. But here at least there is usually an easy remedy: the title deeds may give the answer but, if not, go out into the garden and look at the fence. The law presumes that it will originally have been built up to the very limit of its owner's land. So, if the supporting stake is on your side, the fence belongs to you and you have to maintain it but, if on the other side, the fence is your neighbour's liability. If there are no supports on either side and there is nothing in the title deeds, you and your neighbour share responsibility.

[2] But, Solomon-like, the judge threw out the tree-owner's additional claim that the felling had lopped £10,000 off the value of his £300,000 house.

Barbecues and garden bonfires These frequently cause problems with neighbours. Contrary to what many people may think, the 1956 Clean Air Act does not apply to domestic gardens. So, in the absence of any local by-law, no one can threaten you with prosecution for an occasional smoky bonfire or over-pungent barbecue. But, if you made a persistent habit of it, you could be sued for an actionable nuisance.

Right to light This is what the law calls 'ancient lights' and can only be enjoyed if there is a specific legal agreement to that effect or if you, or previous occupants of your property, have enjoyed it for at least twenty years. This excludes most new properties and many houses on modern estates have a clause in the title deeds preventing a right to light accruing even after twenty years.

But, once the right exists, it is of considerable value. If, for instance, your neighbour builds an extension, even though not large enough to require planning permission, you may well be able to sue. But, as with all actionable nuisance, your inconvenience must not be trivial: your light must have been *substantially* reduced. And it is only light to a building that is protected. You cannot complain merely because there is less sun in your garden.

However, in 1978 the Appeal Court ruled that a garden greenhouse was a 'building' for the purposes of this rule. So a Rochdale house-owner, who had built a fence alongside his neighbour's greenhouse and parked his caravan behind it so that, although the neighbour could still work in his greenhouse, the light was not enough to grow his more exotic plants, had to take down the fence and remove his caravan.

Incidentally, there is a limit to what you can legally do *in your own garden*. You can bury your dead pet there[3] but I know of only one case where someone has been allowed to bury a dead human there. It happened in February 1966 when, after the local planning authority and medical officer of health said they had no objections, the Home Office issued an exhumation certificate to an elderly grieving widower

[3] This long-standing principle of Common Law is now subject to the 1990 Environmental Protection Act which says that where an animal dies on veterinary premises of a highly infectious disease the vet must ensure that it is incinerated as 'clinical waste'. But, if your pet dies at the vet's of old age or some non-infectious illness, you can still bring it home and bury it in the garden.

for him to bring his wife's body back from the local cemetery and rebury it in his garden. I would not advise any further such applications. That was strictly a one-off event.

Sun-worshippers should note that you cannot strip off and sunbathe in the nude in your own garden if there is a risk of a neighbour seeing you from an upstairs window and reporting you to the police for a possible breach of the peace or indecent exposure. And some neighbours would take pleasure in doing so.

Nor can you make love on your own back lawn if anyone can see. 'I love my wife and I cannot see why we should not show some affection to each other,' a 39-year-old instrument-maker in Norwich once told the police. It had been his regular practice to have sexual intercourse with his wife in their bungalow's back garden, as and when the mood took them. Unfortunately, the next-door garden was separated only by a row of flowers, and one afternoon, unknown to them, their neighbour's two small children saw what was going on and told their mother, who promptly called the police.

Local magistrates fined the husband £50 for indecent exposure and gave his wife a conditional discharge for aiding and abetting. Some cases could only happen in Britain.

Noise Of all the reasons for neighbourly dissension, this is far and away the most frequent. Complaints about noisy neighbours have risen over tenfold in the past four years: barking dogs, screaming children, thumping music and DIY noise are the most common cause. After all, when the Americans wanted to winkle out General Noriega from his safe sanctuary in Panama after he had been overthrown, they bombarded him with ear-splitting heavy rock until he surrendered. Not that offending music, as between neighbours, has necessarily to be loud. In one recent case in Leicester when a young single mother was fined for subjecting her neighbours to a continuous stream of music from BBC Radio One, the actual decibel level of the noise was not so great but, as a local environmental health official explained, 'There is a peculiarly irritating characteristic of music coming through a wall, particularly if it has lyrics. The brain cannot help latching on to them. A 10-decibel level against background hum isn't irritating. A singer at the same level is.'

Parties These are a particular noise menace. If an excessively noisy party ruins your evening or prevents you sleeping, you can – even on a one-off basis – complain to the police and they will usually send an officer along to knock at the door and ask them to quieten things down. You have the right to demand this as part of the legal duty cast upon the police to keep the peace. This does not happen only in the deprived areas of our inner cities. In July 1993, exhausted neighbours called police to a pensioners' Darby and Joan party in respectable Aylesbury, where the doors were left open because of the heat. The party had started at 5.30 p.m. and was still going strong well after midnight. As a neighbour said: 'We've had Max Bygraves and now we are on to Frank Sinatra.' Later, the police issued a discreet statement: 'When our officers arrived they found the party was still going strong but the noise was not excessive and no action was taken.' Of course, with most people a polite visit from the police will, in itself, be enough to quieten things down.

But, if noisy parties persist, it can amount to an actionable nuisance. Some years ago, at Clerkenwell County Court, a man whose rowdy parties every third Saturday night always disturbed a couple across the street was ordered to stop and pay them £50 damages (now it would be much more).

Burglar alarms are in a special legal category. As a *Times* leading article said in October 1993, 'Burglar alarms have come to epitomise the worst menaces of urban life, malfunctioning at every conceivable occasion, invariably waiting until a Friday night, when the owners are away and untraceable, before unleashing their aural violence.' False alarms have become a curse of modern living – and the law is largely inadequate to deal with them. The names of two key-holders able to reach the property within half an hour are supposed to be lodged with the police and 'it is desirable that' alarms should be fitted with a device that automatically cuts off the sound after twenty minutes, but these requirements do not have the force of law. They are contained in a 1982 'Code of Practice on Noise from Audible Intruder Alarms' of which most people have never even heard.

But the police, though frequently telephoned by anguished neighbours, have no effective or speedy right of forcible entry to turn off an alarm; nor have local environmental health officials; and, of course, neighbours cannot sue for nuisance because the inconvenience suffered, although intense, does not usually last (at the very worst) for all that long and so does not count as 'substantial' within Vice-Chancellor Knight Bruce's 1851 ruling.

Noise from building works is also in a special legal category but here the law is quite effective. Section 60 of the 1974 Control of Pollution Act gives local authorities extensive powers to control the hours within which building work can take place, the type of plant or machinery used and the level of permitted noise. If your life is being made wretched by building work, speak to the site manager or phone up his head office and say that, unless they curb the din, you will complain to the environmental health department at the local council under Section 60 of the Act. You should quote the actual number of the Section and the name of the Act: they will then realise that you know what you are talking about.

Unfortunately, the Act does not apply to the nuisance caused by so many building workers and house decorators, not only those on building sites, who seem unable to work without their radios blasting out pop music at top volume. Some councils have by-laws about noisy radios and stereos, so a complaint to the local environmental health department may bring results, although I doubt it. Our undermanned police will also usually not intervene, even if you say the noise is causing a breach of the peace. They have their own priorities.

But, in general, what are your practical remedies when your neighbour commits nuisance and makes your life miserable?

1. Self-help

Obviously you should begin by politely asking him to stop or tone down whatever he is doing. If that does not work, some people now turn to mediation: you could try telephoning Mediation UK, an independent charitable organisation with some forty mediation services throughout the country, and asking if they have a local branch. The number is 01272–241234.

Yet the law is quite robust. If you do not protect your own interests, when you physically can, you may find yourself penalised in court. Some years ago, a man sued his neighbour in Lowestoft County Court for £500 for damage done to his house by a plant that had encroached from next door. It must have been a ferocious weed, because it grew up through the floorboards and was sprouting through the wallpaper and up the staircase before the neighbour was finally made to remove it with a mechanical digger.

But: 'The plaintiff could have saved himself much money if he had taken steps to deal with the matter earlier,' ruled Judge Evans, and cut his claim to £50.

Yet there is a limit. In June 1993, a scaffolder on night work who could not get to sleep because of his neighbour's blaring pop music finally smashed up his stereo with an axe. The noise had been so loud that the pictures were jumping about on his bedroom wall as he lay awake. Result: he pleaded guilty at Hatfield magistrates' court to criminal damage but the Chairman of the Bench said he had been 'provoked' and let him off with only an order for £25 costs – ignoring the neighbour's request for £1,000 compensation for his ruined hi-fi system.

2. You can sue for an injunction and damages

As we know, this can be expensive and in most nuisance cases you cannot even resort to your low-cost local small-claims court because, although the judge can award up to £1,000 damages, he cannot grant an injunction. This remedy is often more important than money in a case of nuisance. So you must either sue in the county court or even, in a major case, the High Court. Sometimes a strongly worded solicitor's letter will do the trick but with the truly bloody-minded it may be of no avail.

3. You can complain to the environmental health department at your local town hall

In practice, this is what most people do and it is the most cost-effective way of dealing with the problem. Sections 79 and 80 of the 1990 Environmental Protection Act, improving upon earlier legislation, have set up a really good system of 'abatement notices'. It is primarily invoked

201

by people complaining about noise (which includes vibration) but is also available to deal with complaints about smoke, fumes or gases and with dust, steam, smell or other effluvia from industrial premises.

If, after investigation, the environmental health people agree that a 'statutory nuisance' – which is the same as an 'actionable nuisance' – exists, they have no option. Under the wording of the Act, they *must* serve an abatement notice on the owner or occupier of the building requiring him to stop the nuisance. If 'without reasonable excuse' he does not do so, the council will then prosecute him in the local magistrates' court and, if convicted, he can be fined up to £5,000 with a further £500 for each day on which the nuisance continues. In extreme cases, magistrates have even ordered hi-fi sets and stereo units to be confiscated: the first instance was in January 1992 when a sixteen-year-old Liverpool flat-dweller's hi-fi was seized after she had made neighbours' lives wretched for months with loud music blasting out late at night and early in the morning.

The main problem, as so often, is one of resources. Only one in ten councils can afford to pay environmental health officers to work at night. The result is that you can come across zealous officers prowling round prosperous suburbs in the afternoon, trying to find reggae parties, whereas at midnight, when the parties are really getting under way in the inner cities, they are usually at home tucked up in bed.

4. You can bring a 'do-it-yourself' prosecution

Section 82 of the 1990 Act gives a private citizen the right to bring his own prosecution for a 'statutory nuisance' in the local magistrates' court; but most people prefer to go to the council and invoke the 'abatement notice' procedure of Sections 79 and 80 of the same Act.

Visitors

The 1957 Occupiers' Liability Act says that the occupier of premises, both residential and commercial, owes all his lawful visitors a 'common duty of care' to ensure that the visitor will be reasonably safe in using the premises for the purpose for which he is permitted or invited to be there.

What does that tortuous formula mean in practice? A little-known High Court case in June 1975 provides a good example:

The DIY that went wrong

A DIY enthusiast in Hemel Hempstead converted his garage into an extra sitting-room and put in two attractive glass doors. He did not skimp on the job but went to a reputable local firm to buy the doors. Unfortunately, they supplied doors with 3/16th-inch glass, although a trade code of practice specified either half-inch ordinary glass or 7/32nd-inch toughened glass. Oblivious of the need for thicker glass, he was well pleased with his work.

Some time later his neighbours' eight-year-old daughter was watching TV in the converted sitting-room with his own young children, when her mother called, and she ran out – straight into the glass doors. They shattered and she was badly scarred. Suing through her father, she recovered damages against both the firm that supplied the glass *and* the do-it-yourselfer; they had to share the bill.

In his judgment, Mr Justice O'Connor said that the firm was at fault because it had been negligent in supplying glass that was too thin according to its own trade code of practice. As for the unfortunate DIY enthusiast, the judge referred to the 1957 Act and continued: 'Far be it for me to discourage people from "doing-it-themselves". But, if you "do-it-yourself", the law requires that the degree of skill you must bring to bear on the project is the same that a reasonably competent workman would show.' It was no excuse that this particular workman was a well-meaning amateur.

In fact, any prudent householder should make sure that his household-contents insurance policy covers him (at very little extra cost) for legal liability for injury to visitors.

For valid claims can all too easily be made. Every case depends on its own facts and many are settled out of court, but you can be held liable for any failure to take a reasonable care in all the circumstances – by, for example, leaving a child's toy on the stairs when you are expecting visitors, failing to warn someone that the kitchen floor has just been polished and is very slippery or not reminding an infrequent visitor to your house that there is one step down to your ground-floor lavatory.

This question of warning visitors of possible dangers can be tricky. The 1957 Act specifically says that a warning may not be enough, *in itself*, to escape liability. It is merely one factor to be taken into account. You may, for instance, warn a guest staying overnight that the shower mixer in the bathroom is faulty and only hot water comes out, but if the water is so hot that it scalds him you will almost certainly still be liable.

Furthermore, the Act specifies that someone who visits premises 'in the exercise of his calling' must accept any special risk normally involved with that calling. In one case, a window cleaner recovered no damages when a frayed sash cord broke and a window came crashing down on his hand, yet, if the same accident had happened to a non-working visitor, almost certainly there would have been liability.

But few things in the law are simple: if a window cleaner, plumber or similar trade visitor catches his foot in a worn patch of carpet and you should have realised it was a potential danger (but had not warned him), he probably could successfully sue you.

Another special category is children: as we have already seen (at page 57), the 1957 Act says that you must expect children to be less careful than adults. An adult may have his claim reduced because of his own 'contributory negligence' in not taking reasonable care for his own safety: e.g. in not looking where he was going. With child visitors, it is different: what would not be a potential danger for an adult could easily be so for a child. Obvious examples are the sharp corner of a table left uncovered or a carving knife left lying around.

So much for lawful visitors; what about the unlawful variety: trespassers? As we have already seen (at page 59), the garbled wording of the 1984 Occupiers' Liability Act has attempted to impose liability on occupiers to give some sort of 'reasonable' protection to uninvited guests but there still has been no authoritative court ruling as to exactly what that means. It is hardly a practical issue, though: unless you grab a Kalashnikov rifle and shoot a trespasser between the eyes at point-blank range (which most people would agree was illegal), he is hardly likely to sue over a mishap on your premises.

In fact, in December 1994, a burglar, suing with the help of legal aid, was awarded £4,000 damages by Mr Justice Rougier for injuries sustained when an 82-year-old pensioner, driven to sleeping in a shed to protect his frequently vandalised allotment, shot at him blindly with a single-barrelled shotgun through a hole in the shed door. The decision caused a public outcry and, although the judge took the unusual step of defending his decision in letters to *The Times* and the *Daily Telegraph*, it was soon announced that the pensioner was appealing to the Appeal Court.

Pets

Animals cause a lot of problems between neighbours. If the next-door cat attacks your chickens, you will not be able to sue. Why? Because in 1926, when a suburban houseowner in the Midlands with a chicken-run in his back garden sued a neighbour whose cat had slaughtered some of his chickens, Lord Justice Atkin ruled: 'The owner of a cat is not rendered liable by the mere fact that the animal does damage in following a natural propensity of its kind to do damage.' The 1971 Animals Act was intended to remove the legal immunity of cats to roam wild and unrestrained; but it has not worked out like that. I know of no single case, ancient or modern, where a cat-owner has been held liable to compensate anyone for damage or injury caused by his pet. Cats remain the spoiled darlings of the law.

It is very different with dogs.

For a start, if a dog belonging to your neighbour (or anyone else) attacks your chickens – or your own dog or any other animal – the neighbour will have to compensate you, if he has been negligent in controlling his pet. Indeed, the judges accept that some breeds are more dangerous and require more control than others: for instance, at Birmingham County Court in March 1992, Judge Toyn awarded damages to an old lady whose dog had twice been savaged in her own back garden by a Rottweiler from next door, and there have been similar cases involving Alsatians and Jack Russell terriers.

When it comes to attacks on human beings, many people still quote the well-known old phrase 'Every dog is allowed one bite'. In fact, that is now totally out of date and the legal thinking behind it was abolished by the 1971 Animals Act. For nearly three hundred years, ever since Chief Justice Holt, obviously an early dog-lover, laid down in 1699: 'The law takes notice that a dog is not of a fierce nature but rather the contrary,' the Common Law maintained that a dog-owner was only liable to compensate someone bitten by his dog if it had bitten someone

205

else at least once before (hence, 'one bite') and he therefore knew of its specific vicious propensity.

But the 1971 Act altered that charming simplicity. Section 2 says that the keeper of any domestic animal[4] is *automatically* liable to pay compensation when his or her pet causes damage 'of a kind which (a) the animal, unless restrained, was likely to cause or which was likely to be severe; (b) that likelihood was due to characteristics not normally found in animals of that species or only in specific circumstances and (c) those characteristics were known to its keeper or his servant or member of his household under sixteen'.

This remarkable verbiage (and my version is cut down from the original) was criticised by the judges and for nearly twenty years had little effect in practice. But then two Appeal Court decisions, one in November 1989 and the other in May 1990, belatedly revealed that a fundamental change in the law had taken place. As a result, it is now clearly established that the 1971 Act has made it much easier to sue a dog's keeper for an attack on a human being: the victim no longer must prove that the animal had already had one bite. *Any* potentially very dangerous 'characteristic' is enough.[5]

So, in the first Appeal Court case, when a normally placid bull mastiff leapt at and bit a ten-year-boy who called it while it was being loaded on to the back of a Land-Rover, the Appeal Court ruled the dog's owners were automatically liable, even though the animal was on a lead. They knew their animal regarded the back of the Land-Rover as part of its own territory – and that it was likely to react fiercely when defending its territory. So the boy's parents did not have to prove that the bull mastiff had attacked anyone else before.

In the second Appeal Court decision, a man was walking his dog along a street in Woking when another dog, also being taken for a walk, lunged at it and knocked him down in the process, breaking his

---

[4] The Act imposes liability on an animal's 'keeper'. This is not only the owner. It can also be someone who has temporary charge of the animal or who heads a household where an under-sixteen-year-old owns or is in charge of it. How many people realise they are legally responsible, if their child under sixteen owns a dog – or any other domestic pet?

[5] Yet, as in the old Common Law days of 'one bite', it still remains inadvisable to put on your front gate a warning notice: 'Beware Dangerous Dog'. You are in effect admitting in advance that you know your animal has a dangerous propensity! You are only making it more difficult for yourself if it then bites a visitor.

leg. Both dogs were on leads but the Appeal Court overruled a High Court judge's dismissal of the injured man's claim and awarded him £7,203 damages plus interest. Lord Justice Neill said that the owner of the attacking dog, a large mongrel named Sam, knew his pet was likely to go for other animals. He also knew of the risk of another dog-owner being hurt in any rescue attempt, and that was enough to incur liability under the 1971 Act.

It would be as well to keep these two decisions in mind. Taking your dog for a walk can have legal complications nowadays. I always keep a firm grip on my own dog's lead when I see another dog approaching.

A word about guard dogs: The 1975 Guard Dogs Act makes it an offence to have a guard dog on commercial or industrial premises without warning notices, a full-time handler or unless the dog is satisfactorily tethered. But this does *not* apply to your home or any other residential premises.

The 1991 Dangerous Dogs Act Many people are confused about the effect of this piece of legislation that was rushed through Parliament in the summer of 1991 because of several highly publicised attacks on people by vicious dogs. In fact, it not only bans the breeding or sale of 'any dog of the type known as pit-bull terrier' (which loose phraseology has cost a fortune in interpretation in the courts) and says that it must be registered, insured and kept on a lead or muzzled in a public place. It also made important changes to the existing law on dangerous dogs – of all breeds.

It amended the old 1871 Dogs Act in order to enable magistrates to declare a dog of any breed dangerous and order its owner to keep it under proper control or be destroyed – *without proof that anyone has been injured.* (Another nail in the coffin of the old 'one bite' ideal!)

And it also created a new offence imposing severe penalties on an owner or anyone in charge of a dog who allows it to be 'dangerously out of control' or injure someone, whether in a public or private place. He or she now faces a substantial fine and/or up to two years' imprisonment. For the first time ever, if your dog snaps at visitors on private property you can now end up in the dock of a criminal court rather than merely having to pay damages in a civil court.

Dog collars, dog leads and dog excreta   The 1992 Control of Dogs Order, updating a 1930 Order, says that every dog out in public, whether or not with its owner, must wear a collar with its owner's name and address – but not necessarily the dog's own name.

Many modern local by-laws make it an offence for a dog to be out without a lead, even though wearing a collar, on specific town streets named in the by-laws and identified by a small metal notice attached to lampposts. This offence is committed even when the animal is out with its owner.

Many by-laws also make it a criminal offence to allow a dog to foul the footpath of any street or public place; again, a small metal notice on lampposts identifies the specific streets or public place. The High Court has ruled that 'footpath' does not include a grass verge and public parks have their own dog rules in the large notices of park regulations displayed near all major entrances.

What about those selfish people who habitually allow their dogs to wander into the front gardens of private houses and deposit their excreta there? Because that is not a public place, local by-laws do not apply, but if an aggrieved householder could prove any one person was regularly allowing his pet to defecate in his front garden he could, in theory, sue him for damages and an injunction for an actionable nuisance – but I know of no actual case.

Stray dogs   Bits of the 1906 Dogs Act and bits of the 1990 Environmental Protection Act must be read together to discover the legal system for dealing with stray dogs, although it is difficult to see why Parliament did not simply repeal the whole of the old Act and put the whole thing together in one new Act – but then that is how legal 'reform' so often works in this country.

Anyway, this is the basic framework of how the system works: a stray dog can be seized by either the police or a dog warden employed by the local council, who must give the owner a chance to reclaim his animal. If he cannot be found or does not want the dog back, it will be sold or destroyed. If a private citizen finds a stray dog, he cannot just keep it for himself straightaway. He must either return it to its owner (if, for instance, the name and address are on the dog's collar, as they should be) or take it to the nearest police station or give it to the local dog warden and tell them where it was found.

If he says he would like to keep the dog permanently, the police or warden will allow him to take it home for at least a month and, if during that time its owner does not claim it, he will be allowed to keep it permanently and become its new legal owner.

Taking a dog into a public house, wine bar, restaurant or shop   There is no law which says specifically that dogs can – or cannot – be brought on to trade premises. In each case, the management can make its own rules and there is no legal requirement to provide a small ring outside the entrance to which a customer's dog can be tethered.

But, where food or drink is served, the 1970 Food Hygiene (General) Regulations specify that food (which includes drink) must be protected from risk of contamination. Most pubs, wine bars, restaurants and food shops interpret this to mean that dogs should legally not be allowed on their premises, although to the best of my knowledge no court has ever ruled on the legal correctness of this common interpretation.

However, as far back as September 1976, the Department of Health and Social Services (DHSS) circularised local authorities recommending that an exception should be made in the case of guide dogs for the blind because: 'They do not urinate or defecate while wearing harness and they ignore interesting smells. Thus they present less of a risk to food hygiene than dogs generally.'

That is why many notices on the doors of food shops specifically say that guide dogs *are* allowed.

Part Four
YOUR CAR

THIRTEEN

Motoring Law

Motoring law is totally different from any other part of ordinary, every-day law dealt with in this book. With all other aspects of 'ordinary' law, most people have, at best, only a somewhat hazy idea of what the law has to say and what precisely are their rights.

But, with motoring law, those who need to know – the country's 28.1 million drivers (the official Transport Department figure) – already have a pretty good idea of what the law is and what their rights are. The Highway Code's latest (1993) edition not only outsells the Bible: it also contains, in addition to the Code itself, a simple yet compre-hensive guide to the basic law. At 99p a copy, it is truly remarkable value.

Besides, you cannot be a motorist nowadays without automatically knowing a lot about motoring law. It would be like a cook not having his or her own private storehouse of recipes or not knowing the basic rules of cookery.

So the shape of this chapter is different from all the others. There is no point in telling readers what many of them will already know: i.e. the main framework of the system and its fundamental principles. Instead, I have selected ten specific topics of everyday importance to motorists where the law is always changing and developing – and where sometimes even the experts do not know all the answers.

1. *Learning to drive*

Most people, of course, know that the basic minimum legal require-ments are that a learner cannot drive on a motorway and that he must be at least seventeen, with a provisional licence and L-plates displayed on the car, back and front.[1] Furthermore, the accompanying driver must be at least twenty-one and have held a British licence to drive that type of car for at least three years.

But there is much more to it than that.

The accompanying driver is not just there for the ride. Professional driving instructors must be registered by law if they receive payment for their work. But even non-professionals cannot simply sit back and let the learner get on with it. They have a job to do: they must supervise the driving of the novice at the wheel.

If not, they can *both* find themselves in trouble with the law. Back in the early months of World War Two, in 1940, when there was still a fair amount of traffic on the roads, a learner driver, overtaking on a bend, ran into a heavily laden lorry coming the other way. It was not entirely his fault. His fully qualified friend sitting beside him should have warned him not to overtake but to wait until they had first gone round the bend. He did not: so local magistrates convicted the learner of careless driving and his accompanying driver of aiding and abetting him.

On appeal to the High Court in London, the formidable Mr Justice Hilbery upheld both convictions and laid down this classic statement of the law: 'It is the supervisor's duty, when necessary, to do whatever can reasonably be expected to prevent the driver from acting unskilfully or carelessly or in a manner likely to cause danger to others.'

This basic ruling still applies across the whole gamut of possible motoring offences. Technically the supervising driver may even be guilty of aiding and abetting – and therefore, also liable to be fined – when a learner commits a simple parking offence.

There has even been a case, in October 1980, when Judge Henry Kershaw ruled at Burley Crown Court that a driving examiner had rightly been convicted by local magistrates of aiding and abetting a driving-test candidate to drive without due care and attention while actually taking his test. The young learner had misunderstood the examiner's instructions and turned the wrong way into a one-way street but the examiner had said nothing – until they crashed into an

---

[1] There is no legal mystique about buying manufactured L-plates in a motor-accessory shop. You can make your own: provided they comply with the specific requirements of the 1981 Motor Vehicles [Driving Licence] Regulations: i.e. a red letter 'L', 4 inches high by 3.5 inches wide by 1.5 inches thick, on a white card that is 7 inches square.

oncoming car. Judge Kershaw said: 'While examiners are not in the same category as supervisors or instructors neither are they merely passengers. If a candidate is so incompetent that to continue the test would be a serious danger to the public, the examiner must terminate it.'

Similar considerations apply to the question of civil liability. Other road-users must be protected. The standard of driving on the road has to be objective. A learner's inexperience is no excuse if his negligent driving causes an accident and, if the accident could have been averted by the accompanying driver using reasonable supervision (grabbing the wheel, applying the brake, even just shouting out), he will have to share the bill for damages.

Can the supervising driver himself sue, if injured, or will he be met by the defence that he knew the risk he was letting himself in for? After all, *volenti non fit injuria* ('to the consenting there is no injury') is a general rule of the Common Law. The Appeal Court supplied the answer in 1971 in *Nettleship* v. *Weston*:

The case of the supervising driver

A woman in Sheffield wanted to learn to drive. Her husband did not want the job but he was quite happy to let her use his car. So a family friend agreed to give her lessons. She was a careful pupil and was doing well, but on the third lesson she failed to straighten out after taking a left turn. She panicked. Her hands 'seemed to freeze on the wheel'. The friend grabbed hold of the handbrake and tried to control the wheel with his other hand but could not stop the car slamming into a lamppost. He broke his leg and sued for damages.

The Appeal Court upheld his claim. Lord Denning ruled that the woman learner was guilty of negligence: 'It is no answer to say, "I was a learner driver under instructions. I was doing my best and could not help it." The law requires the same standard of care as from any other driver. He may be doing his best but his incompetent best is not good enough.'

As for the *volenti* defence, the family friend had specifically asked beforehand whether she was insured against injury to passengers (which she was), and that was sufficient to show he had not legally accepted the risk of being driven by her. Lord Justice Megaw went even further: 'The mere fact that the passenger knows of the driver's inexperience is not enough' – without any need to ask about insurance.

215

Even so, for their own protection, anyone today going out with a learner (whether as supervising driver or ordinary passenger) should first check that he or she will be covered by insurance. This is so that they can later *beyond doubt* refute the defence: 'You agreed to the risk of an accident'.

One final point: a learner driver cannot always count on being fully insured. If the car-owner's policy allows 'any authorised driver' to drive the vehicle, he will be covered, although a claim may be subject to a substantial excess. But, if the policy only allows a 'named driver', a claim may be rejected completely unless the policy-holder has informed his insurers and given them the opportunity to charge an increased premium for having a learner at the wheel.

Many people are not sufficiently aware of what they are taking on when helping a relative or friend to learn to drive.

2. *Seat belts*

Ever since 1965, the law has required all new motor vehicles to be fitted with front seat belts. But surprisingly it is only since 1983 that it has been an offence, with certain exceptions (when reversing, a pregnant woman with a medical certificate, taxi-drivers and minicab drivers, etc.), not to wear them.[2] Indeed, the Automobile Association calculates that a life a day is saved through 'belting up'.

Over the age of fourteen, it is the responsibility of the passenger, not the driver, to ensure that he is belted up. In fact, the value of wearing a front seat belt has been obvious for so long that back in July 1975, before wearing was even made compulsory, the Appeal Court ruled in the classic case of *Froom* v. *Butcher* that an unbelted driver or front passenger injured in an accident caused by another driver's negligence might have his damages cut because of his or her own 'contributory negligence'. As you will already know from earlier chapters, the law says we all must take reasonable care for our own safety.

So Lord Denning laid down: 'The judges should say plainly that it is sensible practice for all drivers and passengers in front seats to wear

---

[2] No baby under twelve months is allowed to travel in a front seat, even if securely held by an adult, unless every other seat is occupied. Children between one and fourteen are only allowed to with a proper restraining device (adult belts are not enough).

seat belts.' If not, and their injuries would have been the same despite the seat belt, their damages will not be affected. But, if wearing a seat belt would have saved them from *all* injury, their damages will be cut by 25 per cent – and by 15 per cent if the injuries would have been 'a good deal less severe'.

Since then the law has moved on. Since 1986 rear seat belts have had to be fitted to most new cars (*not* 'motor vehicles', as in the earlier Regulations, so that minibuses, coaches and ambulances are not included and, although some are fitted with rear seat belts, there is no legal compulsion) and since September 1989 it has been an offence to drive a car in which a child under fourteen is being carried in the rear without wearing a suitable seat belt or 'appropriate child restraint'.

But it is only since July 1991 that the marvellously entitled Motor Vehicles (Wearing of Seat Belts in Rear Seats by Adults) Regulations make it an offence for adults not to wear seat belts in the back of a car as well as in the front. A maximum fine of £500 is specified.

Yet how many rear-seat passengers in fact bother to belt up? How many even know that they can be fined if they do not? The Automobile Association knows of cases where front-seat passengers have been badly injured by head butts from the rear when an unbelted back-seat passenger has been thrown viciously forward by the impact of a collision.

Yet the question has not yet been authoritatively decided in the courts whether the reduced rate of damages laid down in *Froom* v. *Butcher* should apply if an unbelted rear passenger, as distinct from front passenger, is injured. There simply has been no case reported since the new law was introduced. But if the line of judicial reasoning in the 1991 Appeal Court case of *Eastman* v. *South West Thames Regional Health Authority*, decided before the change in the law, is followed, the answer will probably be 'Yes':

The case of the injured ambulance passenger

Mrs Eastman was allowed to accompany her aged mother-in-law to hospital in the back of an ambulance. A sign stated: 'For your own safety, use seat belts provided'; but she did not do so. The driver braked hard to avoid a cyclist and she was thrown from her seat and injured.

The Appeal Court threw out her damages claim. It ruled that the health authority was entitled to leave to an individual passenger of mature years the decision whether or not to use the seat belt and it was not unreasonable for the ambulance crewmen not to tell her to use the belt or to point out the warning notice.

This ruling would also seem to apply to those London taxi-drivers (and no doubt taxi-drivers in other cities) who, when the 1991 Regulations came into force, warned passengers to wear seat belts but no longer bother to do so. It was at one time thought that an unbelted rear passenger could sue them if he was injured in an accident. That would now seem to be not the case.

3. Traffic lights

Three common situations are of interest.

(i) *The traffic lights do not work*   If you disobey an official set of traffic lights, whether working properly or not, the 1981 Traffic Signs Regulations and General Directions make it an offence for which you can be fined up to £1,000, have your licence endorsed and get three penalty points.

But there is a nuance: if the lights are jammed at red, you must either turn round and find another outlet or else stop – and remain stopped until a policeman or traffic warden comes along and countermands the red light by beckoning you forward.

However, a judge commented many years ago in a case at Hertfordshire Quarter Sessions (the equivalent of a modern Crown Court) that, if a motorist edges forward carefully in such circumstances without causing any damage or injury, the appropriate sentence should usually be only an absolute discharge. So, in practice, you are unlikely to be charged with any offence.

But, if the lights fail completely and no colour whatsoever is shown, you are legally better off. You can treat the junction as uncontrolled and commit no offence whatsoever, even technically, in carefully edging forward.

(ii) *Traffic lights at road works*   What is their legal status? Some motorists believe that they are only advisory and that, even when they are showing red, you do not have to stop if you can safely see your way ahead. That is simply not so. The 1981 Regulations give portable temporary lights at road works and temporary road-traffic-control schemes equal legal validity with permanent traffic lights. If they show red, you must stop – even if you can see the way ahead is clear.

(iii) *Aggressive windscreen-cleaners at traffic lights* How does the law treat this new curse for motorists? In nothing like so tough a way as it treats the long-suffering motorist himself. Consider this court case in Brighton in July 1993:

The driver who hit back

The owner of a BMW was sitting in the driving seat of his car stopped at traffic lights. A burly youth approached him and started wiping his windscreen without saying anything. The driver ignored him, but the youth put his head inside the car and swore at him.

As the driver later explained, 'If someone puts their head in my car window and shouts threats at me I am going to defend myself, and that is what I did. I got out and grabbed hold of him. It was a push rather than a slap. Within fifteen minutes I went to a police box and reported what had happened.'

What happened next? No prizes for guessing that it was the motorist, not the foul-mouthed washer boy, who ended up at Brighton magistrates' court charged with threatening behaviour, contrary to Section 4 of the 1986 Public Order Act, for which he could be fined up to £1,000.

In fact, the magistrates threw out the case without the motorist even being called to give evidence and awarded him £300 costs. But a local police inspector told a *Daily Telegraph* reporter: 'We get complaints about washer boys *but criminal law does not cover that area.*'

That is absolute nonsense. Aggressive washer boys commit, *at the very least*, the very offence with which the Brighton motorist was charged: threatening behaviour, contrary to Section 4 of the 1986 Act.

And if they continue to use foul language when told by a police officer to stop it comes within Section 5 of the Act, which creates the more serious offence of 'threatening, abusive or insulting words or behaviour with intent to cause a person to believe that immediate unlawful violence will be used.' This offence carries the increased penalty of a maximum six months' gaol sentence or £2,500 fine, or both.

Yet I know of no prosecution brought anywhere in the country against aggressive washer boys under either Section 4 *or* Section 5 of the 1986 Act.

4. *Speeding*

Everyone knows that nowadays you can temporarily lose your licence for speeding – but when exactly is this likely to happen?

The 1988 Road Traffic Offenders Act, which lays down the penalties for speeding – the most common single motoring offence – is of no help. It says that you can be fined up to £1,000, must be given three to six penalty points and have your licence endorsed – but that disqualification is merely 'discretionary'. What does that mean? The Act gives no guidelines as to how magistrates' courts, who alone deal with these cases, are to exercise their discretion.

So the Magistrates' Association has had to resort to self-help. As part of their general sentencing guidelines sent to its members nationwide, there is a specific section on speeding, although the Association emphasises that their 'suggestions' are only to be used as starting points.

Benches are advised to 'consider disqualification if 30 m.p.h. over limit', whatever that limit may be. So that someone travelling at over 60 m.p.h. in a built-up area where the speed limit is 30 m.p.h. is as likely to lose his licence for a short while as someone travelling at over 100 m.p.h. on a motorway where, of course, the speed limit is 70. The guidelines continue with this sliding scale of increased seriousness:

30–34 m.p.h. over the limit: six penalty points, £210 fine and seven days' ban.

35–39 m.p.h. over the limit: six penalty points, £240 fine and fourteen days' ban.

But, when the speed is forty miles or more over the limit (e.g. 70 m.p.h. in a 30 m.p.h. area or 110 m.p.h. on a motorway), it is suggested that Benches show 'a sharp increase' in penalty and disqualification, with a minimum of twenty-one days.

These suggestions are reflected in current practice. As the old *News of the World* advertisements used to say, 'All human life is there.' When it comes to pleading guilty in a magistrates' court for a really bad case of speeding, most of us are at risk. But you are only likely to end up in court if yours is a fairly serious case anyway.

For, under Chief Constables' guidelines, if you are up to 10 m.p.h. over the limit, you will probably receive only a warning or rebuke and, if over 10 m.p.h. but less than 25 m.p.h., the police officer will probably offer you a fixed-penalty fine – which, as a general rule, you should accept; it is almost certain to be lower than if you go to court. Only if you have been driving at more than 25 m.p.h. will you usually be given no option and a court summons will arrive in due course. Two members of the Royal Family, Prince Michael of Kent and Viscount Linley, have both briefly lost their licences in this way, and there are many other examples involving well-known people, such as Neil Kinnock MP, actors Adam Faith and Daniel Day Lewis and ex-world featherweight boxing champion Barry McGuigan.

For the sake of completeness, I should add that there is another way in which a speeding motorist can be banned: under the totting-up procedure laid down by the 1988 Road Traffic Offenders Act.

This applies irrespective of your actual speed on this last occasion. Even though your latest offence may merit only the minimum three penalty points, if that brings your total for the past three years to twelve points or more (not necessarily all for speeding) you will be banned for at least six months, unless a court considers there are strong mitigating circumstances – which seldom happens.

5. Accidents

When do you have to stop in the event of an accident and what precisely are you supposed to do? This is possibly the most misunderstood aspect of everyday motoring law and is, in fact, surprisingly complicated.

Section 170 of the 1988 Road Traffic Act spells out what you must do. Your first duty is to stop. Obviously you must use discretion: if possible, you should not stop in the middle of a busy road but try to pull in to the kerb.

If another motorist is involved, he too must stop but the police need only be called if someone has been injured. If not, your only obligation is, 'if required by any person having reasonable grounds to do so' (e.g.

the other driver or the owner of damaged property), to give your name and address, those of the owner of the vehicle if it is not your own, and its index number. Of course, this applies vice versa to any other motorist involved.

Many drivers think they are entitled to demand driving licence and current insurance certificate; but Section 170 says nothing at all about a driving licence and stipulates that a motorist only has to show his insurance certificate in case of injury.

But not every accident brings with it the duty to stop and give particulars. That only applies when someone besides yourself is injured, *another* vehicle or property is damaged, or any animal (except a cat!) not being carried in your own car is injured.

If you do not give particulars at the time, perhaps because no one was there to ask for them (for instance, the absent owner of a damaged parked car), it is no defence to say no one was around. You must report the accident at a police station or to a police officer 'as soon as reasonably practicable and in any case within twenty-four hours'.

The High Court has ruled that those words mean exactly what they say. You must not put off reporting the accident for up to twenty-four hours: you must do it as soon as 'reasonably practicable'. Only if it is not possible to report the accident promptly do you have up to twenty-four hours in which to do so.

Furthermore, the High Court has ruled that you cannot simply telephone a police station to report. You must do it in person. Failure to stop and give particulars to anyone reasonably requiring them is one offence and failing to report to the police is another, separate offence. You could, if really unlucky (or stupid), find yourself convicted of both. Neither is a laughing matter: for each carries a maximum six months' goal sentence or £5,000 fine (although I know of no case where the offender has been punished so severely) and five to ten penalty points.

The only exception to all this is if you can convince a Bench of cynical magistrates that you genuinely did not know there had been an accident. This is unlikely when there has been an accident on the open road but, where you are trying to manoeuvre in or out of tightly parked cars, it is not entirely impossible. Some years ago, the Queen's cousin Lord Harewood was acquitted at Bow Street magistrates' court in central London when he successfully claimed that he had not realised he had backed into a parked car because he was listening to a Mozart wind serenade on his car radio. He explained that he might have confused the sound of a burglar alarm, set off on the parked car, with a sustained note on the clarinet.

But there is a limit. In 1989, a driver tried to avoid being convicted of failing to report by saying he did not realise there had been a mishap until fifteen minutes later. But it did him no good. The High Court ruled that a driver does not have to realise an accident has occurred *at the time*: later will do.

(**Note**: Because a cat is not an 'animal', as defined by Section 170, do not make the common mistake of thinking that you can drive on with impunity. If there was a reasonable chance of helping it, you must stop; otherwise, if you were spotted, you could be reported for causing it unnecessary suffering, contrary to the 1911 Protection of Animals Act, which *does* define a cat as an 'animal'.)

6. *Drink-driving*

You could write a whole book about drink-driving offences, and some people have; but the general requirements of the law are so very well known that I shall content myself with only one aspect of the problem that is perhaps of special interest.

When can the police breath-test you, once you have got back home? The question is simple but the answer is complex. As Lord Scarman has said, 'Parliament must be understood, even in its desire to stamp out drunken driving, to pay respect to the fundamental right of privacy in one's own home, which has for centuries been recognised by the Common Law.' It was, after all, a judge (Chief Justice Coke) who first said, in the early seventeenth century, 'An Englishman's home is his castle.'

Two basic legal propositions are easy and straightforward:

(i) If you were involved in an accident which injured someone else, a uniformed policeman can enter your home by force, if necessary, and request a breath test, with the normal consequences of arrest, fine and disqualification if you refuse.

(ii) At a less serious level, if a uniformed policeman merely has reasonable cause to believe that, while driving, you had alcohol in your

223

body (not even necessarily that you were drunk!) or committed a moving traffic offence (which can be as trivial as one small sidelight not working), he can knock on your door and request a breath test on your doorstep or, if you let him into your house, request the test inside – with the usual consequences for refusal.

The difficulties start if you do not let him in or, once inside, ask him to leave. As any experienced police officer knows (but may not be prepared to admit), that puts him in a very sensitive legal position.

If he persists with his request, and you refuse, he can undoubtedly arrest you on the spot (though even in your own home), take you to a police station and, if you then prove positive, charge you with drink-driving. The actual arrest will have been unlawful because he was a trespasser – but, as the House of Lords ruled in October 1985, that does not matter. 'A lawful arrest is not an essential prerequisite of a breath test,' said Lord Fraser of Tullybelton.

However, he added that, 'if a motorist has been lured to the police station by some trick or deception, or the police officers have behaved oppressively', a court has a discretion to throw out the charge.

Lord Fraser's words, echoed by his fellow Law Lords, have become the basis of a new and often successful defence of 'oppressive behaviour', although practically unknown outside the ranks of barristers and solicitors specialising in this sort of work. Two years later, in *Matto* v. *Wolverhampton Crown Court*, the High Court quashed the conviction of a motorist who had told police that they could not test him on his own driveway, to which a police officer had charmingly replied: 'We know what we are doing. If I wrongfully arrest you, you can sue me. OK?' Lord Justice Woolf ruled that this was 'behaving in an oppressive manner'.

In April 1993, the prosecution itself withdrew a case at Gray's (Essex) magistrates' court when the driver of a police car was accused of having 'tricked his way' into a woman motorist's house by telling her seventeen-year-old daughter at the front door that he was going in anyway when he knew he had no power to do so.

A motorist's home is still – occasionally – his castle, even when he is accused of drink-driving.

7. Motorways (and hard shoulders)

There is not much that the general motoring public does not know about motorways and the special legal rules that apply to them: no learner-drivers, no cyclists, no riders of motorcycles under 50 cc, etc. But doubts persist, even with magistrates, about the exact legal status of a motorway's hard shoulder.

Everyone knows that it is supposed to be used only in emergencies and that in no circumstances (unless directed so to do by official traffic signs or a police officer) can you drive along it or use it as a short cut or overtake on it. But when precisely are you allowed to *stop* on it?

Paragraph 7 of the 1982 Motorways Traffic (England and Wales) Regulations says that you can stop on a hard shoulder 'by reason of any accident, illness or other emergency' but does not say what constitutes an emergency.

In March 1992, Chris Timms, a High Wycombe antique dealer, was returning from a business visit to France. He was driving his Ford Transit van back home from Dover along the M25, having just passed its junction with the A3, when, at around midnight, his eyes 'suddenly started bouncing', as he later told me.

He realised he was a potential danger to other drivers and himself. He thought it was too far to go to the next junction, so he pulled on to the hard shoulder, stopped, turned off the engine – leaving the lights on – and closed his eyes.

Next thing he knew, a policeman was asking why he had stopped. The sequel, despite a vigorous defence by Timms acting as his own lawyer, was a £60 fine at Woking magistrates' court for stopping his vehicle contrary to the 1982 Regulations. In other words, his sudden tiredness was not an 'emergency'.

But Timms was not prepared to accept that. He fought the case himself on appeal to Guildford Crown Court, where, in October 1992, Judge Peter Slot overruled his conviction. Awarding him £30 costs, Judge Slot said: 'I see no reason to reject Timms's evidence that he felt tired after he passed the junction. It follows that what he did was within the law.'

Timms's case has a wider implication for motorists. An anonymous 'legal expert' was quoted in several national newspapers at the time as saying: 'Motorists must understand that the law has not changed. The judge simply made an exception to the rule.'

That is nonsense. Judge Slot did not make an exception to the rule: he applied and enforced it. For, as far back as February 1972, Lord Widgery, then Lord Chief Justice, in the case of *Higgins* v. *Bernard*, brought on an earlier but identical version of the 1982 Regulations, authoritatively defined what is an 'emergency' for tired motorway drivers.

Taking as his basis the dictionary definition of emergency as 'a sudden and or unexpected occurrence', Lord Widgery said: 'Too much stress must not be attached to the word "sudden".' The tiredness does not have to attack the motorist at the very second before he pulls on to the hard shoulder. 'If he gets on to the carriageway at a time when, so far as he could see, it was safe and lawful for him to proceed to the next turn-off point, it is sufficient to show that something intervened which rendered it unsafe to proceed to that next turn-off point.'

So the reason why Judge Slot quashed Mr Timms's conviction was that he only felt tired after he passed the M25's junction with the A3 and he was 'stuck', as it were, on the motorway until the next junction, which was some distance ahead.

8. *Parking*

Most of us know that a single yellow line on the road or kerbside means that you cannot legally park there, within certain restricted hours, during the week (and nowadays sometimes Sunday), except during restricted hours for loading or unloading – which has to be loading or unloading something for which you reasonably need a motor vehicle: a heavy music centre, yes; a fountain pen (as a judge has actually said!), no. We also know that double yellow lines mean that there is a similar ban on all parking for most of the day during the week (and sometimes Sunday) but that the hours allowed for loading or unloading are even more tightly restricted, and that three yellow lines means, in effect, 'Never park here, even for loading, *any* day or night'.

But what exactly are the hours and days when these various restrictions apply? There is a great deal of variety and the motorist all too often genuinely does not know where he can legally park, and for how long.

Warning notices when you enter a controlled parking zone will tell you in general the restricted hours and days for that zone but if, as sometimes happens, the times are different for any particular street within that zone, the 1981 Traffic Signs Regulations and General Directions say that the local council must put a small official plate on an adjacent lamppost or pole spelling out exactly the hours and days for that street.

But what happens if there is no such small official plate? In February 1992, in *Hassan* v. *Director of Public Prosecutions*, the High Court made a ruling that is almost unknown outside legal circles – and not very well known even inside. Yet every motorist driving in town should know about it:

The case of the missing small plate

A motorist in east London saw at about midday on a working Tuesday that a street had a single yellow line – but no official small plate specifying the hours and days when waiting was restricted. So he parked there.

Within five minutes, a traffic warden slapped a parking ticket on the windscreen. The motorist then looked around and found that the times in that street were different from those on the zone entry warning notices. So he refused to pay. But a London stipendiary magistrate ruled that an offence had been committed because the single yellow line was enough in itself.

The High Court overruled him. Lord Justice Nolan quoted from the 1981 Regulations and went on: 'It is plain that the procedure followed [by the local council] to create the conditions in which the offence would have been committed included the placing of the signs indicating the permitted and restricted hours [on that street]. It cannot be said that the condition was satisfied and therefore this appeal must be allowed.'

This logic applies to *all* yellow lines, not merely single ones; so if the official plate is missing, you should be able to argue that your parking ticket is invalid.

9. Clamping

The ultimate curse. There are two kinds: the official one when your vehicle is parked illegally on a public road and its clamping is authorised by a police officer outside London or (since July 1994) by a police officer, traffic warden or local council parking attendant inside London. It will cost £38 (and much inconvenience) to get the clamp removed plus a £60 or £30 parking penalty. But there is the private version when your car is parked without permission on private land and a release fee as high as £100 is demanded by the occupier of the land or contractors on his behalf.

At present, official wheel clamping exists only in London, although there are plans for extension to the major cities. This is not good news, for the law's restraints are almost non-existent. When a policeman or traffic warden clamps (restricted to Red Routes and some main roads since July 1994 when the 1991 Road Traffic Act came into effect), they do so under the authority of Section 104 of the 1984 Road Traffic Regulations Act. This merely says: 'Where a constable (and nowadays also a traffic warden) finds on a road a vehicle permitted to remain at rest in contravention of *any* [my italics] prohibition or restriction imposed by or under any enactment,' he or she may fix 'an immobilisation device' or authorise someone else to do so. In fact, this task is now delegated to two private clamping companies. By the very wording of the Section, they can clamp a vehicle only 'under the direction' of a constable (or nowadays also a warden) and the authorities have always insisted that the mere fact that the actual clamping is carried out by private contractors for profit has not meant that more vehicles have been clamped than should be.

To that, my only comment is that back in 1987, when private clampers first took over from the police, the annual number of vehicles clamped leapt immediately from 32,270 to 111,032. One wonders why.

At all events, contrary to popular belief, clamping is not restricted only to vehicles that have been parked dangerously – or even for a long time.[3] Just look up and down any busy street in London, when

---

[3] By contrast, the 1984 Act says cars can be towed away when 'illegally, obstructively or dangerously parked', and cars are usually only towed away when parked 'obstructively or dangerously'. The recovery fee is £105 (as against the £38 clamping release fee) plus £12 a day storage and a parking fine.

the clampers are about and I guarantee that you will see many vehicles clamped and taking up space that, if only their drivers had been given a parking ticket, would long since have been left empty. I have seen Post Office vans, department store delivery vans and even taxis clamped. In one case a man's car was clamped while he was inside it sleeping!

The only effective restrictions in the 1984 Act are that a vehicle cannot be legally clamped when displaying a current disabled person's badge or when it is in a parking meter bay where less than 'two hours have elapsed since the end of any period for which an initial charge was duly paid at the time of parking.' Otherwise, it is open house.

Since July 1994 the position has become progressively worse – if that were possible. In that month, all London's thirty-three local councils took over enforcement of most parking laws in the capital from the police and traffic wardens. Under Sections 76 and 77 of the 1991 Road Traffic Act, whose vitally important provisions are still barely known by most motorists in the capital, the Transport Secretary, at the request of local councils, has set up special parking areas where the councils' own parking attendants – not the police or a traffic warden – can authorise private contractors to clamp.

The legal restraints on these parking attendants' zeal (with the net proceeds after paying the private contractors going to their council employers) are even less than those imposed on the police or traffic wardens. Section 104 of the 1984 Act does not apply and the only specific restriction that I can find in the 1991 Act (in Section 70) is that vehicles cannot be clamped unless they have overstayed on a meter for at least fifteen minutes. Big deal! As we have already seen, the 1984 Act says that the police or wardens cannot clamp until the vehicle has overstayed for not less than two hours.

At this stage, let me make a quick digression to talk about the new so-called 'user-friendly' system of parking appeals in London. Since July 1994, most illegal parking in the capital has ceased to be a criminal offence tried in the magistrates' courts.[4] They have been decriminalised and turned into a civil matter in which motorists either pay up without challenge and earn a 50 per cent discount if they pay within 14 days with the full amount pursued in a county court, as a civil debt, if they

---

[4] Parking on white safety zig-zags at pedestrian crossings and causing an obstruction remain endorsable criminal offences.

do not pay within a further 14 days. Or they can write to the council whose parking attendant issued the ticket (now officially called a Penalty Charge Notice) explaining why it should be cancelled. If the council does not agree and refuses to cancel the ticket, it must send the motorist a form telling him he can appeal to a panel of independent legal adjudicators appointed by the Parking Committee for London, a body set up under the 1991 Act to co-ordinate the capital's new parking scheme. This is a free and informal service, which you can use either face-to-face (with lawyers actively discouraged) or through the post with everything in writing. For further information, anyone interested can call the Parking Committee for London on 0171–747 4700.

To return briefly to clamping by the police or traffic wardens: the new London appeal system is available not only for motorists complaining about parking tickets but also for those who consider they have been unfairly or illegally clamped – or towed away. Of course, they will have to pay the £38 declamping fee or £105 tow-away fee to get back the use of their car but, if their appeal is successful, that fee will be refunded and the parking ticket handed out at the same time cancelled. So motorists in the capital should bear in mind that the Parking Committee for London has, in an official leaflet, 'Parking in London', publicly declared its policy to be:

> A record of motorists who persistently evade the law will be maintained
> and illegal parkers with outstanding fines will be more likely to be
> clamped where others would simply receive a parking ticket. Vehicles
> causing an obstruction or nuisance – for example, if they are parked
> in a bus lane or are causing a hazard to other road users – will not be
> clamped but towed away.

If you are not 'an illegal parker with outstanding fines' but your vehicle has still been clamped, those words – and their source – could be useful when arguing your appeal.

But what about private sector clamping on private property? That presents its own set of problems. Outlawed in Scotland since July 1992 by a Court of Session ruling as 'extortion and theft', in England and Wales it is alive and well and flourishing. You can be legally clamped if you park on private land without permission *and a prominently displayed notice warns of the risk of clamping and specifies the amount of the release fee*. The legal theory is that you are presumed to have read the notice and agreed to run the risk. There have been several County Court decisions to this effect.

The Government promised as far back as July 1992 that it was 'urgently considering' what proposals to put before Parliament to curb the well-publicised activities of 'cowboy clampers'. In recent years, among other unacceptable antics, they have reduced pregnant women to tears, taken wedding rings and other jewellery as payment or as a token of future payment and held children 'hostage' while parents dashed to get cash from banks.

But how urgent is 'urgent'? By December 1994, the Government had still not produced any draft legislation. Meanwhile the RAC estimates that there are more than 250 private companies clamping 15,000 cars a year in England and Wales. Of course, not all are 'cowboys', but both reputable firms and their disreputable colleagues remain equally legal – until the Government does something about it.

10. *The fixed-penalty system*

On-the-spot fines are the flavour of the decade, and they are still extensively used for motoring offences outside London with the Government planning to extend the system to a wide range of other offences as well. In fact, the system has proved both a blessing and a curse for drivers. It is a blessing because, if you have committed an offence, it provides a genuine soft option. The fixed penalty will always be less than the fine imposed after unsuccessfully fighting the case in court – when you will also have to pay your own and the prosecution's legal costs. It is a curse because, of course, it is so remorseless. In truth, most fixed-penalty notices are justified and many motorists believe it is not worthwhile querying a fixed-penalty notice, even if there is much to be said on their behalf. They pay up and save themselves aggravation.

But, it is possible sometimes to beat the system – by using the system. Let me explain:

It is pointless challenging a fixed-penalty notice on the basis that you did not commit the offence. The fixed-penalty clerk at a local magistrates' court (whose address is on the notice) will merely write back saying you must let the case go to court.

What you *should* do is write admitting that you were technically

231

guilty but explaining why you think the ticket was unfair or unjust. Someone in authority will then reply that your representations are being considered but in the meantime you should pay the penalty, which will be refunded if ultimately they agree that 'the circumstances do not warrant further proceedings'.

You should always comply with such a request for notices are, indeed, cancelled and payments refunded in genuine cases of hardship or serious mitigation. Pregnant mothers who cannot walk too far and have searched in vain for a legitimate parking place or elderly drivers with a similar problem are among those who receive sympathetic treatment.

But there is another reason why we should all, if possible, query a fixed-penalty notice: there is always a chance that the query will disclose a technical fault which would otherwise have gone undetected.

I give an example of my own from early 1994 before the new system came into effect in London:

The fixed-penalty cheque that was returned

At 10.10 on a Monday morning I came down to the Chelsea mews where I live in a small block of flats to move my car into the garage underneath the block only to find a £30 'ticket' slapped on the windscreen for parking on a single yellow line. I had been unable to put the car in the garage the previous evening because the entrance was blocked by a parked car and I could not use my local resident's permit to park in the nearby residents' parking bays since, as often happens, they were occupied by cars with no permit while their owners visited a nearby cinema.

So I wrote to the fixed-penalty clerk asking him to take no further action. I received a formal reply from the Metropolitan Police requesting me to pay the fixed penalty while the matter was considered – which I did – and eventually a further letter arrived saying that my vehicle had been illegally parked and that the notice 'was correct in the circumstances' – but I would still get my cheque back because the issuing officer had made 'an administrative error'.

And that was it! No explanation as to the nature of the error or whether it would have been spotted if I had not questioned the notice. So I wrote back asking those two very questions and received a reply saying that the office copy of the notice had been found to be incomplete because the exact details of the parking restriction were missing: together with this fascinating piece of information was another: 'Upon receiving mitigation from a member of the public a fixed-penalty notice is checked. If it is then noted that the notice was incorrectly completed by the issuing office, it is cancelled.'

So now we know: if you do not query your ticket, they do not check and, if they do not check, you can find yourself paying when there is no legal need to do so. Which goes to show that, if you use the system, you can sometimes beat the system – even if only by a fluke.

Part Five
YOUR LEISURE

FOURTEEN

Holidays

Holidays should be fun. For most of us, they are also something special and should be a well-deserved rest, with no complications. But who ever said life was going to be fair? You may book well in advance, you may look forward to it with eager anticipation – but a holiday can all too easily work out badly.

At least, it helps to know that the law is basically on your side. The tone was set by the Appeal Court back in October 1972, in *Jarvis* v. *Swan Tours Ltd* (reported in [1973] 1 *All England Law Reports*, at page 71), when a young Essex solicitor booked a two-week winter sports holiday in Switzerland. The brochure promised a marvellous time, with a whole gamut of attractions, but it turned out a disaster. When he complained, the tour operator said he was only entitled to some of his money back because he had enjoyed *some* of the holiday and he was not criticising, for instance, the travel arrangements, there and back.

But the Appeal Court ruled that he should receive substantial damages for his 'frustration, annoyance and inconvenience'. Furthermore, Lord Justice Edmund Davies declared in words that should be written over the door of every tour operator's head office:

'When a man has paid for, and properly expects, an invigorating and amusing holiday and, through no fault of his, returns home dejected because his expectations have been largely unfulfilled, it would be quite wrong to say that his disappointment must find no reflection in the damages to be awarded.'

There are two main aspects of the problem to be looked at:

1. Hotels in Britain

Ever since unscrupulous innkeepers in the eighteenth century made it a habit to knock their clients over the head and steal their belongings, hoteliers have been under what Lord Justice Jenkins once called 'a special liability by virtue of the custom of the realm'. Even if you have not made a booking, they cannot refuse room or lodging to a respectable traveller at any time of the day or night if they have rooms available and the traveller can pay their charges. They are also automatically liable for any loss or damage to a guest's belongings – whether or not any member of their staff is at fault.

The 1956 Hotel Proprietors Act exempts your car from this old automatic liability and allows a modern hotel to limit its responsibility for other goods lost or damaged without the hotel's fault to £50 for any one article or £100 for any one guest; but people tend to forget that their own household-contents insurance policy may cover them for some lost items taken with them on holiday (both at home and abroad).

However, this limitation on a hotel's automatic liability applies only if a clearly legible notice headed '1956 Hotel Proprietors Act' is displayed conspicuously at its entrance or near the reception desk: whether or not you have actually read it![1] If the notice is not there, the hotel will be responsible for anything stolen while you are on the premises, even if you cannot prove that any particular member of staff was to blame: a light-fingered chambermaid or waiter or an inattentive reception clerk not keeping a careful eye on the room keys.

But they may be able to reduce your compensation because of your own 'contributory negligence': for instance, in leaving expensive jewellery in a dressing-table drawer instead of putting it in the hotel's safe.

Some hotels put up a notice in the room itself saying they will not accept liability for goods lost or stolen unless left for safekeeping with the management – a notice similar to the kind one finds in many foreign hotel rooms. But in England and Wales this has no legal effect. As the Appeal Court ruled in 1948, the hotel guest has by then booked in, signed the register – and completed his contract. The hotel cannot then try to impose new terms into that contract.

---

[1] Some older hotels think it more 'atmospheric' to display a notice under the 1863 Innkeepers Liability Act, an earlier version of the 1956 Act. They are foolhardy: it has absolutely no legal effect.

If it wants to limit its liability for valuables only to those left in its safe, it should clearly say so in a notice near the reception desk: so that you can see it when checking in.

Another important notice that you should look for in the reception area is a list of room charges. The little-known 1977 Tourism (Sleeping Accommodation Price Display) Order says that any hotel or establishment in the business of providing sleeping accommodation (those two words 'or establishment' broaden the scope to include boarding houses, private guest houses and even bread-and-breakfast places) must give details of prices plus VAT for all accommodation, including any service charge, provided it has at least four bedrooms or eight beds.

In practice, many establishments do not display this notice. If so, they commit an offence for which they can technically be fined up to £2,500 – *but* the Order does not say that they have to display the price of any individual room in the room itself, as in many other countries.

You are, of course, legally entitled to expect that you will get what you pay for. And this applies both in criminal and in civil law:

In *criminal law* hotels and boarding houses etc. come within the 1968 Trade Descriptions Act, which makes it an offence (with a fine of up to £5,000) to apply a false trade description to the supply of goods and services. So a West Country landlady who wrote to a would-be customer that her boarding house was 200 yards from the sea was fined in the local magistrates' court when a trading-standards officer found the real distance was 801 yards; another West Country hotel has escaped prosecution for claiming that it was only a stone's throw from the beach by employing a Hampshire fast bowler to throw a pebble on to the beach from its front entrance; and a hotel company in Bayswater, London, has been fined for claiming in its brochure that it was 'newly opened' and 'modern' when in truth it had opened six years before and the building was about eighty years old, although a lift had been installed and the building had been extensively modernised. Other examples abound.

As for the *civil law*, back in 1951, in an early test case, the Appeal Court ruled that a holidaymaker, who had booked a 'superior room with a sea view' in a Jersey hotel and was then given a room that was neither superior nor had a sea view, was entitled to damages for his 'appreciable incovenience and discomfort'. And there have, for instance, been decisions that a room from which you can see the sea

239

only by going out on to the balcony is *not* a room 'with a sea view'; that the term 'a lounge' in a hotel brochure does not apply to a room in which meals are served and that accommodation in an annexe will suffice only if it is near enough to the main building and if its amenities (including the provision of meals) are reasonably acceptable.

In all these cases the disappointed holidaymakers won damages in a civil court, but that is not the only remedy available. If, when you arrive at a hotel or similar establishment, you are not offered the type of room you booked (and you should always keep a copy of the filled-in booking form, your booking letter or your written confirmation of a telephone reservation), you can insist on their giving you what you asked for. If they do not, you should reclaim your deposit and walk out: provided, of course, you are reasonably sure you can get what you want elsewhere! If your new hotel costs you more than the original one because you cannot find anything suitable in the same price category, you can reclaim the difference: pursuing your demand, if necessary, into a small claims court.

(Surprisingly I can give no practical advice as to how large you can expect a 'double room' to be. Neither Parliament nor the judges have laid down any precise measurements. When the Appeal Court was faced with the problem back in 1962, it ducked the issue. It was in a case where a South Coast three-star hotel had given a couple a 15 ft. × 8 ft. 6 in. 'double room' hardly big enough to hold a double bed, a chest of drawers and a built-in cupboard, but the appeal judges ruled that complied with the description in that particular hotel and at that particular price and refused to lay down any general guidelines.)

Cancellation

What is the law on cancelling a booking? The best-laid holiday plans can easily go wrong even at the last minute. But that does not entitle you to write, as many people do, to the hotel cancelling your booking because of illness or 'unforeseen circumstances' – and then expecting they will not claim compensation.

A hotel booking is as much a legally binding contract as any other commercial agreement. Just as the hotel cannot go back on its contract, neither can you. Unless you stipulate when making your booking that you reserve the right to cancel in the case of illness or some such cause, which is highly unlikely, neither party to the contract can terminate it off their own bat.

On the other hand, a hotel is not entitled to present you with its bill at once. The management should write a 'holding letter' saying that you have forfeited any deposit but they will try to re-let the room and, if they fail, they will hold you responsible. If they then re-let the room for the same price, they have no case, since they have lost nothing (although they are usually able to keep the deposit).

Even if they have not re-let, they still cannot claim the whole cost of your cancelled booking. They must knock off a third for the food you have not eaten. They cannot, as it were, make a profit out of your breach of contract. In logic and in law, a forfeited deposit is not so much a profit to them as the price to you of cancelling when the contract gives you no such right.

2. Package tours abroad

The twelve million Britons jetting off on holiday abroad every year nowadays enjoy greater legal protection than ever before. Until recently the law had not kept pace with this massive, fast-expanding industry that a bare thirty years ago did not even exist. Various Acts of Parliament and test cases in the courts had built up a partial armoury of legal rights. But that was all part of general consumer-protection law.

At last, there now is – almost unknown to the general public – a detailed set of legal provisions that specifically applies to package tours: the clumsily titled Package Travel, Package Holidays and Package Tours Regulations that came into effect on 31 December 1992. That was literally the very last day by which the British Government could comply with an EC directive dating back to June 1990 ordering all Common Market countries to enact their own package-tour laws. Some lawyers and consumer-rights experts claim these Regulations do not go far enough.

But at least they are a beginning. This is how they (and other laws) work:

(A) *Before you leave Britain*

(i) *Surcharges* These used to be a curse and now are creeping back. But the 1992 Regulations allow no price increases whatsoever within thirty days of departure – and before that they must be tied to increased transport costs.

(ii) *Overbooking* It is usually only a problem on scheduled flights where airlines would habitually 'bump off' passengers with virtual legal immunity because they had sold too many seats. It can now cost them money. For, if the flight originates in an EC country or was booked through an EC travel agent, the EC's 1991 Denied Boarding Regulations say you can demand on-the-spot compensation. If you have a confirmed reservation and have presented yourself for check-in 'within the required time limit', you are entitled to 150 Ecu (about £120) for a flight of up to 2,175 miles and 300 Ecu (about £240) for longer journeys. These amounts are halved if you are offered an alternative flight with an arrival time only delayed by two hours for a flight of up to 2,175 miles and with an arrival time delayed by four hours for longer journeys.

(iii) *Airport delays* Every summer we read of outward-going passengers stranded for hours and even sometimes days.

What are your rights? They are surprisingly few, even today: despite the 1992 Regulations. Most package-tour brochures (which provide the legal basis for your contract) provide adequate safeguards against changes from day flights to night flights but they usually give little or no compensation for mere delay. Tour operators and airlines provide food and drink vouchers or free accommodation for delayed passengers entirely at their discretion. The Airline Transport Users Council used to say that after two hours an airline should give you free refreshments or a meal and, if you were kept waiting between midnight and 4.00 a.m., they should put you up in a hotel.

But in October 1993, in their latest booklet, *Flight Plan, A Passenger's Guide to Planning and Using Air Travel*, they climb down and merely say tamely:

'The airline is not obliged to provide food, drink or overnight accommodation while you wait, *however long the delay* [my italics]. Some airlines do so though and if you are on a package holiday the tour operator will *often* [again, my italics] provide refreshments or hotel accommodation if necessary.'

Some people may consider this appallingly inadequate but it is a correct statement of the law.

Most tour operators nowadays insist on your having holiday insurance and it is always to be recommended. If possible, you should shop around for the best deal. Costing £20 to £30 per adult for a two-week trip, it will give you comparative peace of mind – and includes compensation for airport delays.

But do not cheer too loudly. Usually you will get nothing if delayed for less than twelve hours (or six hours with more expensive European holidays). The clock starts ticking at £20 for that first twelve hours with a measly £10 for each subsequent twelve hours – up to £60 per adult for two and a half days' delay.

What if you want to call the whole thing off and go back home and sunbathe in the garden? Your brochure usually gives you no such right. But insurance does. Even so, you must usually first endure at least twelve hours of airport hell.

(B) *On arrival at the foreign airport*

Missing luggage Until the 1992 Regulations, brochures normally excluded liability for lost luggage and said you must claim on the airline or on your own insurance. Many still try the same tactic; but the Regulations say that the tour operator is ultimately responsible for proper performance of his contract – which includes getting luggage to its destination on time. This provision has not yet been tested in the courts and it will be interesting to see how it works out in practice.

If you claim on the airline, they are bound by international agreement only to pay out £13.60 for every kilo of luggage damaged or lost. And even insurance companies do not pay out for mere delay as against total loss.

In fact, most luggage turns up within twenty-four hours and the insurance offered by some tour operators gives up to £100 to buy essential items after only twelve hours – and you can get the money on the spot from their local representative. You really have to read the small print before deciding which tour operator to go with.

(C) On arrival at the hotel

The hotel and amenities are nothing like the brochure description This is the most common complaint of all – with the strongest protection from the law. Everyone has read horror stories about 'luxury' hotels next to a sewer or 'sea view' rooms half a mile from the sea. But ever since the 1968 Trade Descriptions Act was passed disgruntled holidaymakers on their return can complain to trading-standards officers at their local Town Hall and tour operators have been fined heavily in the local magistrates' court for false trade descriptions. The 1992 Regulations have extended this offence to descriptions that are merely 'misleading' without being downright 'false'.

And, of course, the disappointed holidaymaker can also often sue for damages in a civil court. I wish that more people in the package-tour industry knew the powerful words of Mr Registrar Delroy in the Manchester District Registry in April 1985: 'A tour operator sells a dream. If he sells a dream, he must make it come true. This is fragile; therefore it imposes on him a great obligation to take care.' For those who are interested: the name of this most useful case is *Harris* v. *Torchgrove* and it is reported in (1985) *Current Law Year-book* at paragraph 944).

Brochure conditions often claim that the tour operator has the right to change the resort, flights and accommodation, and to limit the compensation if it makes such a change. But these clauses are only valid if a judge says they are 'fair and reasonable' under the 1977 Unfair Contract Terms Act. If you persevere, you may well find their bite can prove much less than their bark.

The tour operator will often meet your claim with an apology and a host of excuses. They will blame the hotel or say the problem was not within their control. But, if your complaint is reasonable (backed up with photographs, details of complaints to their local courier – *very important!* – and receipts for extra expenses), they may offer compensation or, at the least, private arbitration.

But if your claim is under £1,000 (and each one in a party can separately claim up to that amount), your local small claims court will have jurisdiction and you should strongly consider arguing your case there. Although only another kind of arbitration (with a district judge instead of a private arbitrator in the chair), this procedure has the great tactical advantage (for you) that, since it is a court, you can make public the result. Faced with a fight in a small claims court, many tour operators cave in and offer an out-of-court settlement to avoid unwelcome publicity – but you must have a case they think you are likely to win!

(D) *Your tour operator goes out of business*

It is the ultimate horror to discover that your tour operator has gone bust and you are stranded far from home.

There used to be a vital distinction between holidays booked through non-members of trade organisations and members of the Association of British Travel Agents (ABTA), Air Travel Organiser's Licence (ATOL) or Association of Independent Tour Operators (AITO). Their logos on premises or stationery were essential. They meant that, if the company went bust, you would usually still be covered: you would get your money back if you had not left or would be brought back safely if you had already gone.

For all members of these premier organisations must be fully 'bonded' against adversity: i.e. the company will have lodged a bond with an insurance company or bank sufficient to bail out its customers in the event of financial collapse.

The 1992 Package Tour Regulations were intended to improve the situation. Now *all* tour operators and travel agents commit a criminal offence if not bonded or fully insured. In theory, there should be no more disasters. But in practice I still have my doubts.

The problem is that, despite intense pressure by consumer groups while the Government was framing the Regulations, no new agency was set up to enforce them. The job was thrown back on to harassed trading-standards officers already fully stretched enforcing the wide range of existing consumer-protection laws.

So there is virtually no checking *beforehand* to ensure that bonding or insurance arrangements have been made. Enforcement is primarily on an *after the event* basis. If a company goes bust and it transpires that it was not bonded, trading-standards officers may well prosecute – but what good will that do you? Holidaymakers are still stranded or their holidays cancelled and the travel companies are anyway bust – so they do not even have the resources to pay the fine!

Self-help is still the safest remedy. Despite the 1992 Regulations, it is wise to look around for those essential ABTA, ATOL and AITO logos – *and* check that the company is fulfilling its membership duty and is, indeed, bonded or insured against failure. You should not be too embarrassed to ask.

FIFTEEN

Restaurants, Wine Bars and Discos

Many years ago, I was interviewing over lunch in an expensive restaurant Hugh (now Lord) Scanlon for an article I was writing for a Sunday magazine on the nature of power. I was a young man at the time and he was then one of the most powerful trade-union leaders in the country.

When I tasted the wine that I had ordered, I was not sure but I thought that it might have been off. It seemed corked. What should I do? I did not want to make a fool of myself in front of Scanlon but at the same time I did not see why we should drink wine that was perhaps questionable.

So I called over the wine waiter and he was most unpleasant at the mere suggestion that something might be wrong.

Reluctantly, he tasted the wine – and immediately apologised profusely and brought another bottle. 'That's what I call power!' said Scanlon.

It helped, of course, that I knew I was legally in the right. Food and drink served in a restaurant, wine bar, or public house, for that matter, must be reasonably fit for human consumption and of the quality you are entitled to expect in an establishment of that category. You should never forget that, even in this modern era of the over-hyped 'celebrity chef' or the 'absolutely fabulous' wine bar, you are the client and, as such, you have considerable rights.

Restaurants and wine bars

We are primarily going to look at the law on restaurants, but, as you will see, many aspects also apply to wine bars:

Getting in

If you have made a booking, even if only over the telephone, a restaurant is in breach of contract if it does not honour it – and you can (politely) threaten to sue them, for damages for a spoiled evening, in their own local small-claims court. They will then usually find you a table. (An unscrupulous friend of mine does this quite often – and gets his table – even when he has not made a booking.)

But, if it is vice versa and you have let *them* down, they can sue you for the lost business. This actually happened back in 1988 when a London advertising agency booked a table for 1.00 p.m. for five people at Mijanou, a small but very successful restaurant in Pimlico, central London, and cancelled at 1.35 p.m. on that very day. The meeting had gone on too long and the client did not want to eat.

It was an all-too-familiar scenario for the owner, Mr Neville Blech. 'As always, I was a bit upset,' he told a reporter. 'We only seat thirty so that's a sixth of our seating, and I had turned people away.' The agency refused compensation. So he sued and the judge ruled that, *since it was lunchtime and the table could not be rebooked*, they should pay his loss of profit on the meal plus his legal costs.

But please note the words in italic. They mean that, if the restaurant is not out of pocket perhaps because it is very busy or very large and has immediately seated waiting customers at your empty table, they have lost no profit and have nothing to sue about.

Even so, all restaurant-owners understandably do not like last-minute cancellations or 'no shows' and some of the better-known establishments can afford to draw up their own private blacklist of people from whom they will not accept bookings. They are perfectly entitled to do so. The management of a restaurant, wine bar or public house can always refuse admission at their complete discretion – except on grounds of racial or sex discrimination.

Hence, they can lawfully refuse admission because they say you are 'improperly dressed': no jacket and tie, or torn jeans (however

248

fashionable), for a man or any kind of trousers for a woman – or whatever. On one occasion, a bishop, wearing clerical dog-collar and purple robe, was turned away from a smart central London restaurant and his three-page letter of complaint was to no avail.

But there is a nuance: if they have accepted your booking without warning of their dress code, they cannot legally refuse a table (though not perhaps in the best position). They should have told you of their special rules. In practice, you will avoid a lot of embarrassment by asking them over the phone, when making your booking, if they have a dress code and then choosing either to accept it – or to eat elsewhere.

The menu

Whether in English, phoney French or, even worse, dog-Spanish, this is a vital legal document. The 1979 Price Marking (Food and Drink on Premises) Order says that a restaurant can be fined up to £5,000 for not displaying a full menu (or at least thirty selected items, if the menu is mega-large), including prices and VAT, outside or immediately inside the door, so that potential customers know in advance what they are committing themselves to.

This specimen menu does not have to include a full wine list: whether for restaurant or wine bar. The Order only relates to table wine anyway and stipulates that, if fewer than six kinds of table wine are supplied, the description and price of each kind (white, red or rosé) shall be given but, if more than six, the price and description of only six (again, broken up into white, red and rosé) need be given. It is fascinating to walk out into your local High Street or 'restaurant row', as I have just done, and see how few establishments comply with these strict legal requirements. Some restaurants give no wine at all, table or otherwise, some wine bars give their entire wine list, while others limit themselves to table wine and 'champagne and other sparkling wines'. Yet I know of no prosecutions for breach of the wine provisions of the 1979 Order.

It is an offence against the 1968 Trade Descriptions Act for any food establishment (including restaurants, wine bars and public houses) to give a false trade description to any of their food. Everything must be what it claims to be. *Pâté maison* or *pâté du chef* must be home-made, or at least made on the premises, and not come from a factory or bought in from outside. Fresh fruit salad must consist of fresh fruit and not be tinned fruit freshly mixed. Welsh lamb must be an animal raised or at least born in Wales.

You also have to be careful about scampi. A lot of what masquerades as scampi on many restaurants' menus and tables is nothing of the kind. Genuine scampi should consist only of the tails of Dublin Bay prawns fried in batter but much of what passes for 'scampi' today – especially at the lower end of the market – is often bits of fish minced and bound together with starch or cereal. Prosecutions for breach of the 1968 Act are not unknown. But Roast Aylesbury Duck or Norfolk Turkey do not have to come from Aylesbury or Norfolk: they are merely the names of breeds.

The same principle applies to wine. If they bring you a vintage different from that stated on their wine list, they are not only cheating you but committing an offence against the 1968 Act. With a quality wine, it is always worth checking the cork as well as the label: I once made a restaurant change a wine on which the château named on the label was different from that on the cork!

A menu does not legally have to spell out whether 'liver' is that of a calf, pig or lamb. If you ask the waiter or waitress, their only obligation is to give you a truthful answer. And, if you have a taste for 'bangers and mash' (which you can sometimes find on the menu in even the most fashionable restaurants), you cannot count on the sausages tasting as meaty as those at home. The meat-content regulations that apply to sausages sold by retail to the general public do not apply to the catering trade.

On the other hand, if you pay twice or three times as much in a trendy restaurant as you would pay for sausages and mash in a transport café, and the sausages taste as you would expect to find in a transport café, you may be able to persuade a trading-standards officer at your local Town Hall to prosecute for a false trade description under the 1968 Act or an environmental health officer in the same building to prosecute for the offence of selling food 'not of the quality demanded' under the 1990 Food Safety Act. Anyone fancy a test case?

You cannot rely on getting bread (or roll) and butter free. A restaurant is entitled to make a cover charge for this, provided it appears in the menu by the door. 'Cover' relates to whatever goes on the table apart from the food or drink that you actually order: i.e. clean linen, silverware, glassware, condiments, sauces and such trendy new fads as olives, sliced raw carrots or gherkins which appear whether you ask for them or not – or whether you like them or not.

A little-known legal quirk is that restaurants which have a liquor licence are legally obliged to serve tap water free. This is because the 1964 Licensing Act says that an implied condition of the licence is that suitable beverages, other than alcohol, including drinking water, shall be equally available with the meal – and habitual breach of this condition is grounds for local magistrates refusing to renew the licence.

Technically, merely because a cover charge is stated on the menu does not necessarily mean that you must pay for it. If any part of the 'cover' has been unsatisfactory (or you have not eaten the gherkins), you need only leave what you think the acceptable items are worth. But, of course, most people do not bother. They simply 'vote with their feet' and do not return to the restaurant because usually that is not the only thing that has gone wrong.

Quality

If the food is not cooked to one's satisfaction: for instance, a steak is well done instead of 'rare', you can insist on their taking it back and supplying what you ordered. If you asked for the steak 'well done' and it arrived rare, it is not acceptable for them merely to put the piece of meat back on the grill and cook it a bit more. A 'rare' steak is a steak that has been cooked 'rare' from raw, not merely reheated. If you complain and the management prove difficult, remind them that the 1990 Food Safety Act makes it an offence, with a maximum fine of £20,000 and/or six months in gaol, to supply food 'not of the nature, substance or quality demanded'.

Of course, if the food gives you food poisoning, not only has an offence against the 1990 Act been committed but, *if you have been to the doctor* (an essential for proving your case), you can sue for damages in a civil court. And this applies to any kind of restaurant, irrespective of where it is or how much (or how little) the food costs: it was, for instance, a point of honour at one famous central London seafood restaurant that only the best lobsters were served. The head chef told Judge Blagden at Westminster County Court that they were delivered live each day and any Dead On Arrival were returned at once. Yet one day an out-of-town visitor was served an 'elderly' lobster that made her violently ill. There was no way that she could disprove the head chef's confident evidence – but 'Accidents happen in the best regulated families,' said Judge Blagden, and awarded her damages.

Liability is so well established today that insurers often pay out without a case getting so far as the courts:

The case of the school curry

The chefs at an expensive public school in Norfolk were used to preparing food with a special wheat-free diet for a seventeen-year-old day-boy because he had an allergy to all forms of wheat protein. But in March 1992 he was served a beef curry – and the curry contained flour: kitchen workers had forgotten they had used flour to thicken the sauce.

Result: the curry gave him stomach pains and severe headaches that persisted for eight months. He blamed this illness for his poor A-level results. He sued the school and, in July 1993, the school's insurers paid him £3,000 in an out-of-court settlement.

The £100,000 pay-out

In July 1991, two cricket teams in Suffolk were hit by food poisoning after tucking into sandwiches during the tea interval at a friendly match between a law firm and an accountants firm. Nine solicitors, ten accountants and a number of spectators went down with severe diarrhoea, headaches, vomiting and stomach cramps.

It transpired that mayonnaise used in the sandwiches supplied by a Colchester sandwich bar was infected with salmonella. The sandwich-bar owner had been morally blameless (the salmonella had come from raw eggs used in the mayonnaise and supplied from a batch of chickens later destroyed), so local magistrates gave her a conditional discharge and ordered her to pay £500 costs for offences against the 1990 Food Safety Act.

But a personal-injury specialist with the law firm took up a civil case on behalf of his cricketing colleagues and the worst-affected other victims and in May 1994 the sandwich bar's insurers finally agreed a £100,000 compensation package for the seventy-six major sufferers.

Even if the food or drink is not bad enough to make you ill but you merely think it is not up to a reasonable standard for the money, you can send it back and insist on something else or you can make a deduction from the bill. But, if you make a deduction, you should give your name and address and proof of identity (driving licence, for instance), so that they cannot call the police and claim you have committed the criminal offence of walking out without paying the bill.

If they want the rest of their money, they will have to sue you – if they want to risk the adverse publicity. Amazingly, this happened in one superb case some years ago:

The case of the too-expensive tea

A university economics lecturer, charged eight shillings (40p) at a teashop in Hampstead, London, for two slices of apple pie and a pot of tea, insisted on leaving only five shillings (25p).

He gave his name and address and produced his driving licence, so that they could not call the police. But they actually bothered to sue him for the remaining three shillings (15p) in Marylebone County Court – where Judge Leslie ruled that the meal was worth only 7s. 6d. (just over 12p). The lecturer's solicitor then handed over 2s. 6d. (just over 10p), and a crucial legal principle was reaffirmed.

The great wine scandal

For years, the question 'What is a carafe?' remained as unanswerable as 'How long is a piece of string?' Then, in September 1974, almost unknown to the general public, a great legal victory was – more or less – won. A Government Order specified that wine sold *en carafe* for consumption on the premises must be sold by capacity measurement: half a litre, three-quarters of a litre or one litre.

But the catering industry's steady lobbying had not been in vain: under the Order, an establishment did not have to volunteer to a customer how much its carafes held. It merely had to give a truthful answer if asked. It took another fourteen years before the appallingly titled 1988 Weights and Measures Act 1963 (Intoxicating Liquor) Order said that the size of the carafe must be displayed near the bar in a wine bar or public house or on the wine list or menu in a restaurant. But how often does one see it there or even bother to look?

It is worse with wine sold by the glass. The 1988 Order was updated in 1990 so that at last, as of 1 January 1995, wine sold by the glass must be in a 125- or 175-millilitre glass, with a written statement to that effect on a notice by the bar or in the wine list or menu. Until then the law continued to require no uniform measure: one restaurant, wine bar or public house could charge £1.75 for a large goblet of 'house red' while another could charge £2.25 (or whatever) for a much smaller glass: both fully within their legal rights.

But even since 1 January 1995 there is still no control on the price. There is nothing to prevent an establishment charging, say, £2.25 for a 125-ml. glass and another asking £1.75 for a 175-ml. glass. You simply have to shop around to ensure that you are getting good value for money.

Finally, wine bottles vary in size (usually 50, 70, 72 or 75 cls. or 1 litre) and the 1988 Order says that a wine list or menu must specify the actual size of the bottles on sale in that particular establishment. But you should still check your menu or wine list when next you are out for a meal. The size of a bottle of any individual wine or vintage will almost certainly *not* be stated. This part of the Order is hardly ever enforced.

Tipping

Perhaps the most ticklish question of all. Tipping is in fact purely voluntary. Even if warned of a fixed service charge on the menu, you can still (as with a 'cover charge') refuse to pay it – or some of it – if, at the end of the meal, you do not think the service was worth it.

Very many people do not know their rights. In May 1990, a restaurant in west London advertised a 'set lunch for only £4.95' on a billboard outside the premises but it said nothing about a 10 per cent service charge. Trading-standards officers warned the management that this constituted the offence of giving customers a 'misleading price indication', contrary to the 1987 Consumer Protection Act. When on a second visit this hidden extra was still not mentioned on the billboard, the restaurant was summoned in the local magistrates' court. It pleaded guilty, and was fined £500.

A Code of Practice drawn up under the 1987 Act suggests various ways of including 'extras' on the menu. As with the Highway Code and breaches of motoring law, this Code is of importance when the authorities are deciding if a restaurant has broken the law on misleading prices under the Act but it is neither compulsory nor heeded by everyone. 'Discretionary service charges' and 'optional service charges' are often found on menus, although the Code does not like them. In fact, you can legally ignore them if you think the standard of service does not warrant them.

No one wants aggravation when out for pleasure but also no one wants to be taken for a ride. I recently queried a mysterious 'Grat – £2.50' at the bottom of my bill in a quick-food Italian restaurant in the tourist heart of London. 'That is a gratuity, if you want to pay it,' explained the waiter. Perfectly fair, and I was happy to hand over the extra £2.50.

But I wonder how many people paid their bill without question and added 10 per cent for the tip.

Discos

There are only two things to be said about discos in a book of this nature:

1. *Disco law is based on hypocrisy*   The 1964 Licensing Act allows discos where you can drink to operate legally only on Special Hours Certificates issued by local magistrates allowing them to serve drinks beyond the normal hours permitted by their liquor licence: i.e. on weekdays until 3.00 a.m. in London and 2.00 a.m. elsewhere.

But it is a special condition always imposed that the premises must have a music, singing and dancing licence *and* provide 'substantial refreshment' as well as drink. In fact, food – substantial or otherwise – is one of the last things that people go to such a disco for. Yet the High Court ruled back in 1968 that 'the fact that some customers will not take advantage of either the refreshment or the music and dancing facility does not justify refusal of the Special Hours Certificate'. For many youngsters it is merely a legal way to be out drinking into the early hours of the morning.

2. *There is widespread doubt about the minimum age of entry*   In fact,

there is no legal minimum age! It all depends on whether the disco or club is licensed to sell alcohol.

The 1964 Act makes it an offence for a liquor licence-holder or member of staff to sell to a person under eighteen any intoxicating liquor except beer, porter (a type of thin beer), cider or perry sold to sixteen- and seventeen-year-olds with a meal in a normal restaurant or in a restaurant in a pub not forming part of a bar. Clubs and discos make a great deal of money from alcohol sales and most would rather take strong measures (e.g. bouncers at the door) to exclude under-eighteen-year-olds than run the risk of losing their liquor licence.

Also, many clubs or discos do not want too young a crowd and, irrespective of the law, limit their membership to those over twenty-one.

A quick look at raves

No parents, regardless of wealth or social class, can be complacent about where their teenage children go at night, and some are genuinely worried about what might happen if their young son or daughter were found at a rave. Is he or she liable to be arrested?

The answer is 'No'. Only the actual organisers or someone who allows a rave to take place on his premises commit an offence against the 1982 Local Government (Miscellaneous Provisions) Act, as amended by a 1990 Act, which carries an awesome maximum fine of £20,000 or six months in gaol or both. No one else commits a crime and, even if your youngster is found with a small amount of 'soft' drugs on him for his own use, the police will probably only give him a caution for that specific offence.

As for open-air raves, the controversial 1994 Criminal Justice and Public Order Act has important new provisions that you will find on page 294.

SIXTEEN

Sport

Sport is a dangerous pastime. The *Daily Telegraph* has calculated that in an average year the figures for people needing hospital treatment for football injuries add up to 370,000; for rugby, 78,000; for hockey, 20,000; and for basketball, 15,000. And these are all non-professionals, playing the game for fun!

Indeed, the traditional attitude of English (and Scottish) law has always been that anyone engaged in sport is presumed to know what they are letting themselves in for. You are expected to realise that in certain kinds of sport there is always a risk of injury. Very little Parliament-made law exists on the subject but the consistent attitude of the judges, many of whom took part in sport at school and university, has been that by agreeing to participate in a sporting activity you are voluntarily accepting the risk of injury from 'a normal incident of the game'. As the Ancient Roman lawyers said in Latin, and modern British lawyers still do, '*volenti non fit injuria*': 'to the willing there can be no injury'.

In a vague sort of way, there has somehow always been the feeling among the judges that only 'sissies' sue over a sporting injury. It must be all those cold showers at school when they were young; but there is a general notion pervading the judgments in the comparatively few cases where players have sued over sporting mishaps that it somehow 'isn't done' to go to court over such a matter. 'Judo is a robust and manly sport,' said Lord Justice Sellers sternly in the Appeal Court when quashing a £5,500 damages award to a judo novice hurt in his very first practice lesson.

Yet it was this same Liverpool-born Lord Justice who gave us our classic statement of the modern law on sporting injuries. It was back in 1962, in a case where the Appeal Court threw out a claim for damages over an incident involving one of the horses at an international horse competition. Lord Justice Sellers laid down: 'There is no liability unless there is negligence. Provided that the competition or game is being performed within the rules and requirements of the sport and by a person of adequate skill and competence, another player does not expect his safety to be regarded.'

Exactly! In one of my last games of squash before a bad car smash ended my sporting days for ever, three times within forty minutes I hit my opponent with the ball. That was something of a record, even for me. But the galling thing for my opponent was that each time, according to the rules of the game, it counted as my point because my ball was heading for the right section of the front wall and *he* got in the way. Yet, even if he had wanted to, he could not have sued me – however badly I might have 'crocked' him – for I was not playing *negligently*. After more than thirty years, I was still playing with 'adequate skill and competence', although I did not win the game.

What then is negligence in sport? Later in his 1962 judgment, Lord Justice Sellers gave us this answer: 'If the conduct is deliberately intended to injure someone, or is reckless and in disregard of all safety of others, so that it is a departure from the standards which might reasonably be expected in anyone pursuing the competition or game, then the performer might well be held liable for any injury his act caused.'

Until recent years, before the increasing (and frightening) aggression of several professional sports such as football, rugby and tennis began to seep into the amateur sector, almost the only sporting cases that came before the courts involved golf. Why this should be I really do not know. Perhaps the reason is that so many judges have always played this game, which is one that you can continue to enjoy well into late middle age. Or it may be because golfers tend to come from the more prosperous sections of society and are therefore more likely to accept the financial risks of suing; this was certainly so in the years between the 1920s and 1970s, from which most of the reported cases date.

Whatever the reason, these are just three typical British golfing cases:

• In Belfast, a golfer put all his power into a drive but did not shout 'Fore!' until he saw the ball heading straight for the wrong green. By then, it was too late. The ball knocked out the eye of a fellow player trying to sink a putt. The judge ruled that it was 'a clear case of negligence', and awarded damages.

• 'This is the way to do it,' said a woman golfer to her partner, demonstrating a shot – and had to pay damages to the caddy she struck with her club.

• A golfer in the North Country, playing in a foursome competition, sliced a shot and the ball landed smack on the head of a player in a group in front. He had not shouted 'Fore!' and Mr Justice Brabin ordered him to pay £3,333 damages. Brabin was unusually vehement: 'He made the mistake of thinking the party ahead had played their second shots and were moving off. He misjudged the distance. I think it was an idiotic thing to do. He misread the whole scene. He drove the ball at a time when it was dangerous to do so.'

'Duffed' shots, sliced shots, pulled shots: they have all had their sequel in court. In the early Thirties, Mr Justice Swift, himself, naturally, a golfer of some accomplishment, said: 'A ball may be hit without negligence and strike a spectator or a player. But, if negligence could never be brought home to anybody, an injured person could never recover damages. No player or spectator takes the risk of a negligent stroke.'

Even so, most of the cases before the mid-Seventies had something of an old-world grace to them. They were all very gentlemanly affairs. I know of a cricketing incident on a village green some thirty years ago when a batsman made a wild sweep at the ball, knocking it into the crowd and hitting a spectator. He was happy to hand over £25 in cash to keep the matter from going any further: it was a really stupid stroke and he realised the risk of a judge ruling, however reluctantly, that he had been negligent.

Of course, cricket balls then and now are often hit into the crowd and even beyond – but they are normally splendid shots, not reckless play. Consider, for instance, this case in the early 1950s:

The cricket ball that soared over the wall

A woman was waiting at a bus stop outside a cricket ground in Manchester when a ball came soaring over the wall and hit her on the head. As a judge commented in a later case, the batsman had 'received the right kind of ball and dealt with it in the right kind of way'. But the unfortunate woman was badly hurt. She did not sue the batsman but she sued the club for the inadequate layout of its ground.

She lost her case. A club official testified, 'The hit was altogether exceptional', and evidence was produced to show that only about six times in the previous twenty-eight years had a ball been hit out of the ground. So Mr Justice Oliver ruled: 'The possibility of injury occurring was too remote,' and (after the Appeal Court had overruled him) the House of Lords said he was perfectly correct.

But faulty layout *can* make a sporting club responsible, as in this 1930s case of a Northern golf club:

The wayward golf ball

A man was hit by a golf ball when walking along a road adjoining a course and sued the club for its negligent siting of some of its greens. Neighbours came forward to testify that balls were continually being hit out into the road and the club had done nothing about it.

So Mr Justice Croom Johnson ruled: 'The club officials should have realised their course was dangerous and re-planned some of their greens away from the road.' He awarded damages against the club. But the player was not sued – he had merely been enjoying a pleasant round of golf and using all reasonable care.

In the more materialistic times in which we now live, a senior London insurance claims manager tells me that some golfers, knowing that clubs are nowadays almost always insured, claim against even their own club for injuries sustained as the result of alleged negligence in laying out the course: 'The eighteenth hole is too near the fairway on the seventeenth. That sort of thing.' He did not know of any case actually getting to court but he knew of several out-of court settlements: with consequent changes of layout.

Earlier in this chapter I mentioned the increasing (and frightening) amount of violence and sense of aggression that has seeped into some parts of amateur sport from the professional sector. This is particularly true of football and rugby. The very first case in which a non-professional footballer received damages for being injured by a deliberate foul was as far back as 1941, when a Blackburn policeman received £150 for a foul during a wartime charity match. It took another twenty-nine years before the second award was made: in April 1970, when an uninsured plumber was ordered by Mr Justice Rees to pay £5,400 (in instalments over the next forty years!) to a civil-engineering foreman whom he had deliberately kicked during a game at Eastbourne. But the Eighties and Nineties have, sadly, seen several such cases – and they have not been defeated by the defence of *volenti non fit injuria*, because the judges have ruled that, even in today's lower standards, a foul is still not to be treated as a 'normal incident of the game', the risk of which you accept by taking part in the game.

Sir John (later Lord) Donaldson, then Master of the Rolls, made a positive ruling to this effect in April 1985, in *Condon* v. *Basi*, when upholding a £4,900 damages award by a county-court judge to a player whose leg had been broken by an over-the-ball tackle in a local league game in Leamington. Lord Donaldson said: 'The defendant was clearly guilty of serious and dangerous foul play which showed a reckless disregard of the plaintiff's safety and which fell far below the standards which might reasonably be expected in anyone pursuing the game.' In other words, an amateur sportsman does not accept the risk of being fouled or recklessly kicked: not even today.

What about *professional* sport? For a time it was uncertain whether this also applied to professional footballers who lost their livelihood through injury caused by aggressive play by an opponent that was not so bad as a foul and, in fact, some insurance pay-outs were made on that basis. But then, in June 1994, Mr Justice Drake ruled in the High Court that *Condon* v. *Basi* also applied to professional sportsmen and that they enjoyed no higher standard of protection from the law. His decision came in a case where ex-Chelsea player Paul Elliott had sued Liverpool player Dean Saunders over a tackle in a Liverpool–Chelsea match in September 1992 that had effectively ended his career: Mr Justice Drake ruled that Saunders had gone for the ball, not the man, when he made contact with Elliott's knee and that his action was not reckless or dangerous. The conclusive factor was that the referee at the time did not see it as a foul: so why should a High Court judge nearly two years later?

In fact, sporting fouls amount to criminal assaults as well as giving a right to sue, and several football and rugby players, both amateur and professional, have been gaoled in recent years. That is why anyone injured through a particularly bad foul should report it to the police so that he can, like any other victim of violent crime, then claim compensation from the Criminal Injuries Compensation Authority without having to sue in a civil court.

As the Authority's predecessor, the Criminal Injuries Compensation Board, wrote in its 1980 Annual Report: 'We are getting more and more applications arising out of alleged crimes of violence on the field of play itself. There is little problem when there is a proved "off the ball" incident: what raises far more difficulty is the alleged vicious or wild tackle. Here the alleged victim must prove (as when suing in a court of law) either that there was an intention to injure him as opposed to a mere over-zealous desire to get the ball or, and this is a very difficult matter in what is necessarily a "heat of the moment" situation, that the alleged assailant was guilty of "recklessness".'

Nevertheless, it can be done and the Board returned to the subject in its Annual Report for 1987: 'We consider that it is in the interests of everyone that people who commit criminal offences on the playing fields should be prosecuted. Anyone who considers that an injury upon him was caused by a criminal offence should draw the attention of the police to it. If he does not do so, he is unlikely to receive compensation from the Board.'

It is, of course, possible to insure against sporting injuries or loss or theft of sports equipment and any serious sportsman or woman should do so; but, since individual policies vary, you should hunt around for the best cover. And you should not be embarrassed by reading the small print intently before you make up your mind:

The story of the golf clubs and the small print

In January 1994, the *Daily Telegraph* carried the story of a golfer in Surrey who was refused a pay-out after his golf clubs were stolen from a parked car outside a course because the company claimed the clubs had not been removed from public view. In fact, they were on the back seat covered by two kit bags and loose wet-weather jackets.

Yet a company spokesman claimed: 'We have an exclusion which says golf clubs must be in a locked boot and these were in the back seat of the car which was in public view.'

Are golf clubs 'hidden from view' if they are lying covered on the back seat of a car which is *not* hidden from view? It is a nice question. The Surrey golfer was threatening to complain to the Insurance

Ombudsman Bureau. I do not know the outcome; but anyone who considers himself the unjust victim of insurance small print (in a sporting context or otherwise) should write to the Bureau at 31, Southampton Row, London WC1B 5HJ.

The rights of spectators

As a spectator, you cannot complain if you are injured through a normal hazard of the game – for example, a six being swept into the crowd at a cricket match – but you can complain if either (a) the sportsman has been negligent, as in the High Court case in 1981 when a tennis player's racket flew out of his hand at a tournament in Hornsey Town Hall, west London, and damaged a spectator's eye, or (b) the occupiers of the ground have been negligent.

The classic case of occupier's liability was in 1932 when there had been an accident at Brooklands, a famous speed-car-racing track of the years between the two World Wars. A car had run off the track and sliced into a group of spectators, killing two and injuring many others. A test case brought in the High Court against the Brooklands Auto-Racing Club was successful – but on appeal the decision was reversed. Lord Justice Greer ruled: 'The person paying for his licence to see a cricket match or a motor-car race takes upon himself the risk of unlikely and improbable accidents. There is no absolute warranty that the premises are safe but only that reasonable skill and care have been used to make them safe.'

This basic test has now been written into the 1957 Occupiers' Liability Act which, as we have seen in Chapter 12, imposes a 'common duty of care' on all occupiers of land to ensure the reasonable safety of lawful visitors.

The principle of *volenti non fit injuria* does not apply to this liability. As Lord Denning explained in 1972 in a case where a spectator had been killed in a 'jalopy' car race near Gloucester and he was commenting on the earlier Brooklands ruling, 'No doubt the visitor takes on himself the risks inherent in motor racing, but he does not take on himself the risk of injury due to the defaults of the organisers. People go to race meetings to enjoy the sport. They like to see the competitors taking risks but they do not like to take risks on themselves. Even though it is a dangerous sport, they expect, and rightly expect, the organisers to erect proper barriers, to provide proper enclosures and to do all that is reasonable to ensure their safety.

'If the organisers do everything that is reasonable, they are not liable if a racing car leaps the barriers and crashes into the crowd. But if the organisers fail to take reasonable precautions, they cannot excuse themselves by invoking the doctrine of *volenti non fit injuria*.'

Nor can they exempt themselves from liability by claiming to do so on their tickets or on prominently displayed public notices. The 1977 Unfair Contract Terms Act specifically renders invalid any contract term or notice purporting to exclude or restrict liability for death or personal injury caused by breach of the earlier Act's 'common duty of care'.

But note that this only applies to cases where premises are occupied *for the business purposes of the occupier.*

In Lord Denning's 1972 case, a jalopy-racing club had erected at their meeting large notices headed 'WARNING TO THE PUBLIC. MOTOR RACING IS DANGEROUS' and stating that all persons were present at their own risk and that no liability would be accepted for personal injury (whether fatal or otherwise) 'howsoever caused'. A safety rope got entangled in a car's rear wheel and there was a ghastly accident that killed a spectator. But his widow's claim failed because of the notices.

That was before the 1977 Act and the race was in aid of charity. Would a similar case be thrown out today? Probably yes: I cannot see how raising money for charity comes within the phrase 'using premises for business purposes'.

Even when it comes to sport, the law must inevitably concern itself with the proper meaning of words.

Part Six
YOUR
PURCHASES

SEVENTEEN

Consumer Protection

We have already touched on this subject in several previous chapters. In modern law, you can hardly avoid it.

So we have already seen how the 1968 Trade Descriptions Act, the 1977 Unfair Contract Terms Act and the 1987 Consumer Protection Act have a major role to play in the law dealing with holidays, restaurants and admission to sporting events. But there are also other recent Acts and statutory regulations that we now have to consider as we study what consumer protection is really all about: i.e. **buying goods and services**.

In Victorian times, there was precious little to be said and the little that there was, of course, was said in Latin: *caveat emptor*, 'let the buyer beware!' Many people still use the expression; but they are totally out of date except in the much more casual sense that you should always be careful when spending your hard-earned money to ensure that you are getting what you really want. The maxim no longer means that you have to watch out for yourself because the law gives you precious few rights or even none at all.

Far from it. Nowadays the purchaser of goods (or services) has extensive legal rights. Consumer protection has been virtually a growth industry over the past thirty years or so, with Parliament constantly enacting new and ever-stronger legislation to counterbalance the built-in preference of the old judge-made Common Law for the sturdy entrepreneurial instincts of industry and commerce. As Lord Chancellor Lord Cairns said in a classic mid-Victorian judgment in 1867: 'Some allowance must always be made for the sanguine expectations of the promoters of a commercial adventure. Some high colouring and even exaggeration may be expected.'

267

That has now all changed. Modern consumer law takes a much more vigilant stance to protect the interests of the public. A buyer must still, to some extent, 'beware', but mainly in the sense that he should be alerted to what his rights are – and how best to achieve them.

We shall first look at buying goods and then, to a lesser extent, at services.

(A) Buying goods

Your basic rights are contained in the 1979 Sale of Goods Act, a somewhat belated update by Parliament of the late-Victorian 1893 Sale of Goods Act. This reforming Act, as reinforced by other modern statutes, says that:

(1) *The goods that are sold must be the seller's to sell*

That may seem obvious but it needs to be spelled out. In my young days at the Bar, I used to do a fair amount of work defending people charged with 'receiving stolen goods'. Nearly always the defence was that the items had been bought for cash, at a good price, without a receipt, from a man in a public house. Few of my clients were convicted – for it was then, and still is today, with the modern offence of 'handling stolen goods', for the prosecution to prove positively that you actually knew or believed the goods were stolen. Suspicion was – and still is – not enough.

Yet it is the civil and not the criminal law that, in practical amoral terms, should make one wary of buying possibly stolen goods: for the simple reason that, in the vast majority of cases, you do not become the legal owner.

The law says, again in Latin, *nemo dat quod non habet*: 'no one gives what they have not got'. If the person selling you the goods is not the owner or has not the owner's authority to sell, he cannot legally transfer the ownership.

So you will be at risk for at least the next six years – the relevant Limitation Act period – of the true owner claiming the goods back from you; and you will not have a legal leg to stand on. It does not even matter that both you and the person you bought them from were totally innocent. The villainy of the original thief affects you all.

But there are two exceptions to this rule. The first is ancient and the other modern.

(a) *Exception no. 1* If you buy goods innocently 'in market overt' (an old Common Law phrase meaning 'a market that is open') from a shop in the City of London dealing in that type of goods or from *any* shop or stall on a market day in a market or fair established by charter or custom anywhere in England (but not Wales), the sale is legally valid: even if the seller was not the owner nor authorised by him.

However, there is an important limitation. A case decided in 1596 established that this only applies to a sale 'between the hours of sunrise and sunset' – so that everyone can see what is going on! This 1596 decision (*Market-Overt Case*) in the reign of Elizabeth I was solemnly applied by the Appeal Court in 1973 in the reign of Elizabeth II:

The man who got back his candelabra

In December 1969, thieves broke into a Lloyd's underwriter's home in Chelsea, London, and stole a pair of elegant Robert Adam cut-glass candelabra. Two months later, in February 1970, an art dealer spotted the candelabra in a cardboard box at the famous New Caledonian Market in south London. As Lord Denning later said in the Appeal Court, 'The market is open every Friday from 7.00 a.m. onwards. But dealers go there before that time so as to get the best prices. It is the early bird that catches the worm.' This particular early bird was there after 7.00 a.m. and before sunrise at 8.19 a.m. In Lord Denning's words, 'It was still only half-light. The sun had not risen.'

The dealer bought the candelabra for a fraction of their true value, and the question later arose whether it was a valid sale. The Appeal Court followed the 1596 'Market-Overt Case' and ruled the answer was 'No'. The sale had taken place before sunrise. The Lloyd's underwriter got back his candelabra – and, so far as I know, the art dealer never got back his money from the man in the market who had long since disappeared.

BUT – 'market overt' was abolished by the 1994 Sale of Goods

(Amendment) Act with effect from 3 January 1995. It remains in force, however, for any transaction before that date.

(b) *Exception no. 2*   This relates solely to cars, motorbikes and other motor vehicles. Normally anyone buying goods on hire purchase has no legal right to sell them until they are fully paid off: they still belong to the finance company.

But the 1974 Consumer Credit Act says that any private person (*not* a dealer) who buys a car, motorbike or other motor vehicles for £15,000 or less without knowing of the existence of a hire-purchase agreement or that it has not been paid off gets a good legal title, even though, as always with hire purchase, it was not the hire purchaser's to sell but still remained (until the very last payment) the property of the finance company. In such a case, the company's sole remedy is against their own customer: if they can find him and he is worth pursuing through the courts.

That is not all. A dealer, even though innocent, will not get good title but, if he sells on to an innocent private person, that private person will become the new legal owner. It is only the dealer who is penalised. That is why, in practice, dealers usually check with a company set up by the finance companies and called HPI (Hire Purchase Information) which has a register of all current motor vehicle hire-purchase agreements.

(2) *The description of goods must be accurate*

Again, this is obvious: a shirt sold as 100 per cent cotton should not be a mixture of cotton and polyester and a '1991' model of a car must first have been registered in that year and not in 1990. It does not matter if you have selected the goods yourself, as in a supermarket: if the wrapper on prepacked bacon says that it is Danish, it must come from Denmark. There is still no statutory definition of 'Blue Stilton': if ever there were a prosecution, a Bench of magistrates would have to consult a dictionary and decide for themselves what the phrase means. It used to be the same with 'organic': there was only the *Oxford Dictionary* definition, 'produced without artificial fertilisers or pesticides'. But, since January 1993, 'organic' is legally defined as 'food produced in accordance with the European Community Regulation 2092/91', and several traders have already been warned by trading-standards officers for using a false trade description by calling food 'organic' although not produced according to this Regulation.

Indeed, the requirement by the 1979 Sale of Goods Act that 'goods must correspond with their description' is not merely a matter of civil law. The 1968 Trade Descriptions Act also comes into it: car dealers have been prosecuted for selling cars with 'rolled back' mileometers or falsely stated year of manufacture; tour operators have been convicted of inaccurate descriptions in package-holiday brochures; there has even been a prosecution for 'crab sticks' which contained only 3 per cent crab, and another in East Anglia when Tydeman's Late Orange Apples were sold as Cox's Orange Pippins, although both brands looked very much alike and the trading-standards officer making the purchase was himself not sure which was which.

The 1984 Food Labelling Regulations also specify in great detail the legal description under which most ordinary foodstuffs can be sold, with a maximum fine of £5,000 for breach. You may be interested to know that it is these Regulations which give statutory force to the 'Use by' and 'Best before' labels which we are all used to seeing on food displayed in supermarkets and elsewhere.

What exactly do these expressions mean? 'Use by' (until the Regulations were amended in 1992, the formula was 'Sell by') means: 'The date up to and including which the food, if properly stored, is recommended for use' and relates to food 'which, from the microbiological point of view, is highly perishable and likely after a short period to constitute an immediate danger to human health'. The Regulations – typically – do not define the meaning of 'highly perishable' or 'short period'. It is left to the discretion of the individual packer, although the label must state 'any storage conditions which need to be observed'. 'Best before [a specified date]' relates to all other food, including frozen food, and the stated date is one 'up to and including which the food can reasonably be expected to retain its specific properties, if properly stored'. This label also must state 'any storage conditions which need to be observed'.

Surprisingly, it is not an offence to have foodstuffs still on display after the 'use by' or 'best before' date but it *is* an offence (maximum penalty: £5,000) to sell any such food. In practice, a supermarket manager or owner would be an idiot to keep any food past its proper date still on his shelves, once a customer had pointed it out to him. Incidentally, the two other labels which one often sees ('eat within' and 'display until', specifying period or date) do not come within the Regulations and have no legal status, although they provide useful information.

This is an expanding part of the law. Estate agents describing homes with more regard to fantasy than reality did not come within the Trade Descriptions Act because the Act does not apply to land, only to goods and services. However, that omission was finally remedied by the 1991 Property Misdescriptions Act, which came into effect in April 1993 and says that an estate agent who makes a false or misleading statement about any property commits an offence for which he can be fined up to £5,000. The only defence is that he took all reasonable steps and exercised all due diligence to avoid the offence. Merely claiming 'it was a mistake' will usually not be enough, as when Bedford magistrates recently fined a local firm £250 with £250 costs after one of its staff mistakenly described a house built in the 1860s as eighteenth-century. 'Des. res.' must now really mean 'desirable residence'.

At this stage, I want to break off the general narrative to discuss perhaps the most difficult question that can arise when considering the Sale of Goods Act requirement that goods sold 'must correspond with the description'. I refer, of course, to **antiques**.

British antique dealers are among the most respected in the world. Perhaps that is why there is no entirely satisfactory answer to the question 'In law, what is an antique?' There is no Act of Parliament and the courts have simply not had sufficient opportunity to pass judgment on the matter: there have been too few cases.

'As to what "an antique" means,' Judge Andrew Phelan told a Crown Court jury in a 1977 case over whether or not an 1860 Colt revolver was an 'antique firearm' so as to require a firearms certificate, 'if one looks at the *Oxford Dictionary*, one gets perhaps a little help because there are phrases there which claim that it means something like old-fashioned, something of long standing, something ancient of bygone days – but it is essentially going to be a matter for you.'

The jury convicted the Colt owner of *not* having an 'antique firearm' so that he did need a firearms certificate but, when he appealed, the

Appeal Court not only refused to say that Judge Phelan's somewhat woolly dictum was wrong they did not supply any replacement definition of their own. In effect, they passed the buck and left it to later judges to decide.

Many people believe that an antique must be at least a hundred years old. But there is no legal ruling to that effect. It is merely a practical yardstick used by H. M. Customs in assessing whether to let an item into the country duty-free or at a lower rate of duty than the normal.

The 100-year rule is also adopted by the British Antique Dealers' Association, whose 450 members represent the better end of the market. Anybody in Britain can call himself an 'antique dealer' without the slightest qualification, training or experience, although a few trading-standards departments nowadays operate schemes where all local dealers must at least be registered with the department and keep records of all sales exceeding £100. If you see a BADA membership certificate or emblem hanging up in a shop anywhere in the country, you will know that the shopkeeper has been established in the antiques trade for at least three years, that he has expert knowledge and that he has bound himself to abide by the Association's strict rules as to integrity and fair dealing.

According to the Association's by-laws, an 'antique' is 'an object which (a) was manufactured more than 100 years prior to the date on which it is offered for sale and (b) is in substantially the same condition as when originally made and has not at any time been added to or altered to any material extent ... except for the purpose of necessary repair'.

This definition would not necessarily be accepted in the courts, and Lord Justice Eveleigh has expressly said in another 'antique firearm' appeal case: 'It has been said that an antique must be over a hundred years old. I do not think it is possible to lay down any such rule. It must vary depending on the article.'

Doing the best I can in a grey area of the law, here are my own guidelines as to the protection you enjoy in English law when you buy an 'antique':

First, irrespective of any specific age, it must genuinely be what the dealer (or stall-holder or ordinary shopkeeper) claims it to be. 'A Chippendale chair' must be a chair actually worked on by the eight-

273

eenth-century craftsman Thomas Chippendale. If, at a lesser level, it is said to be 'a chair from Chippendale's workshop', that is also what it must be. That is why so many dealers play safe and prefer 'in the manner of Chippendale'.

Second, there must still be enough of the original article left to qualify for the description used. Restoration work is, of course, permitted – but there is a limit. Even if the courts were to accept fully the BADA's view on 'necessary repair', the object cannot be 'repaired' out of its legitimate description. It may be 'necessary' to do a great deal of repair work to ensure that a genuine Chippendale chair can still be used *as a chair* – but that still does not automatically mean that its description as a chair *made by Thomas Chippendale* survives.

Third, price is a factor. The amount of restoration you can reasonably expect when you lay out £5,000 is surely less than when you pay £500 – provided the two items are comparable.

Fourth, delay in ascertaining the truth about a false description can deprive you of your remedy. Where both dealer and customer have been equally duped by a fake work of art, the judges tend to shrug their shoulders (in the few cases that have actually come to court) and say that, before he took delivery, the purchaser should have taken more care to ensure that he was getting exactly what he had paid for. This is one instance where *caveat emptor* still applies with much of its old vigour.

'If a man elects to buy a work of art or any other chattel on the faith of some representation, innocently made, and delivery of the article is accepted, then it seems to me that there is much to be said for the view that, on acceptance, there is an end of that particular transaction and that, if it were otherwise, business dealings in these matters would become hazardous, difficult and uncertain,' said Sir Raymond Evershed, when Master of the Rolls, in the Appeal Court in 1950. This was in:

The case of the fake Constable

A London collector bought an oil painting of Salisbury Cathedral as a genuine work by John Constable, only to discover five years later that it was a fake. The truth came out when he decided to sell it and took it to the well-known firm of Christie's to put up for auction, and they told him it was a valueless copy. He took it back to the gallery where he had bought it and demanded they take it back and return his money. They refused both requests, maintaining that it was a genuine Constable.

Eventually a county-court judge, after hearing evidence from experts on both sides, decided that it was not genuine but that the gallery owner had genuinely believed it was and that five years after the event was too late to reopen the transaction. He was upheld on both counts by the Appeal Court.

Of course, where the dealer has been dishonest and knowingly misled his customer, it is not only easier to reopen the transaction in a civil court but a criminal offence may also have been committed. As far back as 1973, when a second-hand car dealer had deliberately misled a customer as to the value of his car ('It's only good for scrap,' he said and paid him £2 although later advertising it for sale at £135), Lord Widgery, then Lord Chief Justice, ruled that the Trade Descriptions Act applied. Defence counsel had argued that the Act only governed people *selling* goods, not those merely buying them. In words that apply equally to antique dealers looking for bargains as to second-hand car dealers with the same objective, Lord Widgery said: 'It seems to me that it is perfectly reasonable when the buyer is the expert and the seller may be the amateur, where the buyer makes an examination of the goods in his capacity as an expert and then proceeds to pronounce on their qualities or otherwise, that he should be as much liable to be restrained in his language as a seller and is to be restricted in any temptation to make false and misleading statements about them.'

One quick word before leaving the subject of antique dealers: when buying a painting – or, indeed, anything else – you should always insist on being given a receipted and dated invoice bearing the firm's name and address and (most important) a brief description of your purchase. Technically a description does not have to be in writing, but it certainly helps! This is vital to protect your interests both at civil and criminal law: so much so that at the famous Portobello street market in London the local trading-standards department has on permanent display a printed notice giving its address and telephone number and stating: 'Always ask for a receipt giving (1) Description of goods, (2) Age of goods, (3) Name of seller, address or stall number, (4) Date of sale.' Also: 'If an item is a reproduction, that word *must* appear in the description.' That is good advice: but I wonder how often people bother?

So much for antique dealers. The role of auctioneers is also of importance, and in 1989 the Appeal Court ruled that an auctioneer can be sued for negligence in valuing an art work brought to him for auction. Unfortunately, the ruling also said that the courts should not be quick to find that negligence has been proved!

As Lord Justice Slade said, 'The judgment may in the very nature of things be fallible and turn out to be wrong. Provided that the valuer has done his job honestly and with due diligence, the court should be cautious before convicting him of professional negligence.' So, despite Lord Justice Slade's 'sympathy', an elderly couple in Surrey lost their award of £76,222 damages against local auctioneers who failed to identify two oil paintings of foxhounds as attributable to the famous eighteenth-century painter George Stubbs and sold them for £840 – only for the lucky buyer to sell them five months later at Sotheby's in London for nearly £90,000.

Auctioneers were also in the legal limelight the following year, when, in June 1990, the High Court ruled in *Derbyshire County Council v. Vincent* that the Trade Descriptions Act applied to them just as much as to antique dealers and other retailers. Until then it had been generally believed that the normal disclaimer in auctioneers' catalogues that all goods are bought as viewed and that they are not responsible for errors or mis-descriptions meant that no description could be the basis of a criminal prosecution. Now we know this not to be so. Indeed, an auctioneer in the Midlands has been fined £100 and ordered to pay £50 costs after an art dealer paid £3,250 at auction for a landscape allegedly by Thomas Girton, the well-known Georgian artist, whereas it was really by William Pearson, a follower of Girton, and worth only £400.

Now let us return to the basic requirements of the 'ordinary' law of the sale of goods:

(3) The goods must be of merchantable quality

They must also be reasonably fit for the purpose for which they were bought, having regard to their description and the price.

This is perhaps the most important part (Section 14) of the Sale of Goods Act and no amount of small print in the contract, whether in the order form, invoice, delivery note or elsewhere, can take away this basic right. It is, in fact, a full statutory guarantee.[1] Too few consumers appreciate the protection given them by Section 14: they are ensnared by the lavish promises of manufacturers' guarantees and overlook the rights that Section 14 gives them *against the shop where they bought the goods*. Have you ever noticed that little phrase 'This guarantee does not affect your statutory rights' amid all the glib PR verbiage on manufacturers' guarantees? That statement is not there out of the goodness of anyone's heart. It is because the 1976 Consumer Transactions (Restrictions on Statements) Order pronounces it a criminal offence to make any statement about a consumer's rights relating to quality and fitness without informing him at the same time that his statutory rights are not affected.

Nothing is for nothing in this world. You cannot expect caviare for the price of fish paste. But, however lowly priced a washing machine, electric toaster or whatever may be, it must still work reasonably well for the money. The same applies to second-hand goods and goods bought from a charity shop. They are all supposed to work reasonably well.[2]

If not, *and you act promptly*, you can take it back to the shop and demand a replacement or full refund. They cannot fob you off with a credit note or say, 'It's the manufacturer's fault.' (It would be different if you were claiming under a manufacturer's guarantee, but we will come to that shortly.) They can keep it for their own people to check the fault but you should make clear that you have rejected the goods as faulty and are only leaving them on that basis. Demand a receipt and write on both copies (theirs and yours): 'Left for checking but rejected by the customer.'

With all immediate payment purchases (whether by cash, cheque or credit card), you cannot complain merely because you have changed your mind or decided that you did not like your purchase once you got it home. But, if you are buying goods for £15,000 or less by hire purchase or other credit agreement, the 1974 Consumer Credit Act

---

[1] This vitally important provision is not to be found in the 1979 Sale of Goods Act itself but in Section 6 of the 1977 Unfair Contract Terms Act.

[2] Beware of car-boot sales! You can sometimes get the most marvellous bargains but you should be warned that Section 14 only applies 'where the seller sells goods in the course of a business'. It does not apply to sales between private individuals, such as those at car-boot sales. So you cannot count on goods being of merchantable quality or reasonably fit for the purpose for which they were bought.

says that, if you sign the agreement 'off trade premises', you can cancel within five days: for whatever reason. This is known as the 'statutory cooling-off period' and home-visit agents selling expensive products on credit often suggest that you 'do the paperwork' at their shop or office rather than sign the papers at your home. Beware! They are trying to take away your legal right to second thoughts.

You also cannot complain because of defects or limitations of which the seller *specifically* warns you (for example, 'Do not apply to wheat or barley crops beyond the recommended crop-growth stage' on a herbicide canister in a 1987 case) or which you ought to have discovered for yourself if you had examined the goods. In fact, unless you are prepared to examine goods really carefully before buying them, you should not check them at all. A half-hearted examination may take away your right to complain later about something that you missed but should have spotted.

If you bought the goods as a present for someone else, and they prove defective, technically only you can take the goods back because the contract was only with you. But, if you give the recipient a letter authorising him to return them on your behalf, that will probably suffice. Similarly, if at all possible you should take your receipt with you, but if you have lost it do not be put off by a salesperson telling you that no complaints are accepted without a receipt. Legally they cannot do that. That very statement is, in itself, in breach of the 1976 Consumer Transactions Order and you can justifiably retort: 'Are you calling me a liar? If so, we'll see whom the district judge at your local small claims court believes.'

But please note: once you have, in the legal sense, 'accepted' goods, you lose your right to a full refund or to insist on their being taken back. You can claim *some* of your money back and compensation for any loss or damage (when, for instance, clothes are ruined if a defective washing machine overheats or someone is hurt when a chair collapses) but a total refund is out of the question. Section 35 of the 1979 Act says that a buyer accepts goods 'when after the lapse of a reasonable time he retains the goods without intimating to the seller that he has rejected them'. That vital word 'reasonable' is strictly interpreted. You really must act fast, for look at what happened to the unfortunate motorist in:

The case of the disappointing Nissan

In December 1984, a man in north London took delivery from his local dealer of a new Nissan car costing £8,000. Three weeks and 140 miles later, it broke down on the M3 motorway. The engine seized up due to the camshaft being starved of oil because a blob of sealant had got into the lubrication system. When the motorist finally got home, tired and angry, he immediately rang the dealer to say he was rejecting the car and followed it up the next day with a letter saying: 'I do not regard the car as being of merchantable quality as defined by Section 14 of the 1979 Sale of Goods.'

He seems to have known his law but the dealer did not accept the rejection and had the car repaired without cost so that it was as good as new. But the motorist still would not have it back and sued in the High Court.

Mr Justice Rougier agreed that the car was not of 'merchantable quality' but ruled that the man had lost his right to reject it because he had had it for three weeks and driven it for 140 miles. He was only entitled to a paltry £232.90 damages for out-of-pocket expenses and aggravation.

This case (*Bernstein* v. *Pamson Motors Ltd.*) is important because of the very restricted interpretation that Mr Justice Rougier gave to the definition of 'acceptance' in Section 35:

In my judgment, this section seems to me to be directed solely to what is a reasonable practical interval *in commercial terms* [my italics] between a buyer receiving the goods and his ability to send them back, taking into consideration from his point of view the nature of the goods and their function, and from the point of view of the seller *the commercial desirability* [again, my italics] of being able to close his ledger reasonably soon after the transaction is complete.

But what about the argument that, as soon as Mr Bernstein knew about the defect (i.e. when the car seized up), he at once rejected the vehicle? That did not matter, ruled this judge. 'The nature of the particular defect discovered *ex post facto* and the speed with which it might have been discovered are irrelevant to the concept of reasonable time in Section 35 as drafted.'

It is a shame that Mr Bernstein did not appeal, for this remains the law of England until another High Court judge or (preferably) the Appeal Court pronounces upon it.

(4) The price of the goods, once fixed, cannot be changed – except by mutual consent

This entails the discussion of two main items:

(a) *What is the price anyway?*   Perhaps the most frequent legal question that I have been asked over the years is: can you insist on a shop selling you something at the price in the window?

Before the 1968 Trade Descriptions Act, the answer would have been 'No'. A retailer did not legally offer to sell you goods by displaying them in his window with a price tag. He was merely, in law, inviting you to come into his shop and offer to buy it – an offer which he could then legally decline.

Shoppers have often been met with a downright refusal to take goods out of the window or with a claim that the price tag was 'a mistake' and the real price was very much more – never, it will be noted, very much less. For decades this was perfectly legal and many shopkeepers still think it is; but they overlook – or do not know – that Section 6 of the 1968 Act says, 'A person exposing goods for supply shall be deemed to offer to supply them.' This means that, if they refuse to sell you the goods at the price 'exposed', i.e. in their window, you can legitimately threaten to report them to the local trading-standards department – which may well make them change their mind.

It is also an offence against the 1968 Act if the shop does not have identical goods for sale at that same price inside *or* refuses to sell you those very goods in the window if they have no more left in the shop itself. The only way they can avoid this is to display a conspicuous notice in the window saying something like 'Goods in window are for display purposes only' or 'Goods available in store so long as stocks last'. This brings us to:

(b) *The law of sales*   If you read carefully the small print at the bottom of a sales advertisement in the press, you will often find: 'All offers subject to availability. Some lines only at selected stores.' A similar announcement is often made in television commercials about so-called 'special bargains'. They are there for a reason: to give national retailers vital legal protection to prevent you from going along to any particular store and demanding, as a matter of right, to buy goods at the advertised low price. They need that legal safeguard in case stocks run out.

Two further special points arise:

(i) A shop does not have to say why goods have been reduced, except where the reason for the price reduction is that they are substandard. But, even when items are labelled 'shop-soiled', 'slightly imperfect' or 'seconds', they must still be of a reasonable standard: all things considered.

What about those notices one sometimes sees that say: 'No sale goods exchanged or money refunded'? You can ignore them! They are psychological warfare by unscrupulous shop management: without any legal effect.

It goes further than that. The 1976 Consumer Transactions (Restrictions on Statements) Order, which we have already met, makes it an offence to display notices restricting your legal right to return defective goods at sales time or any time. An umbrella-maker in Shropshire has been fined for displaying a sign that read: 'All umbrellas must be checked before leaving cash-till. No returns can be accepted after use.' And a dress-shop owner in Leeds has met a similar fate for putting up a sign: 'We willingly exchange goods but regret that money cannot be refunded.'

(ii) How can you be sure that the price reduction is genuine? Quite simply. Section 20 of the 1987 Consumer Protection Act says that any retailer who gives, by any means whatever, to any consumer an indication which is misleading as to the price at which any goods, services, accommodation or facilities are available commits a serious offence for which he can be fined up to £5,000 in a magistrates' court or without limit in a Crown Court.

And the Act backs this up with a detailed Code of Practice which retailers breach at their peril. It is, for once, written in simple, non-lawyerly language – for example:

> Always make the meaning of price indications clear. Do not leave consumers to guess whether or not a price comparison is being made.

If so, the comparison should always state the higher price as well as the price you intend to charge. Do not make statements like 'Sale price £5' or 'Reduced to £39' without quoting the higher price to which they refer.

Perhaps most important of all, the Code spells out that the higher price of which the sale price is supposed to be a reduction must have been available to customers for at least twenty-eight consecutive days in the past six months. *And*:

(i) that price must have been available in the same shop where the reduced price is now offered (and not at another branch in another part of the country, as used sometimes to be the case); and

(ii) if the higher price was, in fact, only available for a shorter time or in another store, you must be told so by a conspicuous notice saying something like 'These goods were on sale here at the higher price from 1 October to 31 October' or 'These goods were on sale at the higher price in 10 of our 95 stores only'.

(5) *Goods must be delivered within the time agreed*

Delivery dates are usually an essential part of a contract of sale and, if not kept, the buyer is entitled to back out. The problem is that, if instead of cancelling the order you continue to press for speedy delivery, you cannot at a later stage just turn round and refuse to take the goods. By keeping the contract 'alive' after the original delivery date, you have waived your right to claim that time of delivery was an essential part of the contract. So what you should do is give a *new* delivery date, a reasonable time ahead – and confirm it in writing. If that new date is not kept, you can then safely refuse to take the goods.

Finally, going back to what I wrote a few pages ago, what exactly is the law about those tempting guarantees – or warranties, as they are also called – offered by some manufacturers? It is estimated that there are about 10 million currently in force and that one-third of consumers take one when they make a purchase: in addition to their statutory rights under Section 14 of the 1979 Sale of Goods Act it all seems so cut-and-dried, and they can hardly be blamed for doing so.

But I do wish that more people would read the small print. Some guarantees are first-rate; others (as the Director-General of Fair Trading warned in March 1994) are not worth the paper they are written on.

In fact, there are three different kinds: the manufacturer's free guarantee that usually lasts for at least a year and in the event of a breakdown *can* cover the cost of parts and labour (depending on the small print); 'extended guarantees' offered by the shop itself; and service contracts offered by the manufacturer that are supposed to pick up where your statutory rights or the manufacturer's free guarantee leaves off. Provided they are not too expensive, they can be well worthwhile – but they are not really 'guarantees' in any legal sense. They are more truthfully breakdown insurance which is laudable in itself but you really do have to read the small print to see if what you are getting is worth the money they are charging. For example, does it cover you for transport or the cost of delivery to whoever is doing the servicing – and does it cover call-out charges?

So much for buying goods. Now let us turn very briefly to:

(B) Buying services

There is not much to add to what has gone before. A great deal of consumer-protection legislation applies just as much to providing services as to providing goods.

But there is one matter that we should specifically mention: John Major's much-vaunted Citizen's Charter launched in 1991. How does it affect the law? I must say: 'Not a great deal.' It applies to all public services – such as schools and colleges, hospitals, rail services, roads, council services, the Police, the fire services, the privatised utilities, the Post Office and the rest – and about forty individual Charters have been published and much public money spent (some would say, 'Not nearly enough'), with a considerable improvement in general standards and in the quality of service offered.

But, at the end of the day, the Charters have had very little impact on the law. That is not their proper function. As Mr Major wrote in his foreword to the Second Annual Report in March 1994: 'Many public services are already rising magnificently to the new challenge the Charter has set them. I will only be satisfied when all of them are doing so.'

As a lawyer, it does not impress me greatly but it is undoubtedly very good public relations.

STOP PRESS

The 1994 Sale and Supply of Goods Act, a Private Member's Bill that came into effect on 3 January 1995 has abolished the outdated term 'merchantable quality' in the 1979 Sale of Goods Act (see page 276) and replaced it by 'satisfactory quality' for all transactions after that date. This gives a buyer more rights. It means that he or she is now entitled to expect that goods shall be safe, durable and free from minor defects, including mere defects of finish or appearance.

The new Act also softens the rigours of the old law, as shown in the Case of the Disappointing Nissan (*Bernstein* v. *Pamson Motors Ltd.*) at page 279, where the purchaser of a defective new car lost the right to demand his money back because he was deemed to have 'accepted' it by driving it for 140 miles over a period of three weeks. The 1994 Act makes clear that a material question in deciding that a 'reasonable time' has elapsed so that a buyer is presumed to have accepted goods is whether or not he has had a reasonable opportunity of examining them to ascertain that they conform with his contract, including the right to satisfactory quality. If Mr Bernstein had bought his Nissan after 3 January 1995, he would probably have won his case.

Part Seven
YOUR SPECIAL PROBLEMS

EIGHTEEN

Lodgers, Squatters and Other Matters

This chapter and the next one are different from the others that have gone before. They do not contain any major theme but deal separately with some individual topics which, although mostly unrelated to each other, I have found over many years in legal journalism to be of special interest.

Lodgers

Letting out a room in your own home has become much simpler since the 1988 Housing Act came into effect in January 1989. Before then, it was easy enough to take lodgers in but getting them out could be a problem. If their time was up or you gave them reasonable notice and they refused to go, you had to go to your local county court and get an eviction order – which could be time-consuming and expensive.

But now, if they refuse to go, you can simply change the lock on your front door and only let them back in on the strict understanding that it is temporary and solely for the purpose of packing their belongings and leaving for good. Until the 1988 Act, you could not have done this: you would have had to go to court for an eviction order. A lodger, even though not a tenant, was deemed 'a residential occupier' under the 1977 Protection from Eviction Act, and you would have been guilty of unlawful eviction and could have been goaled for up to six months or fined up to £2,000.

Even today, you would be well advised to have a friend present when you expect your ex-lodger to come back after you have changed the lock on the front door, if only for your own protection in case the ex-lodger uses violence, or as a witness, in case he afterwards alleges that *you* used violence (which would be an offence against the 1977 Criminal Law Act).

There used to be a vital legal distinction between a lodger and a tenant. A lodger is someone who does not have the right to exclusive possession of any part of your home, not even his own room to which he usually does not have a key. Technically, you could walk into his room at any time although usually, of course, you would be expected to knock. As Lord Templeman said in a 1985 case, 'A lodger is entitled to live on the premises but cannot call the place his own.'

On the other hand, a tenant, even though, like a lodger, he may share the kitchen or bathroom, does have the right to exclusive possession of his own room. In addition to a front-door key, he will usually have his own key to that room and is legally entitled to a rent book. With all letting arrangements made with a resident landlord since 15 January 1989, his position in law is nowadays little different from that of a lodger – except that it tends to be more formal and there is usually a written 'tenancy agreement' spelling out all the terms and obligations on both sides.

Yet, even with a 'mere' lodger, it is better to have written rules. The minimum basic set-up is a furnished bedroom with access to kitchen, bathroom and living-room. But there are many variations: with price usually a determining factor. Some people offer only bed and breakfast, others an evening meal and perhaps Sunday lunch as well; some clean the lodger's room, others merely supply weekly clean linen. There are no legal restrictions as to what a landlord can charge and he is perfectly entitled to take up references before letting a stranger into his home and to insist on a refundable deposit against breakages that amount to more than 'reasonable wear and tear'.

All lodgers usually have their own front-door key and can come and go as they please – but some landlords insist on no noise between 11.00 p.m. and 7.00 a.m. and ban smokers, pets or overnight visitors. Some may allow local phone calls free but usually all insist on international calls being paid for there and then. The reason is simple: too many landlords receive nasty shocks when their phone bill comes in after a lodger has left and they find several international calls charged to their account. They are legally liable to pay although, if the position is explained, the telephone company will usually allow extended time for settlement of the account in case the money can be recovered from the departed caller.

I have said there are no legal restrictions as between you and your lodger; but this is not so as between you and other people. If you rent the property or have a mortgage, your lease or mortgage will probably say you must first obtain the consent of your landlord or building society. In fact, it will nearly always be granted, but, with such a personal arrangement, few bother to ask and, to be honest, the worst that can happen to you, if found out, is that you will have to tell your lodger to go. Usually no lasting damage will have been done.

Insurance can, however, prove a problem. Rules differ from one company to another but they all stress that you should let them know if you are taking in lodgers. The reason is simple: as a spokeswoman for Legal & General, one of the major companies, has told the *Daily Telegraph*, 'Landlord and lodger rarely know each other in advance, and people are often more careless about security if they do not own the house themselves.' The result is that most companies will exclude cover for theft or accidental damage on a home contents policy once you tell them you have lodgers – or refuse to pay out in the event of a claim if they later discover the truth. In practice, many people take a chance and simply say nothing – which may be ethically wrong but makes a certain kind of pragmatic good sense.

You are also supposed to tell the Inland Revenue that you have lodgers because – obviously – any profit derived from them should be disclosed as part of your income. To encourage honesty and discourage unlawful tax evasion, the Inland Revenue have been operating since 1992 a scheme called 'rent-a-room relief'. Under this system, you can earn *gross* up to what is currently a threshold of £3,250 a year from lodgers without paying any tax on it. The granting of the relief is automatic. If rents received are less than that figure (or whatever it may be in future years), you simply tick the relevant box on your annual tax return and that is the end of it. On the other hand, it may be more advantageous, in any given year, to opt for what is called the 'alternative basis'. In this event, tax will be charged on the excess of gross rents over £3,250. So if you estimate that, after deducting all your legitimate expenses, you have made in any one year more than £3,250 *net* profit, you should disclose that full figure as part of your overall income.

It all depends on how the figures work out: for example, if you have received in any one year total rents of £3,800 but incurred expenses of £150, your net income from lettings would be more than the permitted tax-free threshold. It would, in fact, be £3,650. So you should elect for the 'alternative basis' and you will be taxed only on the excess gross rents over the threshold: i.e. £3,800 minus £3,250 equals £550. The subject is somewhat complicated but the Inland Revenue has a helpful leaflet, IR87 *Rooms to Let*, obtainable at most tax offices.

One final point: what about Council Tax? Who has to pay: you or the lodger? It is difficult to find any clear answer in the available literature so I asked my own local authority at Kensington and Chelsea in London, and this is what a helpful official had to say:

> Many people are still very confused. They still mix up the situation with what it used to be under the old Poll Tax where there was a counting of heads and, as a general rule, each adult living in a property – including any lodger – had to pay his own Poll Tax. It does not work like that any more. Only one person in any property is responsible for paying the Council Tax and that is usually the 'head of the household'. The amount is solely based on the value of the property, not upon how many people may be living there.
>
> Taking in lodgers does not affect a householder's Council Tax at all – except in the one case where until a lodger was taken in the householder was living on his or her own and claiming the normal 25 per cent discount for sole occupancy. Once they have a lodger, they should tell us because they are no longer entitled to the discount. Do they make the lodger make up the shortfall? We never get involved in that: it is entirely a matter for the householder and lodger to sort out between themselves. So far as we are concerned, no lodger has to pay Council Tax.

Squatters

It is a national disgrace that, despite all the old-fashioned notices that still threaten 'Trespassers Will Be Prosecuted', trespass is *not* a criminal offence. In December 1984, well over a year after Michael Fagan had caused a public outcry by breaking no law when getting into the Queen's bedroom in Buckingham Palace because he had not broken or damaged any part of the structure (he had merely shinned up a drain-pipe and pushed wider open an already partly opened first-floor window), Leon Brittan, then Home Secretary, announced that the Government was going to make trespassing on residential property a criminal offence. This was just one more unfulfilled political promise. Despite the assurance of his successor-by-two, Michael Howard, to cheers at the Conservative Party Conference in October 1993 that the Government was at last going to get tough with squatters and others who take advantage of our archaic laws on home protection, the Criminal Justice and Public Order Act, which received the Royal Assent in November 1994, still does not make it an offence for an unauthorised intruder to enter your house or property *so long as he does not use force* – which has always been the case.

It still remains the law that strangers can walk uninvited into your house through an unlocked door or clamber in through an open window, read your letters and open your drawers and commit no offence – so long as their intention is not to steal, damage or rape.[1] You can use 'reasonable force' to evict them; but that is all. If any of us should wake in the night to find an intruder sitting on the edge of the bed, and that person has not got in through force, we could seek no recompense in our legal system for the sense of terror, violation and anger we would all feel. The police would not even be under a legal obligation to come and help you evict them. *No crime has been committed.*

An even more bizarre (but little-known) fact is that a foreign ambassador and his family enjoy greater legal protection than the rest of us. In 1977, after a series of embassy break-ins, the Callaghan Labour Government passed through Parliament the Criminal Law Act which makes it a criminal offence for a trespasser to be found in the home of a foreign ambassador – but still today not in yours or mine. The wife of the ambassador of the smallest country is safer in her bedroom than the Queen.

---

[1] A recent example of this was when a young Tory aide and two friends, who had been drinking, were discovered in Tony Blair's office at Westminster shortly before Christmas 1994. They claimed they had lost their way – despite 'Leader of the Opposition' clearly written on the unlocked door. Police said they were not treating it as a criminal matter. The truth is that it was not a crime!

Squatting in someone else's property remains, despite all Mr Howard's rhetoric at the October 1993 Conservative Party Conference, a civil wrong and not a criminal offence. Ninety per cent of squatting is said to occur in public-sector housing and 9 per cent involves commercial property, usually vacant shop premises. Squatting in private homes amounts to only about 1 per cent of the total but, as Mr Geoffrey Cutting, chairman of the Small Landlords Association, has said, 'There are dozens of cases of people whose vacant home is up for sale, and cases where someone has gone to hospital or has died, and their home has been squatted in.' Yet they cannot call the police for help unless they can prove that violence or damage has been used to gain entry, which is virtually impossible.

In practice, until Mr Howard's 1994 Criminal Justice and Public Order Act came into effect, the only remedy for anyone who, say, returned home from holiday to find his home taken over by squatters was to sue them in his local county court for an eviction order which the court's bailiff would enforce.

But now Section 73 of the 1994 Act has reformed the law in two important respects, as from later this year:

(i) Aided by new court rules to be brought in by Lord Mackay, the Lord Chancellor, it will simplify the procedure of suing for an eviction order. Now it takes several weeks to get an order at a cost of several hundreds of pounds which you will stand almost no chance of getting back. Under the new system, you will be able to go immediately to the local county court and, at comparatively little expense, obtain an interim order within a day. There will no longer be any need for the squatters to be present or represented in court.

If the squatters then do not go within twenty-four hours, the criminal law will at last come into it. They commit the offence of 'adverse occupation of residential premises'. You can report them to the police and they can be gaoled for up to six months or fined up to £5,000 or both.

Once the squatters have left, they will be able to apply for a full court hearing. Few are likely to bother but this is a necessary safeguard to protect the very few alleged intruders who are, in fact, tenants in arrears with their rent whom unscrupulous – or perhaps desperate – landlords have categorised as squatters to get rid of more easily.

(ii) The 1977 Criminal Law Act is amended so that if the squatters are in your home – but not on business premises – and you are Rambo-minded, you no longer need to go to court in the first place! You can chuck them out yourself or employ someone else to do so – using no more than 'reasonable force'. Liberty, the leading civil-rights organisation, has said: 'This removes the security of the front door' – but whose front door is it: the squatters' or the rightful owners of the property's?

New Age travellers

The summer of 1992 was a nightmare for many people living in the country. So-called New Age travellers seemed able to flout the law with impunity. They camped illegally on farmland, desecrated huge areas with their rubbish and excreta, cut down trees, knocked down fencing, allowed their dogs to savage sheep, pilfered from villagers' cars and urinated in their front gardens.

A few were arrested for drugs and vehicle offences but that was about all. The police were sometimes able to prevent trouble in one area by putting up roadblocks; but it usually only served to divert the travellers elsewhere.

The existing legislation, contained in the 1986 Public Order Act, was too cumbersome and took too long to enforce to be properly effective. So, at the October 1993 Conservative Party Conference, Michael Howard, again to cheers, promised sweeping changes in the law. The relevant sections of his Criminal Justice and Public Order Act are now in force.

Whether it will be sufficient to bring back peace to the countryside, only time will tell. But these are the Act's main provisions:

(i) It creates the new offence of 'aggravated trespass' by 'disruptive trespassers'. The problem is that it does not do so cleanly or by using simple, direct language. It takes the somewhat convoluted course of first postulating that someone is carrying on some 'lawful activity' in the open air and then gives a uniformed policeman the power to arrest without warrant any 'disruptive trespasser' who does anything intended to intimidate, obstruct or disrupt that activity. Magistrates can then gaol the trespasser for up to three months or fine him up to £2,500 or both. But I wonder how many successful prosecutions will in fact be brought. The agonised wording of Sections 68 and 69 of the Act is full of potential loopholes.

(It is to be hoped so for, despite the Government's denials, many people fear the provisions could be used to stifle traditional rights of peaceful protest – nothing to do with controlling the excesses of Travellers.)

(ii) Section 70 gives the police new power to ask local authorities, or, in London, the Home Secretary, to ban open-air 'trespassory assemblies' of twenty or more people on land to which the public has no right of access or only a limited right. These are defined as assemblies likely to be held without the lawful occupier's permission and which may result in 'serious disruption to the life of community' or which may damage a public monument, such as Stonehenge. There is no right of appeal and anyone breaking the ban can be gaoled for up to three months or fined up to £2,500 or both.

(iii) It makes it a criminal offence not to leave land if ordered to do so by a police officer when damage has been caused or more than six vehicles are on the land (the 1986 Public Order Act only gave this power when there were more than twelve vehicles on land).

Open-air raves

Open-air raves – or 'outdoor music festivals', as the 1994 Act calls them – are another curse of the modern countryside. But now Sections 63–66 make illegal all open-air gatherings of 100 or more persons (*whether or not trespassers*) at which amplified music is played *during the night* and causes serious distress to local inhabitants.

A police superintendent can order the ravers to leave and, if they disobey, they can be arrested and magistrates can gaol them for up to three months or fine them up to £2,500.

What is 'music' in this context? For the first time in British legislative history, the Act defines pop music: 'Sounds wholly or predominantly characterised by the emission of a succession of repetitive beats.' So now we all know.

The police can turn back people within a radius of five miles whom they reasonably believe to be attending a rave. And they can seize vehicles and sound equipment which a magistrates' court can then order to be confiscated.

Let us hope that Sections 63–66 work – and that the police and the courts do their traditional balancing act of weighing the rights of the community as a whole against those of a minority who regard themselves as merely 'doing their own thing'.

Legal tender

What does this well-known but elusive term mean? It is not the same as 'cash' or 'money'. It refers to that unique form of cash which *must* be accepted in payment of a debt – as distinct from any other form of payment, such as a cheque or credit card, which the other party may refuse. He cannot say 'No' to legal tender, if you are within the rules.[2]

Those rules are deceptively simple:

• £1 coins are legal tender up to any amount. You can insist, if so minded, on paying a £10,000 debt in £1 coins – and cannot even be compelled to provide a suitcase for it!

• 50p and 20p coins are legal tender up to £10;

• 10p and 5p coins are legal tender up to £5;

• 2p and 1p coins are legal tender only up to a measly 20p.

There is a quirk about banknotes. The Bank of England notes – £5, £10, £20 and £50 – are legal tender only in England and Wales. But three Scottish banks also issue notes – the Royal Bank of Scotland, the Bank of Scotland and the Clydesdale Bank (with the Royal Bank of Scotland still issuing a £1 note, although the English £1 banknote ceased to be legal tender back in March 1988). But these are legal tender only in Scotland, although an English bank will, in practice, cash a Scottish banknote for you, if you have been mistakenly handed one – and vice versa. There is no Scottish coinage.

Jersey and Guernsey in the Channel Islands and the Government of

---

[2] Yet, if a shop or restaurant displays a notice on its front door or window indicating that it accepts a particular credit card or bank switchcard, it must do so: provided, of course, that the card is valid and in funds. But this has nothing to do with legal tender. It is merely part of the ordinary law of contract.

the Isle of Man issue their own banknotes *and coinage* – but, like Scottish banknotes, these are only legal tender locally.

If you pay by legal tender, there is no legal right to demand change. This stems from the old Common Law rule that when I owe you, say, £5.55, I am under a duty to hand over exactly that sum. It is for me to find notes or coins of the correct denomination.

Similarly, although I can, for instance, pay for a £3.50 tub of quality ice cream with exactly £3.50 worth of 50p, 10p or 5p coins, the principle does not work the other way. Those stories that we have all heard about being able to insist on a bus conductor having to accept a £10 note for a 25p ticket are hogwash. He would be perfectly within his rights (although remarkably cavalier) in refusing to give you change and, unless you give him 25p in coins, in asking you to get off his bus.

The reason is that coins or banknotes are legal tender *up* to a certain amount. They are never legal tender *down* to a certain amount, if you see what I mean. I told you the rules were 'deceptively simple'.

Beating a credit 'blacklist'

Contrary to what most people believe, there is no such thing as a credit 'blacklist' – but, in practical terms, it amounts to much the same thing. Credit reference agencies, of which there are three main ones in the United Kingdom, collect and file both good and bad information on your credit history and, if you have a good track record, this can stand you in good stead just as much as a bad credit history will work against you.

Sadly, we have long passed the stage when you could count on banks, finance houses and retail organisations respecting the confidentiality of your financial arrangements or transactions. Some still do; many do not – and readily pass on information about their financial dealings with you to the agencies.

There is nothing very much that you can do to stop that but, under the 1974 Consumer Credit Act, you can at least ensure that the information that the agencies keep on file about you is accurate. This is how it works:

If you are refused credit for £15,000 or less, you should write to the shop or finance house or whatever it is within twenty-eight days, asking why they refused you credit and asking for the name of any credit reference agency they consulted. If they do not wish to do so, they do not have to say why they refused credit but they must within seven working days give you the name and address of any agency they used.

Section 158 of the Act then gives you the right to write to that agency asking to see a copy of your file. You should state that you are writing under Section 158 and enclose a £1 fee,[3] your full name and your current and previous addresses over the past six years. The agency has seven working days from receipt of your letter to send you a copy of your file or else tell you, if that is true, that it holds nothing on you.

If you see that any details are wrong or misleading, you can then write back asking them to correct or remove the error, which they must confirm they have done within twenty-eight days of receipt of your letter. If not, you have a further twenty-eight days in which to send your own note of correction in not more than 200 words.

If the agency then refuses to accept your correction or you hear nothing for a further twenty-eight days, complain to the Office of Fair Trading at Field House, 15–25 Breams Buildings, London EC4A 1PR (Tel: 0171–242 2858), sending full details and copies of all correspondence. They will then intervene for you.

Once their file is amended, the agency must send the corrected details to anyone who has asked for information about you during the last six months, and continue to use them in future.

The process is complicated but effective.

Liability for jury service

Until 1974, juries were chosen on an outdated property qualification but nowadays everyone aged eighteen to seventy, apart from those in certain privileged professions such as lawyers, doctors and MPs, is liable to be called to sit in judgment on his or her fellow citizens. Every year an estimated 300,000 people receive a letter summoning them for jury service for an average of two weeks. Their names have been selected

---

[3] The 1984 Data Protection Act gives you the same right but, perhaps because it is a later Act, the fee is increased to £10. That is why you should make clear you are applying under Section 158 of the 1974 Act.

at random from the electoral register by a clerk at their local Crown Court.

Jury service used to be regarded as an important duty, undertaken willingly in the cause of justice. But nowadays many potential jurors view it as a burden: costly, inefficient and time-wasting, or simply unimportant. In September 1992, for instance, a judge at Newcastle-upon-Tyne Crown Court had to dismiss a woman juror for thumbing through cheque stubs and filling in a job application form while evidence was being given.

Jurors earn a modest recompense which many observers consider totally insufficient for the major upheaval at home and at work that may be entailed: a daily allowance of up to £41.40 (to a maximum of £77 after ten days) for loss of earnings, plus expenses that are tightly budgeted. Yet even today few people would want to get out of their jury service entirely – although many would probably like to put it off for a while, especially if that little buff envelope drops on to their front doormat at a particularly inconvenient time.

What hope of success do they have? More than you might think, especially if you write back at once requesting postponement and explaining exactly why. Court officials are fully aware of the yardstick laid down by Lord Justice Lawton in a 1977 Appeal Court case:

> Those summoned to serve as jurors are entitled to such consideration
> as it is within the power of the courts to give them. If the administration
> of justice can be carried on without inconveniencing jurors unduly, it
> should be. An aggrieved and inconvenienced juror is not likely to be
> a good one.

Even so, mere inconvenience will usually not be sufficient: the courts still rightly regard jury service as a public duty. But holiday arrangements that cannot easily be altered, professional or university exams, pregnancy, a forthcoming long-awaited visit from close relatives living abroad or a major and important industrial fair for a business executive: these are all excuses that will receive sympathetic treatment; and it always helps to make the point that you would be only too willing to do your jury service at some later stage when this immediate difficulty has been overcome.

You would be very unlucky not to be excused for some such reason – at least, first time round.

Shoplifting

This is the one offence with which most innocent people can wrongly be charged. It is always serious. Do not be influenced by a 'friendly' police officer advising you to 'get it over with in the magistrates' court' or accept a police caution, which not enough people realise can only be given on the basis that you admit your guilt. You should not let your feelings of embarrassment and distress persuade you to deal with the matter as quickly as possible. If you truly are innocent – and only you can know that – you really should use your right to insist that your case be tried by a judge and jury in your local Crown Court.

It does not matter that little may be involved in purely financial terms. Your honour is beyond price to defend. And I am convinced, after defending people I believed innocent both in magistrates' courts and at Crown Courts, that the best hope of success lies in the understanding and compassion of twelve other ordinary people who could so easily find themselves in the dock instead of the jury box.

Shoplifting is theft. A major survey by the British Retail Consortium reported in January 1994 that, with 1,516,481 annual shoplifting incidents and 1.2 million customers arrested, it is costing Britain's shopkeepers a staggering £516 million a year. The retail industry cannot be blamed for responding with more sophisticated closed-circuit television cameras, security guards, store detectives, hi-tech labels and other electronic gadgets.

But innocent shoppers still have their rights. For a start, to secure a conviction it is not enough for the shopkeeper merely to prove that someone left the premises without paying. As the late Mr Eric Guest, a highly experienced London stipendiary magistrate, once said when throwing out a case against an elderly woman: 'Of course, it is proved beyond peradventure that she walked out with some biscuits for which she had not paid. But, in addition, it has to be proved beyond doubt that she did so fraudulently – that is to say, with criminal intention. It is absolutely essential to examine these cases with a microscope.'

It is so very easy for harassed shoppers inadvertently to put wares in the wrong bag. Or not to notice that their small child has stuffed a chocolate bar into their open shopping bag. As far back as April 1975, in the case of *R. v. Ingram*, the Appeal Court warned that the defence of 'absent-mindedness' must be taken seriously:

The case of the absent-minded lawyer

A store detective in a supermarket saw a young lawyer, who was a Cambridge University research student, take two packets of ham from a refrigerated cabinet, put them in his jacket pocket and leave without producing them at the check-out. But he paid for other items which he had put into a wire basket.

When stopped, he said that he remembered handling the ham but not putting it in his pocket. He must have done so in a moment of absent-mindedness.

A clearly unsympathetic judge told the jury that, when testing this defence, they should decide his alleged state of mind by looking at what he actually did. They convicted – but the Appeal Court quashed the conviction and said the judge had been too cavalier. 'The temptation to regard this defence sceptically must be resisted. A trial judge should sum up to the jury fairly in the clearest terms, balancing the case of the prosecution against that of the defence.'

Contrary to popular myth, a store detective does not have to wait until you have left the premises before he can stop you. He can stop you at any time after you have passed the spot where you should have paid for the goods, even though you may still be in the store. But, wherever he stops you, you should always ask him why. You are entitled to know what you are supposed to have done – and he has to be discreet in what he then says and does. If not, you can sue for slander, as did a wealthy racehorse owner and breeder who in April 1984 in the High Court was paid £1,500 agreed damages by an Oxford Street store after she had been 'humiliated' by being publicly questioned and her handbag searched in front of other shoppers and onlookers in passing buses in this premier London shopping street.

You do *not* have to 'come with me to the manager's office', as store detectives often say, simply because they ask you to. You can refuse and immediately put them on the spot. For they must then decide whether to let you go – or physically arrest you. They are not police officers.

300

They are only private citizens and, as such, can only make a 'citizen's arrest'. This means that you can sue them and their employers for substantial damages for wrongful arrest and false imprisonment, *if it turns out that you did not steal anything.* Successful claims are not uncommon. (Police officers have greater powers: they can arrest on reasonable suspicion, even though later it is shown no offence was committed.)

Furthermore, if you do return with them to see the manager, please remember it is still not too late to avoid a prosecution. You can give him your version of events and it will be his decision whether or not to call the police. A good store manager does not necessarily accept every word his own detectives say: he knows they can be mistaken.

A word of caution: anyone can be unnerved in such circumstances. You may say something you really do not mean. Such as 'I'm sorry. I didn't mean to do it,' meaning only that you did not mean to leave without paying. But it will not sound good in court.

If wrongly charged with shoplifting, it can sometimes help to telephone a special hotline staffed by the Crisis Counselling for Alleged Shoplifters (CCASS) on 0181–958 8859, 0181–202 5787 or 0171–722 3685. This London-based organisation, set up by the National Consumer Protection Council in the Eighties, has a network of local counsellers inside and outside London whose advice and assistance can be invaluable especially for someone without a sympathetic or experienced solicitor to turn to.

One final matter: most shoplifting prosecutions nowadays are brought by the Crown Prosecution Service and not privately by the shop itself, as used to be the case. But in recent years there has been a new development: in more than a third of all cases, the shop does not prosecute suspects nor hand them over to the police. Instead it bans them from its premises and circulates their names among other retailers. Estimates of people blacklisted in this way by national retail chains vary between 38,000 and 50,000 a year. This is most disturbing. It means that large numbers of shoppers are being victimised without their guilt being proven in a court of law.

But the practice, however regrettable, is legally permissible. The public has no automatic right of entry to a store. Customers are there by invitation. And that invitation can legally be withdrawn at any time: however unfairly.

NINETEEN

Police Powers, Patients' Rights, Libel and Slander

Police powers

The police have always had an ambivalent position in society. On the one hand, they are society's principal protection against the forces of crime and lawlessness. On the other hand, they have enormous power, the use of which can sometimes be suspect.

Quis custodiet ipsos custodes? (Who guards the guards?) is a question that has been asked since Roman times. The working classes in Britain have always had a much closer grasp of police reality but in the Nineties, where miscarriage of justice and abuse of police power seem to occur with sickening frequency, a new antipathy has set in between the police and the middle classes, which is a section of society where hitherto they enjoyed most respect and support.

At the Association of Chief Police Officers' annual conference at Eastbourne in June 1992, Mr Kenneth Clarke, then for a brief while Home Secretary, slated the police and urged them to concentrate on winning back the support of 'the solid citizens of middle England', whose confidence had been shaken, so he rightly said, by rising crime and miscarriages of justice. Four months later, in a response that only a few years earlier would have been thought impossible, Sir Peter Imbert, then Metropolitan Police Commissioner, took the opportunity when addressing in London an international police conference to accuse the middle classes of self-interest and hypocrisy in their approach to policing. He openly accused them of breaking the law when it suited them.

'They are not above ignoring motorway speed limits,' he said, 'walk-ing the narrow line between tax evasion and tax avoidance or neglect-ing to pay a fine when the opportunity arises. Yet they demand guarantees of safety for property and person without always recognising the competing demands placed on the police.'

No sensible person could ever deny the debt that we all owe to the dedication, sense of duty and at times physical bravery of the vast majority of police officers in this country. But that does not alter the fact that nowadays even the most law-abiding citizen, of whatever social class, can all too easily come into contact with an individual police officer who is brash, rude and acting far in excess of his or her legitimate powers.

Ten years ago, in a book of this nature, I would never have thought of including a section headed 'police powers'. Nowadays, sadly, I think it may well be of value.

So what is there to say?

Most of us know that the 1984 Police and Criminal Evidence Act, generally known as PACE, and the detailed Codes of Practice made under it, lay down complex rules as to how the police are to conduct their interviews, arrest and detain suspects, carry out identity parades and search property and persons. I could almost fill a whole chapter with these requirements. Police cells must be adequately heated, clean and ventilated. Access to toilet and washing facilities must be provided. There must be at least two light meals and one main meal each day. The suspect must be allowed at least eight hours' rest each day. Inter-view rooms must be properly heated. Suspects are not to be made to stand. There must be a break from interviewing at normal meal times and, as a general rule, there should be short refreshment breaks every two hours, etc., etc.

But what concerns the average law-abiding person is fourfold:

(i) *When can a police officer stop you in the street or other public place and ask your name and address or demand to know what you are doing?*

The leading case is *Rice v. Connolly*, decided by the High Court in May 1966. Its name is known only to experts in criminal law but the principal judgment by Lord Parker, then Lord Chief Justice, is a classic statement of our rights. What happened was that, on a night in Grimsby in an area where several premises had just been reported broken into, the police were out looking for possible suspects and they noticed a man loitering in the shadows. They asked him where he was going, where he had come from and his name and address, and he replied: 'Give me a good reason why I should.'

They then saw that he had a cut on his finger, so one of the policemen asked him again for his name and address. He had to ask it twice and then the man said, 'Rice, Convamore Road,' which afterwards proved to be true. The policeman then said he wanted his full name and address, the man refused to give them and refused to accompany him to a police box to confirm his identity, saying: 'Look, son, I am not moving from this spot. If you want me, you'll have to arrest me.'

So they did. And he ended up being convicted by the local magistrates of obstructing the police in the execution of their duty – even though he was never charged with any of the breaking offences in the area that night. His appeal to the local Quarter Sessions (now Grimsby Crown Court) was dismissed – but, on further appeal to the High Court, three judges agreed that he had been wrongly convicted.

In particular, Lord Parker restated this essential principle of our ancient Common Law – which has not been affected by the subsequent 1984 Police and Criminal Evidence Act:

> It seems to me quite clear that though every citizen has a moral duty
> or, if you like, a social duty to assist the police, there is no legal
> duty to that effect, and indeed the whole basis of the Common Law is
> the right of the individual to refuse to answer questions put to him
> by persons in authority, and to refuse to accompany those in authority
> to any particular place; short, of course, of arrest.

And, of course, as we shall see in a minute, if the police choose to arrest you and they get it wrong you can sue the individual police officer and his bosses, the local police authority, for a great deal of money for wrongful arrest or false imprisonment.

The police are our servants not our masters, and they sometimes need reminding of this. When I was out shopping some time ago with my son, who had just moved into his first flat, we were coming back to my car briefly parked illegally on a double yellow line in Chiswick High Road, west London, when a young policeman appeared and, with an imperious flick of his hand, said: 'You – move on!' My reply was: 'The first thing you do, officer, is call me "Sir" and then you politely tell me to move my car because I am parked illegally' – which, in surly fashion, he then did.

My son, who was then a despatch rider, harassed like most of his fellow bikers by the police on an almost daily basis, was most impressed. 'I'd have called him a filthy pig and told him what he could do with himself,' he said. Arrogance breeds intolerance.

In particular, the police often seem to think that they have a general right to arrest people simply because they refuse to give their name and address. This is just not so. Section 25 of the 1984 Act allows them to arrest someone on this ground only in the very limited circumstances that they have told him that they reasonably believe he has committed a minor offence (which they must designate) for which they would normally report him to be summoned to court, e.g. most motoring offences, and so they need his name and address for a summons to be served on him. *And that is all.*

The 1987 case of *Nicholas* v. *Parsonage* is a perfect example of what I mean:

The cyclist who would not give his name

A young man was stopped by two policemen for riding his cycle dangerously. Neither constable knew his name and address. They asked for his name as he was riding his cycle in a dangerous manner. He refused, was warned that he could be arrested under the 1984 Act and was asked again for his name and address. He again refused and one constable told him he was being arrested for failing to give his name and address. He tried to ride away, the constable tried to stop him and the cyclist assaulted him.

Local magistrates convicted the cyclist of riding his bicycle without due care and attention and of assaulting the constable in the execution of his duty. He appealed to the High Court against the assault charge, and this required a judicial examination of Section 25 since, if the police had not been acting lawfully, the cyclist could not be guilty of assaulting him *in the execution of his duty*.

The conviction was upheld. The High Court ruled that Section 25 is complied with 'if, a short but reasonable time before the arrest, it is indicated the nature of an offence in respect of which a name and address are required'.

The decision is important. It emphasises that police have no power to ask for your name and address without good reason – which they must specify to you at the time. We do not live in a police state.

I wrote those last words before Parliament enacted, in November 1994, Section 60 of the 1994 Criminal Justice and Public Order Act. This Section was totally ignored by the media at the time and its potential threat to traditional liberties scornfully dismissed by a Tory backbencher with whom I tried to raise it during a discussion on the Act in the Richard Littlejohn Show on Sky TV in which we were both taking part. Yet it presents a dangerous extension of police powers, albeit restricted – in name – to combating offences of serious violence.

For, in summary, this is what it says:

> Where a police superintendent or, in his absence, a chief inspector, reasonably believes that incidents involving serious violence may take place in a locality and it is expedient to prevent their occurrence, he may authorise his uniformed constables to stop and search persons and vehicles within that locality for up to twenty-four hours (capable of being extended for a further six hours).

A constable's power of search under this Section is limited to looking for offensive weapons or dangerous instruments, and not all that many people would disagree with that; but what I find totally objectionable – and so, I think, would many readers – is that the Section goes on to specify: 'A constable may stop any person or vehicle and make any search he thinks fit, *whether or not he has any grounds for suspecting that the person or vehicle is carrying weapons or articles of that kind.*'

How on earth can the words that I have italicised be justified? Random police powers to stop and search private citizens should not be acceptable in a civilised democracy.

(ii) *When can a police officer ask you to come to the police station 'and help with our enquiries' – and how long do you have to remain there?*

The police can ask you whenever they think it is necessary: whether you have to go is a different matter. As we have already seen, a past Lord Chief Justice (Lord Parker) has said: 'Though every citizen has a moral duty, or, if you like, a social duty, to assist the police, there is no legal duty to that effect.' A suspect would be within his rights in refusing to go to the police station and challenging the police to arrest him there and then – which would probably be very foolhardy on their part because, at that stage, they almost certainly would not have sufficient evidence to do so. That, of course, is what they hope to obtain by questioning him at the police station.

Furthermore, you do not have to remain at a police station 'helping with enquiries' for a split second longer than you want to. Clause 3.15 of the Code of Practice under the 1984 Act is quite specific:

> Any person attending a police station voluntarily for the purpose of assisting with an investigation may leave at will unless placed under arrest. If it is decided that he should not be allowed to do so, then he must be informed at once that he is under arrest and brought before the custody officer who is responsible for ensuring that he is notified of his rights. If he is not placed under arrest but, at some stage in the questioning, it becomes clear that there are grounds for suspecting him of having committed an offence, he must be cautioned: 'You do not have to say anything unless you wish to do so but what you say may be given in evidence.'[1]
>
> The officer who gives the caution must at the same time inform him that he is not under arrest, that he is not obliged to remain at the police station but that if he remains at the police station he may obtain free legal advice if he wishes. [Please note that this is not the same kind of 'caution' that we have already met on page 299, where shoplifters are given a 'caution' instead of being taken to court.]

What about seeing a solicitor? From the very first moment that a person voluntarily helping the police with their enquiries enters a police station, he has the right to telephone his solicitor, ask him to come to the station and sit in on the interview – and to say nothing until he

---

[1] The 1994 Criminal Justice and Public Order Act has restricted the traditional Right of Silence, enshrined in this wording of the caution. With effect from an (as yet) unspecified time in 1995, it is proposed to change the wording to: 'You do not have to say anything. But if you do not mention now something which you later use in your defence, the court may decide that your failure to mention it now strengthens the case against you. A record will be made of anything you say and it may be given in evidence if you are brought to trial.'

arrives. Clause 6.1 stipulates: 'Any person may at any time consult and communicate privately, whether in person, in writing or on the telephone, with a solicitor.' Annexe B of the Code says there is an exception: if the offence is 'serious' (generally speaking, where the maximum sentence is at least five years' imprisonment), a police superintendent may deny access to a solicitor if he thinks that would interfere with the evidence, alert other suspects or hinder the recovery of stolen property. Clause 6.6 also says that, whether or not the offence is 'serious', someone who wants legal advice may be interviewed without talking to a solicitor or one being present if a superintendent has reasonable grounds for believing that 'delay will involve an immediate risk of harm to persons or serious loss of, or damage to, property – or awaiting his arrival would cause unreasonable delay to the process of investigation'.

Unfortunately, nowhere does the Code spell out that you can refuse to answer questions, whatever the circumstances, until your solicitor arrives and you have taken his advice.

What happens if you do not know a solicitor or cannot afford one? Everyone is entitled to free legal advice at the police station, *whatever their capital or income*. An independent duty solicitor, not employed by the police, is available twenty-four hours a day and you have the right to ask the police to contact him on your behalf. Indeed, the police should give you an information sheet telling you about your rights at the police station.

If you end up being taken to court, legal aid is available on a more generous basis than in civil cases. The court itself, whether Crown Court or magistrates' court, will grant you legal aid if it decides that you need financial help in meeting the legal costs of your defence and, in the words of Section 22 of the 1988 Legal Aid Act, it is 'in the interests of justice' to do so. In practice, this phrase means that, if anyone is likely (if convicted) to go to gaol or to lose their job, legal aid will be granted. So, at least at magistrates' court level, accused motorists or suspected shoplifters generally do not qualify, although in the Crown Court – where by definition the offence tends to be more serious – legal aid is much more readily granted; and it has been said that over 97 per cent of all Crown Court defendants are legally aided.

This is not a pleasant time for anyone and it is easy to panic; but it may be a comfort to remember that there are no upper income or capital limits for *criminal* legal aid – although you will probably be ordered to make a contribution (which may be substantial), if your disposable capital is over £3,000 or your weekly disposable income exceeds £46.

(iii) *When can a police officer actually arrest you – and what are your rights upon arrest?*

A policeman can always arrest when he has a warrant from a magistrate, which will be issued only if there is sufficient evidence *on oath* to justify it; but the overwhelming number of arrests take place without a warrant. This is most often when the police reasonably suspect someone of having committed a serious offence and when they see someone committing a breach of the peace or acting so that a breach of the peace is likely to occur, being drunk and disorderly in a public place or driving while disqualified or committing other major motoring offences.

Once arrested and held in custody at a police station, the 1984 Code gives you the right to have 'one person known to you' informed and, if the person cannot be contacted, you can name up to two alternatives. (This right does not exist if you are merely voluntarily at the station helping the police with their enquiries, although there is nothing to prevent you making a phone call before you go off with them.) If you have not yet exercised your right to see a solicitor by the time you have been arrested, you should certainly do so now.

For, once arrested, you move on to the next stage: that of actually being charged with an offence. Arrest is merely a stage in the process. Most people do not appreciate that you then go on to be charged with a specific offence – when again you must be told that you do not need to say anything but, in the words of the new caution, if you do, it will be taken down and may be given in evidence if your failure to mention it now strengthens the case against you.

You cannot just remain at the police station indefinitely after you have been arrested. The arresting officer must take you 'as soon as practicable' (Section 37 of the 1984 Act) to the station's custody officer who is, at least, a sergeant and he will have to decide whether or not there is sufficient evidence to charge you with the offence in connection with which you have just been arrested. If he thinks there is not yet sufficient evidence, he can (a) question you further himself, or (b) if he reasonably believes it necessary to secure or preserve evidence he can order you to be kept longer in custody, or (c) he can release you on bail to come back to the station at some future date for further questioning: hence, the term sometimes seen in the press, 'police bail'.

If, on the other hand, as most often occurs, the custody officer thinks the evidence justifies your being charged, he will charge you at once and then either grant 'police bail' himself or tell you of your right to ask the local magistrates' court for bail when you are brought before them at their next sitting, as must happen.

No one in this country can be charged by the police without being taken before the next sitting of the local magistrates' court for his case to be made public and for the magistrates to decide whether he is to be given bail or sent to a remand prison to await trial ('remanded in custody'). Nowadays magistrates usually only withhold bail when there is a real risk that you may abscond before trial or may interfere with witnesses. It is even granted in murder cases, which never happened when I was first called to the Bar and the seriousness of the charge was always a factor.

What happens if the police reasonably believe they have sufficient evidence to arrest you (i.e. reasonable grounds for *suspecting* that you have committed an offence) but not sufficient evidence to charge you with it (i.e. sufficient *proof* to obtain a conviction)? How long do they have to improve their case against you?

Section 40 of the 1984 Act says that, with ordinary offences, they can keep you at a police station for only up to twenty-four hours without charging you but, when 'serious' offences are being investigated and an officer of at least the rank of superintendent reasonably believes that extra time is necessary, he can authorise detention for a further twelve hours and then, if more time is still required, he can authorise detention for a further thirty-six hours. But after that the police must apply to the local magistrates' court for a warrant authorising a final extension of up to another thirty-six hours and they will get it, if the court accepts that the investigation is being conducted diligently and more time is, indeed, needed.

Yet, on any basis, the total period of detention between arrest and being charged cannot be more than 96 hours (eight days) from first arrival at the police station.[2]

(iv) *What are your rights, if wrongly arrested?*

In theory, they are considerable: in practice, you must be articulate, determined and persistent. You can sue in the courts for wrongful arrest or false imprisonment or for malicious prosecution if the police, without what the Common Law calls 'reasonable and probable cause', actually carry things so far as to charge and prosecute you and a jury eventually acquits you – although not every acquittal (or even most) means it was wrong to charge you in the first place.

You can also – or instead – complain in writing to the Metropolitan Police Commissioner or local chief constable. Serious complaints are supervised by the Police Complaints Authority but all cases are investigated by other police officers and the success rate is not high.

You stand a much better chance by suing in court than by following the official complaints procedure. The case of Mrs Cheryl Holland, to whom the Metropolitan Police agreed to pay £25,000 damages in Lambeth County Court in October 1993, is a good example of this:

The case of the missing tax disc

In March 1989, Mrs Holland, a British Telecom manager, called at her mother's florist shop in south-east London to collect a chequebook before going on to buy flowers for the shop. While she was inside, two policemen spotted there was no tax disc on the Renault car she had recently bought. Although she claimed that she gave them her name and address and said she had applied for the licence, they told her she was being arrested for 'having no tax' – which is not an arrestable offence. While she was in her mother's shop trying unsuccessfully to telephone the car dealer to verify her story, a police van arrived and she was bundled into it and taken to Kennington police station,

---

[2] The time limits are different for those arrested under the Prevention of Terrorism Act. Once arrested, a person can be held for up to forty-eight hours and then for a further five days with the consent of the Home Secretary. There is no absolute right to see a solicitor until after forty-eight hours from arrest and the right to have someone informed of your arrest can be delayed even beyond this period.

311

where she was detained for four hours before being charged and released on bail.

Her solicitor told Lambeth County Court that, following her arrest, the two officers made written statements in which they falsely alleged that she had pushed an officer in the chest, sworn and used abusive language and refused to leave the shop, forcing one of them to speak to her through the letter box in the shop door.

She pleaded guilty at Horseferry Road Magistrates' Court to failing to display a tax disc, for which she was fined £15, but her 'not guilty' pleas to failing to give her name and address and using threatening, abusive and insulting words and behaviour were rejected. She was convicted and given a six-month conditional discharge.

She had the guts to appeal to Inner London Crown Court, where her barrister called a local postman to prove that her mother's shop had no letter box! Her convictions were quashed and Judge Rucker commented: 'It is clear that the officers were lying. It makes my blood run cold to think that police officers are willing to perjure themselves over a matter as trivial as this.'

But a Scotland Yard spokeswoman later announced that the Director of Public Prosecutions and the Police Complaints Authority had investigated whether the officers should be charged with perjury and had concluded that the evidence did not justify criminal proceedings. 'Both officers were severely admonished by their chief superintendents,' she said.

It was left for Mrs Holland to sue for damages for assault, false imprisonment and malicious prosecution and four years after the original incident her case was settled on the basis of the Metropolitan Police Commissioner paying her £25,000 damages and her costs estimated at about £7,000 – with no admission of liability and no apology.

Patients' rights

There are four main matters to be considered:

(i) *The legal standard of care you are entitled to expect*

It is obvious that no doctor can legally guarantee a cure or that you will not continue to feel pain despite all his treatment; but the law says that he is under an obligation to treat you with reasonable skill and care. If he fails to do so, you can sue him personally, if he is a private doctor, or, if he is a NHS doctor, you can sue his employers (the local health authority or a NHS trust) for damages for his negligence.

The yardstick of medical care was laid down a long time ago by Mr Justice McNair, in February 1957:

> The test is the standard of the ordinary skilled man exercising and professing to have that special skill. A man need not possess the highest expert skill at the risk of being found negligent. It is sufficient if he exercises the ordinary skill of an ordinary competent man exercising that particular art.
>
> A doctor is not guilty of negligence if he has acted in accordance with a practice accepted as proper by a responsible body of medical men.

Not every bad diagnosis amounts to negligence. As a Scottish judge has said:

> In the realm of diagnosis and treatment, there is ample scope for a genuine difference of opinion and one man is clearly not negligent merely because his conclusion differs from that of other professional men.

But there is a limit. A doctor who failed to diagnose a broken kneecap in a man who had fallen 12 feet on to a concrete floor has been ruled negligent, and a successful woman sales executive from Colchester, Essex, whose life was blighted by a wrong diagnosis of cancer after her name was mixed up with test results from a genuine cancer victim has been awarded over £200,000 damages. The hallmark, as so often with the law, is reasonableness: a patient who, for instance, visits his GP because he is experiencing irritation in his eye cannot expect him to have the skill of a specialist eye consultant but he would have a legitimate grievance if the GP failed to refer him to such a consultant – if his condition would have made a reasonable GP suspect that something might be seriously wrong and the patient needed specialist attention.

The law does not expect supermen or superwomen. It *does* expect reasonable professional competence. And the standard of competence is the same for private medicine as it is for the NHS. There may or may not be a two-tier NHS, but there is definitely no two-tier legal standard of medical care in the sense of the actual level of competence that you are legally entitled to expect from doctors, surgeons, nurses, anaesthetists and other medical professionals. There is no difference, in that vital respect, between what you pay for and what you do not.

Doctors, lawyers and politicians sometimes need reminding of the classic statement of the law by Lord Denning in *Cassidy* v. *Ministry of Health* in the Appeal Court in February 1951, back in the early days of the NHS:

> If a man goes to a doctor because he is ill, no one doubts that the doctor must exercise reasonable care and skill in his treatment of him, and that is so whether the doctor is paid for his services or not. If, however, the doctor is unable to treat the man himself and sends him to hospital, are not the hospital authorities then under a duty of care in their treatment of him? I think they are.
>
> Clearly, if he is a paying patient, paying them directly for their treatment of him, they must take reasonable care of him, and why should it make any difference if he does not pay them directly but only indirectly through the rates which he pays to the local authority or through insurance contributions which he makes to the State in order to get the treatment? I see no difference at all.

To be sure, there are some legal variations. The NHS patient has no contract with his doctor or surgeon and may be operated on by any surgeon employed by the local health authority or NHS trust: he has no legal choice in the matter. A private patient has a contract with his chosen doctor and only he, or a specifically agreed substitute, may carry out any treatment or surgery.

But, as Professor Margaret Brazier says in her book *Medicine, Patients and the Law,* 'NHS and private doctors are both obliged to do their best,' and I would add that their 'best' must be of the same legal standard of reasonable professional competence and skill.

Yet only a fool or a Government minister would deny that there are the most appalling differences between the level of medical treatment that is available privately or on the State. Long waiting lists, over-worked, overtired and sometimes grievously inexperienced doctors and nurses, inadequate or out-of-date equipment, wards closed because the funds are simply not there to keep them open: none of these blemishes on a civilised service will you find in the private sector. But still the judges do what they can to enforce the law with an even hand. It has, for instance, been held no defence to a claim for medical negligence that a hospital doctor was overworked or inexperienced. As Professor Margaret Brazier has written, 'Judges sympathise with hard-pressed doctors. But a doctor who carries on beyond the point when fatigue and overwork impair his judgement remains liable to an injured patient.' In fact, in December 1990, the Appeal Court ruled that young doctors whose own health is threatened by the impossible work demands made on them can sue their own health authority for damages.

If there is a mishap in a NHS hospital, you may not be able to pinpoint the particular member of the 'team' who was at fault. That does not matter. As Lord Denning said in 1950, in the same judgment from which I have already quoted, 'The hospital authorities accepted the plaintiff as a patient for treatment and it was their duty to treat him with reasonable care. They selected, employed and paid all the surgeons and nurses who looked after him. He had no say in their selection at all. If those surgeons and nurses did not treat him with proper care and skill, then the hospital authorities must answer for it, for it means that they themselves did not perform their duty to him.'

The same argument probably applies to private hospitals, except that there you will have a separate legal contract with your surgeon and your anaesthetist and, if they were negligent, you could sue them personally: irrespective of any possible liability on the part of the hospital for, say negligence by a member of their nursing staff. Incidentally, if you are being treated privately by your own surgeon in a NHS hospital and, as usually happens, the hospital allocates staff to look after you, the result is the same: if you suffer injury through the surgeon's negligence, you sue him personally but, if it is the hospital staff who have been at fault, you sue the local health authority or NHS trust. They remain liable for their employees' failings – even though you are a private patient!

(ii) *What can you do, if you suffer injury through medical negligence?*

Obviously, you can sue – if you have a good enough case and you think you can afford it, always remembering that the Medical Defence Union and the Medical Protection Society, the two major defence organisations for doctors, tend to encourage their members to settle out of court if it looks as if they are likely to lose, although they often leave it until very late in the day in the life of a lawsuit before any substantial offer is actually made. Your own resistance is more likely to be worn down by then and you are more likely to settle for less.

You must issue your High Court writ or County Court summons within three years, and this is one thing that you cannot undertake on your own. Anyone who thinks that he has suffered injury through medical negligence should consult a solicitor, preferably someone specialised in that field (your local citizens advice bureau may be able to help with some names) and he will ask the doctor or hospital for your medical records. He will then send them to an independent specialist for assessment. This independent specialist will also examine you himself and it will be upon the basis of his opinion that the lawyers (your solicitor and probably a specialist barrister he has called in) will be able to advise you whether or not to proceed.

But not everyone wants to sue. Some people just want to be able to complain: to get their grievance off their chest and perhaps to ensure that an incompetent or uncaring doctor or nurse is suitably reprimanded. The NHS Patients Charter, with the typically joyous prose only found in television commercials and Citizen's Charters, says breathlessly:

'*Charter Rights*. These are guaranteed. If you think that you are being or are likely to be denied one of the National Charter Rights, you should write to Duncan Nichol, Chief Executive of the NHS, Department of Health, Richmond House, 79 Whitehall, London SW1A 2NS. Mr Nichol will investigate the matter and, if you have been denied a right, he will take action to ensure that this is corrected.'

The reality is sadly very different. In May 1994, an official review committee under Professor Alan Wilson set up by the Department of Health itself reported: 'Complainants can face an uphill struggle when using NHS complaints procedures: firstly, in making their views known; and, secondly, in receiving the sort of response they would wish for.' As Mary Ann Sieghart commented in a moving article in July 1994 in *The Times*, in which she recounted her protracted and ultimately unsuccessful attempts to find redress within the system for the rudeness and incompetence of the GP treating her two young daughters, 'A doctor's terms of service are so narrowly defined as to make it almost impossible for a patient to win a case.'

But the most damning indictment of the turgid over-bureaucratic official complaints system – written complaints to the local Family Health Services Authority about GPs and a complex system of 'hospital complaints procedure' and 'clinical complaints procedure' about hospitals – was provided by Mr William Reid, the National Health Service Ombudsman, in his annual report published in July 1994:

'I cannot emphasise too strongly the importance of a strong and clear commitment from the top, particularly from chief executives and non-executive members of NHS authorities, boards and trusts. Unless that is recognised and put into practice, much-needed improvements in dealing with complaints will not happen.'

(iii) *Do you have the legal right to change your NHS doctor? When can he strike you off his list?*

You can change your doctor at any time, and without giving reasons. But, in sheer prudence, you should first make sure that another NHS doctor is prepared to take you on. Once you have found him or her, your medical card outlines the official procedure: either you can change at once by asking both your new and your present GP to sign your card or, if you do not want to involve your present doctor, you can send it, together with a letter saying that you want to change, to the local Family Health Service Authority which administers GPs' services in your area and whose address you will find on your card. In that case, you will not be able to see your new GP for fourteen days.

Likewise, GPs do not have to give a reason for removing patients from their lists, and in July 1994 the family doctors' watchdog organisation, the Association of Community Health Councils for England and Wales, reported that thousands of patients were being removed from their GPs' lists against their wishes. Almost predictably, the most affected were the old, the chronically sick and the mentally ill, whose need for care was the greatest.[3]

Some fund-holding medical practices do not favour the elderly or the chronically ill. They make too great a demand on their financial

---

[3] In November 1994, doctors were urged by the British Medical Association, in new guidelines, to write to struck-off patients explaining their reasons. But Mrs Linda Lamont, Director of the Patients' Association, said she feared doctors would develop a standard form of words for telling people why they were struck off. The basic reality of the situation sadly seems unlikely to change.

and economic resources. Guidance issued by the General Medical Council in May 1992 made clear to GPs that they should not discriminate against patients on the grounds of the amount of work they were likely to generate by reason of their clinical condition. Even so, Dr Brian Macwhinney, then Health Minister, greeted the watchdog association's report with the chilling observation: 'The Government believes it is important there should be no more restrictions than are essential on the freedom of both parties.'

But what is the 'freedom' of the elderly, the chronically ill or the mentally sick to find another doctor to take them on?

(iv) *The hazards of private healthcare and small print*

Private health care is Big Business. Fears over the future of the National Health Service have led to a big rise in recent years in spending on private medical insurance – especially among the middle-aged and elderly. In 1993, it surged from £1.3 billion to £1.6 billion.

As with any other growing business, where profit rules and 'market forces' prevail, all too often financial considerations can affect the quality of the service provided. In July 1994, the *Sunday Times* reported that medical-insurance companies were not only increasingly relying on the small print of policies to find an excuse to reject claims outright, they were using delaying tactics in settling even the claims that they accepted, hoping their worn-down customers would eventually accept less than the full amount. A medical-insurance broker was quoted as saying: 'Insurers are looking for ways to reduce costs. They have cut back on cover and are much harder on claims than they used to be.'

I was not at all surprised to read that. The process has been going on for the past few years. Far too many people do not read the small-print exclusion clauses in their policies until they actually want to make a claim – and then they discover that they cannot claim at all or for only a very limited amount. These clauses have always excluded things such as chronic or incurable conditions, normal pregnancy and childbirth, normal dentistry, Aids, cosmetic surgery, infertility treatments and conditions caused by dangerous sports.

But the mid-Nineties have brought a new nuance: for instance, some exclusion clauses used to say bluntly 'alcoholism' as a condition with regard to which the company would not accept a claim, so at least everybody knew where they stood – that is, if they bothered to read the policy. But now you will often find the bland phrase 'addictive condition' instead. It means the same but is not so obvious. *The only answer to small print is to read it.*

Then, when you have read it, you must stand by your interpretation of what it means. For instance, the *Sunday Times* has told the story of a 38-year-old pregnant secretary who lost her baby after developing septicaemia and whose claim for medical expenses was rejected by BUPA, Britain's biggest medical insurer, because they said she had had a 'normal pregnancy' and the claim was therefore excluded. Yet she persisted and after a six-month battle BUPA paid up. 'I believe I only got paid because I wasn't prepared to give in,' she said. 'I contracted septicaemia, lost my baby and nearly died. If that's a normal pregnancy, what would BUPA consider an abnormal one?'

If you are battling with a company over an interpretation of their rules, your best ally is your GP. In August 1992, a survey by *Which?* magazine showed that, of 660 patients with health-insurance claims, one in seven had had to pay part of the cost. It told of a patient from Norfolk who developed complications during prostate surgery and urgently needed twelve pints of blood. BUPA agreed to pay the cost of the operation with no difficulty but refused the extra cost of dealing with the complications which amounted to £2,000. The patient's GP then intervened on his behalf – and they paid up.

Sometimes the support of your GP, or even a consultant, is not enough. Then, if the amount involved is large enough, only the courts or arbitration can resolve the dispute. I do not know of one major dispute that has got so far as a full court hearing. But I am sure that some have been started, although no one can say how many, and then settled before coming to trial: no leading insurance company would welcome the bad publicity of a defeat in open court.

Arbitration, though, is a different story: it is not in public and is very much cheaper than litigation. Perhaps that is why the two leading British medical insurance companies, BUPA and PPP, state in their Rules that any dispute is subject to the jurisdiction of the courts 'or, at the election of both parties, to arbitration under the rules of the Personal Insurance Arbitration Service of the Chartered Institute of Arbitrators'. A helpful official at the Chartered Institute has told me that it has been approached by other medical-insurance companies with a view to starting similar schemes for their own customers.

Here is the story of one such arbitration. Sadly, it is not binding (unlike a judge's ruling, an arbitrator's award creates no legal precedent for other cases), but it points the way that other decisions may go. It concerns the vital question: Whose clinical judgement of a patient's condition is to prevail, that of the insurance company or the patient's own medical advisers?

The case of the rejected £11,806 hospital bill

In December 1990, 83-year-old Mrs Joan Lyall, who had for years paid the then top annual London BUPA rate of over £1,000, spent six weeks in the private Lindo Wing at St Mary's Hospital, Paddington, after a stroke. She had first been admitted to the NHS part of the hospital because no bed was available in the Lindo Wing but she had asked to be moved.

Her daughters telephoned their local BUPA office and were told that their mother would be covered for up to three months, provided they supplied a letter from her consultant confirming that she was having 'active medical treatment'. The consultant sent the letter within days.

But, when BUPA eventually received the bill for accommodation, consultant's fee and physiotherapy totalling £11,806, they rejected it, saying that, despite the consultant's letter, Mrs Lyall had received only nursing care and not 'active medical treatment'.

After months of wrangling, the claim went, with the consent of both parties, to the Personal Insurance Arbitration Service, which ruled that BUPA should pay the bill. The arbitrator said that the company was not bound by Mrs Lyall's daughters' telephone conversation with its local office, as that merely amounted to a reiteration of its conditions regarding claims, but that it still had to honour the claim because it could not substitute its own clinical judgement for that of the patient's consultant.

Patients' rights are the same as any others: you must be prepared to fight for them.

Libel and slander

Libel and slander cases have largely ceased to be important legal issues strongly debated and explored in court. They have become highly entertaining courtroom theatre where the pay-outs for unfounded and scurrilous accusations can be astronomical – like Elton John's £1 million because the *Sun* said he used rent boys, or fellow pop singer Jason Donovan's £200,000 because the *Face* magazine implied he was homosexual – or a bizarre case nearly three years ago when a dispute between two Syrian businessmen over a letter sent to a Saudi prince earned the financier Wafic Said a staggering £400,000.

Almost alone in civil lawsuits today, libel and slander cases are not decided by a judge alone but by a judge and jury: with juries having the sole right to assess the damages. And sometimes their awards can be so high as to be meaningless:

- In December 1989, Lord Aldington won £1,500,000 damages when wrongly accused of war crimes but then found that the writer concerned, Count Nikolai Tolstoy, could not pay.
- In July 1994, an award-winning yacht designer in the West Country, his wife and their company were awarded £1,485,000 against IPC Magazines for a scathing review of their revolutionary new trimaran in the magazine *Yachting World*, although the judge immediately put a stay of execution on the damages pending a possible appeal.

The Appeal Court does sometimes cut excessive awards. In April 1993, for instance, Esther Rantzen, star of BBC/TV's *That's Life* programme and chairman of ChildLine had the £250,000 damages awarded her by a jury against the *People* newspaper for alleging she had covered up for an alleged paedophile teacher reduced to £110,000. In December 1993 £150,000 awarded by a jury to a woman family doctor accused of saying the male GP male with whom she shared a surgery in East Hunbury, Northamptonshire, had sexually groped her was cut to £50,000.

But the problem lies not only in the disproportionately high awards that are made to winners (not always challenged on appeal, sometimes because of cost) but also in the disproportionately high bills for the legal costs *for both sides* that unfortunate losers usually have to pay.

For, if the stakes are high, so are the fees of the professional players. A leading specialist QC can earn up to £50,000 on delivery of his brief before the case even starts in court, plus up to between £5,000 and £10,000 'refreshers' for every day the hearing lasts.

Specialist solicitors, needed to brief the expensive QCs and their juniors, also earn vast sums. Indeed, many solicitors are not prepared to take on libel or slander cases unless the client pays a very substantial sum up front. No down payment – or collateral – and you run the risk of not being represented: at least, not by a high-flyer.

After all, libel lawyers know that they can very easily get burned. A loser, faced with a combined bill of £500,000 for both sides at the end of a ten-day hearing (not uncommon in a really top-drawer case), may well prefer to go bankrupt – and indeed some have! – rather than pay the full terrifying bill. Sometimes, in the end, 'accommodations' are undoubtedly made.

The idea of being able to sue for libel (or slander, which is the spoken version and much less frequent) is superb, and well-established.

It was back in 1840 that Baron Parke coined the classic definition: 'a false statement of fact that holds the plaintiff up to ridicule, hatred and contempt among right-thinking members of society generally'.

Unless, which seems highly unlikely, the Government introduces a law of privacy, taking the offender to court remains the only way of protecting one's reputation from hurtful and untrue attack. (The Press Complaints Commission, with no legal authority or power, cannot adequately protect the Royal Family's privacy let alone anyone else's.)

If a newspaper or magazine genuinely makes a simple factual mistake and commits what the law calls 'unintentional defamation', it is not so bad. You can promptly write or fax the editor a letter, quoting the 1952 Defamation Act (one of the few instances of libel law reform), and assert your right to demand a full factual apology – to be given the same prominence as the original offending item. A solicitor's letter may have more impact; but I know of apologies that have been printed on the strength of a letter from the aggrieved person alone.

Otherwise, however, it is a Rich Man's Club. Few ordinary people can afford to sue or, indeed, do so. Although the authoritative Faulks Committee first recommended as far back as 1975 that legal aid should be allowed, successive Governments have steadfastly refused to do any-thing about it. The idea somehow still persists that libel and slander cases are in some besmirched way 'gold-digging' actions, brought because of the hugely tempting awards available if you win. And undoubtedly some cases are. But so what? That is no reason for refusing legal aid to those genuinely in need.

However, as we know, extending legal aid to cover libel and slander would not be enough to bring justice within the reach of most of us. What would help more is for lawyers to put their own house in order. There simply is no justification for the vast courtroom costs in these cases. With all respect to the specialist lawyers concerned, I cannot believe that their fees for this type of work should be, on average, more than double the normal fees for ordinary High Court litigation, which are in all conscience high enough anyway. Fighting or defending a libel or slander case is no more difficult, time-consuming or arduous than any other High Court case where the issue in dispute basically boils down to who is telling the truth.

For most of us, the law's protection is like some splendid stately home lived in by others but only to be walked through and admired by us on special 'Open to the Public' days. By all means, you can write a letter threatening to sue, or pay a solicitor £50–£100 to do so for you; but most high-powered defendants know you will almost certainly not have the resources to persist to the door of a court. You may perhaps get some kind of financial offer as 'nuisance money' and, if that happens, good luck! You should think long before rejecting it. But more than that is unlikely. Sad but true.

STOP PRESS

In late November 1994, Lord Mackay, the Lord Chancellor, announced that he intended to introduce legislation, based upon recommendations two years earlier by a working group headed by Lord Justice Neill, for a faster and cheaper system to deal with smaller libel or slander claims. These reforms would include a new defence to avoid the need for a trial if the defendant was 'prepared to offer amends and pay damages assessed by a judge'. Every claim would also first come before a judge, who would assess whether it was suitable to be dealt with summarily or be sent on for full trial – which could be either in the County Court (not possible under present law) or High Court and with or without a jury. But if the judge dealt with it summarily, he could award damages up to a fixed ceiling – possibly only as low as £5,000.

Although a draft Bill had already been drafted, Lord Mackay's announcement gave no clue as to its exact timing: 'As soon as I have a suitable opportunity,' was all that he said. We may have quite a long wait.

Part Eight
YOUR DEATH

TWENTY

Wills, Intestacy and Death Itself

Recently the Law Society commissioned research into why so many people – at least a third of the adult population of this country – have not made their wills. The answer? Some have never thought about it, some simply have not yet got around to it, many think they are too young (although road accidents and terminal illness are not a monopoly of the middle-aged or elderly), some believe their husband or wife will automatically inherit everything anyway (which is not true), and one in ten did not want to think about dying.

Even multimillionaires can feel this way. When Robert Holmes à Court, the Australian media magnate, died suddenly in September 1990 at the age of fifty-three, leaving a £330 million estate, it was discovered that he had carried a draft will in his briefcase for eighteen months but never signed it.

This is all very understandable – but totally indefensible. If you care about your loved ones and what is to happen to them after you are dead or even, at a more mundane level, what is to happen to your money when you have gone, you simply must make a will. It is your only way of exerting some control over your assets and ensuring that your estate is properly divided up between the people – or charitable organisations – you care about.

If you die intestate (i.e. without having made a will), your estate will be distributed in accordance with fixed rules laid down by two outdated pieces of legislation, the 1925 Administration of Estates Act and the 1952 Intestates' Estates Act. These take no account of your wishes and, indeed, may have exactly the opposite effect. Back in December 1989, the Law Commission called for the law to be modernised and at last, in the Queen's speech in November 1994, the Government promised some reforms, which may or may not take effect in 1995.

So, before we discuss wills, let us look at **the law of intestacy**.

There are two main problems: *one*, the existing rules totally ignore an unmarried partner who has no rights whatsoever although, as we shall see later, he or she may be able to go to court and claim 'reasonable provision' from the estate; and, *two*, even when it is a married person who dies without a will, the widow or widower does not, as many people believe, always automatically inherit all the property. This only happens if:

(i) the total estate is not more than £75,000, which nowadays, with middle-class or middle-income families, is somewhat rare; or

(ii) there are absolutely no other surviving close relatives: no children, grandchildren, parents, brothers, sisters, nieces or nephews – which is even more rare.

In all other cases, the position is complex, arbitrary and can be unjust. All ages and social groups may be affected: a surviving spouse may be forced to leave the family home in which he or she has lived for years, a solitary parent left with young children may lose control of sufficient money to bring them up, even though the deceased in his lifetime may have been comfortably off, an elderly and ailing widow or widower may be left with insufficient income to provide adequately for her or his nursing and other needs, or an unmarried partner may be left with no share whatsoever in the estate of someone he or she may have lived with for years, although, as we will see, an unmarried partner may be able to go to court and claim 'reasonable provision' from the estate.

This is how the rules work:

(a) *A surviving spouse and children or grandchildren* Your surviving spouse inherits your personal 'chattels' (personal possessions including car, jewellery and household goods) and a statutory legacy of £75,000 but only a life interest in half the rest of your property. This means it is put in trust and your surviving spouse merely enjoys the income during his or her lifetime, after which it is shared out between your children or, if any have by then died, their children. What happens to the other half in which the surviving spouse does not have a life interest? He or she has no rights. It is divided between your children or, if any is already dead, their children take their parent's share.

These provisions may put the family home at risk for, as the Law Commission pointed out, there is no law saying that a surviving spouse must be entitled to, at least, the family home (which the Law Commission recommended). Where the house has been in joint names there will usually be no hardship, as the surviving spouse automatically takes the other's interest in the property, but hardship can, and does, occur where they were only tenants in common or the house was in the deceased's sole name. Then the deceased's interest in the family home forms part of his or her estate and, depending on its value in proportion to the total amount of the estate, the home may have to be sold so as to provide the surviving spouse with his or her statutory legacy of £125,000 or the children with their half-share of the total assets.

(b) *No surviving spouse but there are children or grandchildren* Your children share everything equally between them but, if any child died before you, their child or children take their parent's share. Illegitimate and adopted children are treated the same as legitimate children but stepchildren are ignored.

(c) *A surviving spouse but there are no children or grandchildren, only parents, brothers, sisters, nieces or nephews* Your surviving spouse will inherit your personal chattels, a statutory legacy of £125,000 and half the remainder absolutely, not merely a life interest. The other half will go to your parents or, if none survives, down the line to your brothers and sisters and, if any of them is dead, their child or children take their share.

(d) *No surviving spouse nor children but your parents are still alive* Your parents share the whole estate or, if only one survives, he or she takes all. This happens increasingly nowadays and causes injustice when a gay man dies, for instance, of Aids while still comparatively young and without having made a will in favour of his long-term partner and there is a fairly substantial life-insurance pay-out. This will go directly to the parents even though he may not have seen them for years or may even have been rejected by them because of their disapproval of his life style. Yet they will inherit everything with not a penny going to his lover.

(e) *No surviving spouse nor children nor parents but there are certain other relatives still alive* Your estate will be divided equally between your brothers and sisters or, if any has died, their children. If there is no one in this category, then this order of priority applies:

- half-brothers or sisters or their descendants; if none,
- grandparents; if none,
- full uncles and aunts or their descendants; if none,
- half-uncles and aunts or their descendants

(f) *No other surviving family members* Your estate passes to the Crown or, in appropriate areas, to the Duchy of Cornwall or the Duchy of Lancaster although, in practice, the Crown or these Duchies will often pay all or part to someone who seems morally entitled to a share. It is always worth asking.

Who looks after an intestate's estate? The job goes to the 'administrator'. This is the closest surviving relative in order of priority: widow or widower, children over eighteen in order of seniority, parents, brothers and sisters, etc. It is not automatic. This relative has to apply for what is called 'a grant of letters of administration' to his or her local probate registry – whose address and telephone number are in the local phone book or can be obtained from a citizens advice bureau. If the nearest relative does not want to apply, he or she can renounce the right – without forfeiting his or her inheritance – by completing a 'form of renunciation' from the probate registry. Many people ask a solicitor to act for them but, if you want to do the job yourself, the Probate Registry will give you a most helpful leaflet (Form PA 2) which will tell you exactly what to do.

Incidentally, this leaflet also explains that if someone dies with an estate worth less than £5,000 you may be able to wind up the estate without formal appointment as 'the administrator'.

Now let us go back to **the law of wills**.

It is not enough simply to make a will: you must do it properly, and I am afraid that this means you must ask a solicitor to draft one for you. The cost varies from about £50 or £75 plus VAT for the *very* simplest will up to several hundreds of pounds. But it is always money well spent. You are buying peace of mind for yourself and for your loved ones. Even if the solicitor is negligent and makes a mistake – which, with complicated wills, can happen even with an experienced lawyer – beneficiaries wrongfully deprived of their inheritance can sue him for compensation. This has been the law ever since a pioneering decision by Sir Robert Megarry, then Vice-Chancellor of the High Court's Chancery Division, in *Ross* v. *Caunters* in June 1979.

Other less satisfactory options are available: some banks and insurance companies offer a will-writing service but they usually insist on being appointed as executor, who does the same job as the 'administrator' when there is no will: i.e. he winds up the estate. This will almost inevitably increase the cost but, not content with that, they also sometimes try and sell you life assurance. Several large charities publish advice on will-making hoping that you will leave some of your money to them, although they cannot insist on this.

Also in recent years a new breed of professional will-writers has set up in business trying to undercut solicitors; but I would be wary of using them. Unlike solicitors, these people require no legal qualifications and their standard varies considerably. In October 1991, an Institute of Professional Will Writers was established to try to enforce minimum standards – but the organisation is voluntary and many firms are not even members.

The one thing you should definitely *not* do is try to write your own will, although many people still persist in doing this. Inexpensive do-it-yourself will packs and will forms are readily available in the shops, but please do not use them. You could be setting up the most awful problems for your family at a time when they can least cope: in the aftermath of your death. As a judge once said about a do-it-yourself will that ended up in the High Court: 'The testator filled in the will form and signed it, and no doubt thought he had done a good day's work – as for the legal profession he had!'

There are two main hazards:

(i) You will not get the will properly witnessed – which can easily happen despite the fact that the printed form generally spells out how it should be done. Namely, you must have at least two adult witnesses, who do not have to be present when the will is actually written out or typed (in fact, they do not even need to read it: you can cover it up when they appear) but they must both be present when you sign the document and must then immediately sign it themselves.

If you are too frail or infirm to sign with your name, you may simply put an 'X'. This is known as 'making your mark' and, when the will is drafted by a solicitor who supervises the proceedings, it causes no problems.

But neither the spouse nor anyone who is given a legacy in the will should be asked to sign as witness, for that will invalidate the legacy. (It was their negligence in failing to advise their will-making client of this basic legal requirement which made the solicitors in *Ross* v. *Caunters* pay damages to his sister-in-law when she lost her legacy after they allowed her husband to witness the will.)

Technically a will does not have to give the witnesses' names and addresses or state their qualifications, although nowadays it often does; but do not worry if you discover that an elderly relative's will made many years ago does not give these details. The will is still valid. Similarly, it does not matter if, by the time a testator dies, the witnesses are also dead: the validity of the will is not affected.

There is one category of people who do not need to have formal witnesses for their will or even for it to be in writing: soldiers and airmen on actual military service and sailors and mariners when at sea. So long as their words are intended to be a will, they are given the status of a will:

The case of the young army officer

On 6 July 1917, during World War One, a twenty-year-old Army lieutenant told his fiancée: 'If I stop a bullet everything of mine will be yours.' He was then on embarkation leave immediately before being posted to France. Three months later he was killed in action.

Two years later, in the High Court, Mr Justice Horridge ruled: 'It is not necessary, in order to establish the validity of a soldier's will, to prove that he knew he was making a will but merely that he intended deliberately to give expression to his wishes as to what should be done with his property in the event of his death.' He accepted the fiancée's evidence as to what the young officer had said, ruled that while on embarkation leave he was already 'on actual military service' – and upheld the validity of his 'soldier's will'.

This case (*In Re Stable*) still applies today. Lord Denning has said that you can be on 'actual military service' even in peacetime. So soldiers serving in Bosnia or in Northern Ireland, or Army bomb disposal experts trying to make a terrorist bomb safe on the British mainland, all come within Mr Justice Horridge's ruling back in 1919.

(ii) The second main hazard in DIY will-making is that it is so easy to get the wording wrong. Many phrases have a specific legal meaning which you use at your peril: you may think that you know what normal-sounding phrases such as 'money', 'all my personal jewellery', 'all my stocks and shares' and 'all my cash at the bank' mean, but these and many other seemingly straightforward expressions have all led to protracted and costly lawsuits.

It is not only legal terms. The meaning of everyday expressions may also vary depending on the context, and an astute solicitor will be on the alert to pre-empt potential problems. For instance, a legacy to 'the children of Joyce and Hilda' could result in the gift going to Joyce's children and to Hilda's children but it could also go to Joyce's children and Hilda alone. It would depend on what the judge thought the testator intended.

At least, that is the theory. The reality is probably nearer to the famous aphorism of Mr Justice Eve in the early years of this century: 'I shudder to think that in the hereafter I shall have to meet those testators whose wishes on earth have been frustrated by my judgments.' Sometimes they even give up the battle to try to make sense of the will-maker's wishes, as in the case of the elderly lady in Australia, where the law is similar, who left her estate to 'my two brothers, Percy Ernest Evans and Mark Evans'. The trouble was that Percy Evans was her cousin and her only two brothers were Mark Evans and Luke Evans. So who on earth did she mean? The Supreme Court of Victoria ruled the gift void for uncertainty.

Anybody who is over eighteen and of sound mind can make a will. But what does 'of sound mind' mean? The law is remarkably understanding of the frailties of age: an elderly person may have fantasies and delusions about some aspects of reality ('Don't we all?' you may ask) but, so long as they do not affect the subject matter of his will, they will not be sufficient to enable other people disappointed by the will to challenge its validity. As far back as 1870, in *Banks* v. *Goodfellow* Lord Cockburn, then Lord Chief Justice, ruled:

> A form of unsoundness of mind which neither disturbs the exercise of the faculties necessary for such an act, nor is capable of influencing the result, ought not to take away the power of making a will.
>
> In the case before us two delusions disturbed the mind of the testator, the one that he was pursued by Spirits, the other that a man long since dead came personally to molest him. Neither of these delusions had, or could have had, any influence upon him in disposing of his property.

So the will was upheld.

Of course, if a will is made in someone's favour through 'undue influence', it can be challenged and ruled invalid. In 1883, Lord Justice Lindley gave this classic definition of 'undue influence':

> Some unfair and improper conduct, some coercion from outside, some overreaching, some form of cheating and generally, though not always, some personal advantage obtained by a donee placed in some close and confidential relation to the donor.

That is why the judges have often said that, whenever old and infirm people make a will – or, even more so, a new will – their solicitor should ask their doctor to be present and preferably sign the will as a witness: to avoid any subsequent dispute as to their mental condition or any undue influence. Of course, difficulties may arise if the doctor himself benefits under the new will, as the courts tend to view with suspicion new wills made by elderly people disinheriting close family members in favour of their doctor, solicitor, nurse, housekeeper or any other newly acquired confident. But, as a solicitor friend of unimpeachable integrity has told me, 'If I see that the doctor himself benefits under the terms of the will, I always ask for a second opinion.'

Wills and families

A death in the family can bring out the best – and the worst – in human nature. Sometimes 'grieving' relatives do not even wait for the body to be cold before arguing over their inheritance or stealing a march over their rivals by lifting coveted goods from the home of the deceased. From the beginning of civilised time, this has been the human condition and from the start of will-making as we know it, in Ancient Rome, lawmakers have been concerned to prevent families squabbling over what they consider their 'rightful' inheritance.

That is why Roman law, which is the basis of most modern Western European civil law (and, in this respect, Scottish law as well), laid down a *jus uxori*, a widow's right to a fixed proportion of her dead husband's estate. The same applied to children. A man could not disinherit his family: whatever his will said, they were entitled to something. It was their inalienable right. Eventually this also became true when it was a woman who died.

But, until 1938, English law knew no such restrictions on a person's freedom to leave his assets to whomever he liked. Hence Shakespeare's famous will showing his wife Anne Hathaway exactly what he thought of her by leaving her only 'my second-best bed'. That was completely legal in 1616 and, depending on the circumstances of their marriage, could still be so now.

For even today if you want to disinherit your spouse or partner or children that still remains your prerogative. No one can tell you what you should or should not do with your own property. If no one complains, the will is valid.

But Parliament by several Acts starting in 1938 and culminating in the 1975 Inheritance (Provisions for Family and Dependants) Act now gives substantial protection to these groups of people: a surviving spouse; a divorced spouse (if not remarried); a child of whatever age (whether illegitimate, adopted or 'treated as a child of the family', which includes stepchildren) and a dependant maintained by the deceased immediately before his or her death (which includes both a mistress, who may well not have actually lived with the deceased, and an unmarried partner who probably did).

If any in this category considers they have been unreasonably treated by a will – *or by the fixed intestacy rules, if there is no will* – they can go to court (whether County Court or High Court) and ask a judge to make 'reasonable provision' for them out of the estate. Contrary to popular belief, grandchildren do not qualify, nor nieces and nephews. And surviving spouses generally fare better than other dependants, for 'reasonable provision' in their case means a fair share of the family assets, while for others it only means reasonable provision for maintenance – which is a lower yardstick.

How does a judge decide what is 'reasonable'? It is a typically English compromise. It is left to his individual discretion. He must 'have regard to' the testator's reasons in acting as he did, whether explained in the will itself or in an accompanying letter, but he is not bound by them. In one notable case, a husband left his wife nothing because, as he explained in his will, he believed she had committed adultery. She complained to the court. A judge heard the evidence, ruled that the dead husband had been wrong and his wife had not been unfaithful – and awarded her half the estate.

In another case, a 54-year-old spinster who devoted fifteen years of her life to her ailing mother won an extra £7,000 and £800 a year after Mr Justice Megarry was told that the spinster was left with only £7,500 worth of assets, while most of the £112,000 estate went to her mother's favourite daughter. A young second wife who left her husband of more than twice her age at the onset of his final illness was awarded only £2,000 after he chose to leave his entire estate to his two children by his first marriage and a close friend who had nursed him in the last remaining months of his life. A 52-year-old woman who married a retired stockbroker aged seventy-five and left him after only a few months when she found (so she alleged) that he was mean not only with his money but with his sexual favours, received an undisclosed sum from his estate after settling her claim against his daughter.

The first successful case brought by a mistress for a share of her deceased lover's estate was in May 1979. Four years earlier, the 1975 Act had made such a claim possible. The case is pure copybook because it shows that the claimant does not have to be the dear departed's sole dalliance and confirms that she does not need actually to have lived with him.

The case of the Birmingham womaniser

According to his younger brother, a Birmingham insurance broker who died in 1977, leaving an estate of £899,000, had 'lived for women'. He 'usually had four girlfriends on the go at once, a couple of regulars and two casuals'. He also had a wife who was one year older and a Common Law wife who was twenty-four years younger.

When the 1975 Act was passed, the broker told one of his regular girlfriends, a 34-year-old auxiliary nurse with whom he had had an affair for the past ten years, that he was not going to leave her anything in his will – but he handed her a copy of the new Act. 'I think he was too embarrassed to put me in the will,' she later explained, 'but I sincerely believe he expected me to go to court to fight it.'

And, when he died, that is what she did. She qualified as a dependant – it does not have to be a *sole* dependancy – by proving that he had given her a holiday flat in Malta, a white MG sports car and a flat worth, at the time of the lawsuit, some £17,500. Furthermore, she was not an ex-mistress with a dependancy only in the past – which would not count – because this 'generous and considerate' man had continued to pay her a £65-a-month allowance right up to the date of his death.

She was awarded £19,000 from the estate.

All claimants must act promptly. Claims must be made within six months of the grant of probate, which is when the will is officially accepted as valid; and anyone thinking he or she may have a claim should, in sheer prudence, consult a solicitor as soon as possible after the death. The solicitor can then lodge a notice at court ensuring he is notified when probate is granted and the six-month clock starts ticking.

What does it cost? If the estate is not too small, judges usually order a claimant's legal expenses to be paid out of the estate, even if the claimant loses.

Some may doubt whether this is entirely fair, for the estate also usually pays if the claimant wins. So, in a sense, the only one who really loses is the person who made the will: he has to pay posthumously for others to dispute his own final wishes as to what is to happen to his own property.

Wills are a very important subject. In my various legal-advice columns in the press over the years more people have written to me about wills than on any other single topic, so, before we move on, here is a quick résumé of some of the points I have most often been asked about:

• Wills have an obvious value in reducing the impact of *inheritance tax*, which many people still call death duties but experts refer to as IHT. It is currently charged at 40 per cent on estates over £150,000 (due to go up, in April 1995, to £154,000) and, although both are considerable sums, property and investments bought some time ago may have risen in value. This is a highly specialised branch of the law and you really do need a skilled and experienced solicitor's advice on how best to use your will to reduce your IHT burden. For instance, many people think that they merely have to put their home in a son or daughter's name and then survive for at least seven years to avoid IHT being paid on the value of their home. It is nothing like so simple. A gift to a child of your main residence does not save IHT, even if you live for seven years or more – if there is any understanding that you will be allowed to go on living there rent-free. You cannot have what is called a 'reservation of an interest in the property'. But there are still some ingenious manoeuvrings that a specialist solicitor or expert tax-planner may be able to suggest to you.

• If you have young children, it is always useful to name their *guardian* in your will in case you die before any of them reaches eighteen. That, in itself, counts as their formal legal appointment. My wife and I made a will when we were both young for this very reason alone: at that time we had no money or other assets worth worrying about.

• A *codicil* is a useful way of keeping a will up to date without incurring the full expense of a whole new will. For instance, you may wish to increase the amount you have given your grandchildren in your will. You can easily achieve this minor alteration by a short formal document of two or three sentences stating the new amount and confirming that, in every other respect, your will remains the same.

But please do not do it yourself. The exact wording is vital and a codicil must be formally signed in front of two witnesses, just like the original will. A solicitor may charge about £50 plus VAT, but it is money well spent.

• You should *review your will at regular intervals*. Do not go so far as the distinguished old lady who is reputed in her *Who's Who* entry to have stated her hobby as: 'changing my will'. But circumstances change and you should keep abreast of them. The sad fate of Benny Hill's will is a warning to us all.

The case of the famous TV comedian

In January 1992, in a newspaper interview, Benny Hill told a reporter that, as his close family had all died, he intended to make two named loyal fans his principal beneficiaries. 'Sadly all my family have gone now,' he said, 'so I must make a new will and I can safely say they will be No. 1 and No. 2 in it.'

But when he died of a heart attack three months later, aged sixty-seven, no new will could be found. There was only an old will dating back to 1961 in which his £7 million estate was left to his parents, his brother Leonard and his sister Diana Olive – but they had all died before him.

So what happened? His estate was shared equally between his dead brother's two sons and two daughters and his dead sister's two sons and a daughter.

• *Keep your will in a safe place* and tell your nearest relative or closest friend where it is. Many people keep their will in their solicitor's safe or at the bank but there is also an official will-deposit service at Somerset House which not many know about. You can write to the Record Keeper at the Principal Registry, Family Division, Somerset House, Strand, London WC2R 1LP, and he will send you a large envelope and instructions on how to complete it. You then return it with your will and a fee of only £1 and he will send you a deposit certificate which has to be produced before the will can be withdrawn.

• People sometimes say they are going to leave something in their will to someone, who then never hears anything more about it. *How can you find out if you are named in a will?* The original will or a certified copy is always available for inspection at Somerset House – and you do not have to give any explanation. It costs nothing to look at the will but a photocopy will cost 25p per page. If you cannot journey to London, send a £2 cheque to the York Probate Sub-registry at Duncombe Place, York YO1 2EA, giving such details as you can, and you will receive a copy post-free; but there can be a delay of up to four months. (In Scotland, you should write to the General Register House, Edinburgh.)

• How can you *donate your organs* for transplant or your whole body for medical research? You can either state your wishes in the will itself or, with organ donation, sign a donor card and keep it among your effects, or, with a gift of your whole body, contact, in London, the London Anatomy Office at Rockefeller Building, University College, London WC1E 6JJ (Tel: 0171–387 7850). Elsewhere you should get in touch with the anatomy office of your nearest medical school, whose address you can easily get from your local hospital.

But, after you are dead, you do not own your own body or any part of it. In practice, whatever the will or any other document may say, doctors will usually not remove organs or dissect a body if the immediate family objects. By that time, your body no longer belongs to you but to your next of kin;[1] yet this is a grey area within the law and it is by no means clear whether the doctors must first ask the next of kin for their consent before they wield the scalpel or whether, if you have given your own agreement in your lifetime, they can simply proceed assuming that there will be no objection.

• *After divorce*, it is always better to make a new will. The law may be changed in 1995 but, as I write (in December 1994), marriage invalidates a will (a useful point to remember) but, surprisingly, divorce does not have this effect: it merely invalidates any gift to the former spouse or his or her appointment as executor. This can easily throw the whole will off balance. In any event, you may as well have a complete rethink and make a new will.

• Many people name a close relative or friend as their *executor* in the will itself, sometimes without the sensible precaution of first asking if the person wants the job. But, even if you have agreed to be someone's executor while he or she was still alive, there is legally nothing to stop you changing your mind afterwards. The local probate registry will supply you with a simple form to fill in. Some testators name their bank or solicitor as executor (at one time the Government hinted that

---

[1] Technically the expression 'next of kin' only applies to your nearest *blood* relative. If you are married, your husband or wife is legally your nearest relative but not your 'next of kin'. In practice, hospitals and doctors treat as 'next of kin' whomever the patient nominates for that role, irrespective of the nature of their relationship: lover (gay or straight), brother or sister, whomever. You put down on the form that you fill in and sign when admitted to hospital whomsoever you want.

it might also allow building societies and insurance companies to offer this service but so far nothing has come of this).

Solicitors and, even more so, banks can be expensive executors, but solicitors, as in all their non-court work, are supposed to charge only a 'fair and reasonable' fee. So an executor has the same right as any other client, on receipt of a solicitor's bill which he considers excessive, to write to him within twenty-eight days (preferably by recorded delivery) saying he is dissatisfied with the bill, refusing to pay more than half the bill, plus VAT and disbursements – and asking him to obtain a 'remuneration certificate' from the Law Society confirming that it is, in fact, 'fair and reasonable'. The Law Society cannot increase the bill but it can – and sometimes does – reduce it. If you are in any doubt about this, you should telephone the Solicitors Complaints Bureau at its office in Leamington Spa, on 01926–822007/8.

It does not always have to be a solicitor or close relative or friend as executor, as if the two were mutually exclusive. There is nothing to prevent you, as executor, using the specific services of a solicitor as and when you think necessary. His fees will, of course, be borne by the estate but, in this way, it is much easier to monitor the charges, as they occur. That is what I did when I was my father-in-law's executor. The great secret of dealing with solicitors is: Never be frightened to ask 'How much?'

• Getting a will *'admitted to probate'*. This is the first essential step needed to enforce the will as a valid legal document. It is the job of the executor or his solicitor but, if you are doing it yourself, the same useful leaflet (Form PA 2) which you can obtain from your local Probate Registry when applying to be administrator in the case of an intestacy will tell you what to do in these circumstances as well.

• *Living wills*. Technically these are not wills at all. They have no relevance as to what is to happen to your property after death. They merely relate to the way in which you wish to die. The law on 'advance treatment directives', as they are properly called, is still evolving. Only in June 1992 did Lord Donaldson, when Master of the Rolls, first declare: 'Every adult has the legal right and capacity to decide whether or not he will accept medical treatment, even if a refusal may risk permanent injury to health or even lead to premature death.'

Living wills are much more popular in the United States (among other famous people, both Richard Nixon and Jacqueline Kennedy

341

Onassis were allowed to die with dignity because of their living wills) but in this country the Terrence Higgins Trust provides living-will forms and the British Medical Association supports their use. These forms are not restricted to those with HIV infections or Aids and are free to individual applicants, although professional firms are asked for a donation and it might be thought appropriate for a private person to give one anyway. The Trust's address is 52–54 Gray's Inn Road, London WC1X 8JV (Tel: 0171–831 0330).

Now we come to the most awesome topic of all: **Death**.

And, at once, we must face up to the question: when can someone legally say that he or she wants to die and that the doctors and nurses should stop all their efforts to keep him or her alive? Suicide ceased to be a criminal offence in 1961 with the Suicide Act of that year. As we have just seen, Lord Donaldson has proclaimed the legal right of all of us to refuse further medical treatment, even if it means that inevitably we will die.

But what about others: doctor, nurses and, even more heart-rending, loved ones who are asked to assist in the process and positively kill someone who is in pain and despair and knows that he is dying? This is not the place to discuss the medical ethics of 'mercy killing' or euthanasia. The law is quite clear: there is a fundamental difference between killing and letting someone die. The former is murder,[2] the latter is not a crime: indeed, I was in this situation myself over forty years ago when, as a young man of twenty-three, I was called to the London nursing home where my 82-year-old grandmother was living. She had been in failing health for some time and now she had suddenly been taken desperately ill. 'I can let her go tonight or I can keep her for a week,' her gravel-voiced Austrian-born doctor told me. 'What shall I do?' I did not hesitate. I knew my parents were out of town but I did not think of them. I thought only of the old lady lying in front of me, obviously *in extremis*. 'Let her go tonight,' I said and within half an hour she died, as I sat beside her bed.

I have thought about that scene many times and wondered if I did the right thing. I never told my mother, her daughter, what had hap-

---

[2] Although it may be reduced to manslaughter on account of 'diminished mental responsibility' in the case of a husband, wife, lover or child because of the appalling mental anguish they will have endured, this defence is not open to a doctor or nurse: they are supposed to be coolly professional.

pened and, to be honest, I did not even consider what the law would have said. Yet I am now reasonably sure (not that it matters a great deal, I must admit) that neither that pleasant doctor nor I committed a crime.

But what about the situation where a terminally ill patient is in great pain and a doctor knows that certain drugs will alleviate the pain but may hasten death: what is his legal responsibility then? Again, the answer is clear: if the *primary* purpose of administering the drugs is to lessen the pain, then he commits no crime even if the drugs cause death. As a spokesman for the Crown Prosecution Service told the House of Lords Committee on Medical Ethics in June 1993: 'The administering of pain-killing, though life-shortening, drugs to terminally ill patients is rendered lawful if the doctor is acting in the best interests of the patient, despite the fact that the patient will die as a consequence.'

Fine lines are drawn and delicate decisions taken every day in hospitals up and down the country. In a study by Cambridge researchers reported in the *British Medical Journal* in May 1994, almost half the 300 doctors questioned said they had been asked by patients to take active steps to end their lives – and a third had agreed to do so. This is a potentially dangerous area for doctors, as shown by the case in September 1992 of Dr Nigel Cox, a courageous consultant rheumatologist at the Royal Hampshire County Hospital in Winchester:

The case of the compassionate doctor

Dr Cox had cared for seventy-year-old Mrs Lillian Boyes for thirteen years. Finally she was lying dying slowly and painfully of a wasting disease in his hospital. She had borne intense pain with remarkable courage until five days before her death, when she asked him to 'finish her off' with an injection. Reluctantly he gave her twice the lethal dose of potassium chloride and mercifully she died. Her suffering was over.

But the Crown Prosecution Service prosecuted him for attempted murder – and a jury at Winchester Crown Court convicted him. Why? Because his 'primary purpose' was not to relieve his patient's pain but to end her life as the only way of relieving her suffering. Mr Justice Ognall rejected defence counsel's impassioned plea for an absolute discharge and gave the doctor a twelve-month prison sentence, suspended for a year.

'What you did was not only criminal. It was a total betrayal of your unequivocal duty as a physician,' Mr Justice Ognall told him. Not everyone will agree.

In February 1994, the House of Lords Select Committee on Medical Ethics agreed unanimously that there should be no change in the law to permit euthanasia and Dr Brian Mawhinney, then Health Minister, on behalf of the Government, agreed that any such suggestion would be 'unacceptable'.

Now what about death itself? When legally do we 'die'? Perhaps surprisingly, there is no legal definition, neither in any Act of Parliament nor in any pronouncement by a judge. The law, faced with the technological sophistications of modern medical science, throws up its hands and leaves it to the doctors to decide. Nowadays doctors say that we 'die' when our brain stem suffers total and irretrievable damage and can no longer control our bodily functions, even though this may be achieved artifically; and the judges go along with that view.

As Lord Browne-Wilkinson said in February 1993 in the classic case of *Airedale NHS Trust* v. *Bland*, when the House of Lords ruled that the doctors committed no criminal offence in withdrawing artificial feeding from the tragic young football fan, 21-year-old Tony Bland, who lay helpless in his hospital bed in a persistent vegetative state, unable to think, speak, see, swallow or feel anything (including pain or hunger) after his brain and lungs had been damaged in the crush that killed ninety-five others in the Hillsborough stadium disaster nearly four years earlier:

'Until recently there was no doubt what was life and what was death. A man was dead if he stopped breathing and his heart stopped beating. There were no artificial means of sustaining those indications of life for more than a little while. Death in the traditional sense was beyond human control. Apart from cases of unlawful homicide, death occurred automatically in the course of nature when the natural functions of the body failed to sustain the lungs and the heart.

'Recent developments in medical science have fundamentally affected these previous certainties. In medicine, the cessation of breathing or heartbeat is no longer death. By the use of a ventilator, lungs which in the unaided course of nature would have stopped breathing can be made to breathe, thereby sustaining the heartbeat. Those, like Anthony Bland, who would previously have died through inability to swallow food can be kept alive by artificial feeding. This has led the medical profession to redefine death in terms of brain-stem death, i.e. the death of that part of the brain without which the body cannot function at all without assistance. In some cases it is now apparently possible, with the use of the ventilator, to sustain a beating heart even though the brain stem, and therefore in medical terms the patient, is dead: "the ventilated corpse".

'I do not refer to these factors because Anthony Bland is already dead, either medically *or legally* [my italics]. His brain stem is alive and so is he; provided that he is artificially fed and the waste products evacuated from his body by skilled medical care, his body sustains its own life.'

But five Law Lords unanimously agreed that he should no longer be fed and twenty-seven days later he finally 'died' medically and legally when, with his body deprived of all food, his brain stem ceased to function. You could say that the law allowed him to be starved to death; but he felt nothing and knew nothing. He died with dignity and without suffering.

Yet the Law Lords were uneasy, and understandably so. They ruled that in all future cases of withdrawing life-prolonging treatment (such as artificial feeding) from patients in a persistent vegetative state the approval of the courts must first be obtained. They were clearly worried by the serious legal, moral and ethical issues raised by the case and, as Lord Mustill said, 'The whole matter cries out for exploration in depth in Parliament.' This has not yet happened.

But what about the many, many cases when doctors 'turn off the switch' on a life-support machine: do they first have to go and get the consent of a judge? Not at all. People in a persistent vegetative state, as Tony Bland was, are still medically and legally *alive*: part of their brain stem is still working. When doctors 'turn off the switch', the whole brain stem is dead. It no longer functions. The apparent 'life' of the patient is entirely artificial: turn off the switch and *at once* that semblance of life will cease.

As far back as March 1981, in the cases of R. v. *Malcherek* and R. v. *Steel*, the Appeal Court accepted that turning off the switch did not 'kill' a patient: the patient was already dead. In both cases, the patients had been criminally attacked and apparently died from their injuries but, for a while, they had been put on a life-support machine until the doctors satisfied themselves incontrovertibly that irretrievable brain damage had occurred and there was no hope whatsoever of continued life or recovery. Both attackers were convicted of murder and sentenced to life imprisonment but they appealed on the basis that they had not 'killed' their victims: the doctors had done so when switching off the life-support machines.

Lord Lane, then Lord Chief Justice presiding over the Appeal Court, would have none of it. Both murder convictions were upheld. He said:

> Where a medical practitioner adopting methods which are generally accepted comes bona fide and conscientiously to the conclusion that the patient is for practical purposes dead, and that such vital functions as exist (for example, circulation) are being maintained solely by mechanical means, and therefore discontinues treatment, that does not prevent the person who inflicted the initial injury from being responsible for the victim's death.

So much for death itself. I began this book with the law dealing with our bodies before we are born. Now let us end with a brief look at the law dealing with the disposal of our bodies after we are dead. On the whole, it is remarkably straightforward:

(i) *If death occurs at home*

• If a doctor is not already there, call him at once. If he can, he will immediately confirm the cause of death and give you a free medical certificate stating the cause of death in a sealed envelope addressed to the Registrar of Births and Deaths along with a formal notice which says he has signed the certificate and explains the procedure for registering the death. You must take the sealed envelope to the nearest Registrar of Births, Marriages and Deaths within five days (or up to forty-two days for a stillbirth) and register the death. The Registrar will then give you a formal death certificate and a green 'disposal certificate' that allows you to arrange the funeral.

• If the doctor did not see the deceased during his last illness *or* within the past fourteen days *or* he thinks the cause of death is uncertain *or* it was sudden, violent or caused by an accident or industrial disease, he will report the death to the coroner and inevitably the funeral and burial arrangements will be held up.

(ii) *If death occurs in hospital*

• If you were not present at the time of death, the ward sister will telephone you as soon as possible but, if the deceased was brought in as the result of an accident, the police may inform you and ask you to identify the body.

• If the cause of death is clear, a hospital doctor will give you the same free medical certificate and formal notice as when someone dies at home. But, if there is some doubt as to the exact cause of death, he may request your permission to conduct at least a partial post-mortem. You may refuse but, as the hospital will warn you, this means that they must inform the coroner who will arrange for his own post-mortem to be held – and there will be even more delay before you can bury your loved one.

• If the cause of death is uncertain and the next-of-kin will not agree to a hospital post-mortem or the death was sudden, violent or caused by an accident or industrial disease or if it occurred during an operation or while the deceased was under an anaesthetic, the hospital must inform the coroner and again there will be delay.

(iii) *If the coroner is informed*

Despite what many people believe, there does not always have to be an inquest but there will almost certainly be a post-mortem conducted by an independent forensic pathologist reporting directly to the coroner. The next-of-kin cannot object to this, as they can in the case of a hospital post-mortem, although he or she can ask for their own doctor to be present. As with a hospital post-mortem, the whole body does not have to be dissected. There may be a partial examination of the dead body limited only to certain vital organs such as the heart or liver: some grieving relatives find this easier to bear.

If the coroner's post-mortem, whether full or partial, satisfies him as to the cause of death, the coroner – not your own doctor or the hospital's – will supply a cause-of-death certificate and a green disposal certificate for you to register the death and arrange the funeral.

347

However, if despite his post-mortem, the coroner is still not satisfied as to the cause of death or if the death was violent, accidental or resulted from an industrial disease, he may decide to hold an inquest. If this happens, he will normally hold a preliminary hearing within a week or so for purposes of identification only and will then usually release the body and issue the relevant certificates for burial. The full inquest will usually follow several weeks later and relatives have the right to be present and to be represented by a lawyer, although the actual role that their lawyer will be allowed to play in the proceedings is entirely a matter for the individual coroner – and some are very autocratic.

Coroners, who must be either lawyers or doctors (a few are both), are virtually a law unto themselves. They begin by questioning each witness themselves and then it is entirely their own choice whether they allow any questions from anyone else – or even any speech by a lawyer representing interested parties. Sometimes they sit with a jury but, as the late Dr Gavin Thurston, himself a distinguished London coroner, once wrote: 'It is indisputable that juries make no contribution to most inquests. Jurors have been heard to voice the opinion that their time has been wasted.'

Inquests are only as valuable as the quality of the individual coroner, and most people who have any experience of their courts would agree that the standard varies enormously up and down the country.

(iv) *Finally, the very end: burial or cremation*

You may state clearly in your will – or in detailed written instructions in a separate document – your exact wishes as to how you want to be buried or whether and where you wish to be cremated. *These have absolutely no legal effect.* Once you are dead, your body no longer belongs to you and your next-of-kin can arrange whatever lawful kind of disposal he cares for. There are many sad stories of families at last getting their own back on some selfish or domineering old person after death and disposing of the body in ways completely contrary to the deceased's express wishes.

You can be buried in a churchyard you have never heard of, cremated although you were totally opposed to the idea, or buried with great pomp in a magnificent marble tomb although you specifically said in your will that you wanted to be cremated with as little fuss as possible.

The only legal requirement for cremation is *not* that the dead person specifically wanted to be cremated, although in many cases this is undoubtedly so, but that there is no improper reason for wanting the body irretrievably destroyed in the furnace of a crematorium: in other words, you have not been murdered or been caused deliberate physical suffering.

The next-of-kin has, in effect, to prove this by giving a crematorium no less than three signed forms under the 1902 and 1952 Crematorium Acts:

• Form A, which is the formal application for cremation, counter-signed by a householder who knows the next-of-kin personally.

• Forms B and C, which are on the same piece of paper. Form B is completed by the doctor who attended the deceased during his last illness, although not necessarily the one who signed the cause-of-death certificate, and it details the deceased's treatment and states whether the doctor benefits financially from the death. Form C is a confirmatory certificate completed by a doctor who is totally independent, although often recommended by the Form B doctor. He will have seen the body and made a careful external examination (this form is not required where a post-mortem has taken place).

But that is not all. There must also be a fourth form, Form D, which is, in fact, the formal authority to cremate signed by the crematorium's own medical referee after he has read Forms B and C. If he is unsatisfied for any reason, he may refuse authority to cremate or may himself order a post-mortem or refer the matter to the coroner. The relatives have no right to prevent this. If they do not want a post-mortem, they will have to forgo cremation and have the body buried instead.

No one's body can just be left to rot. If your next-of-kin chooses to bury you rather than cremate you, he can assert your legal right to be buried, if there is room, in the graveyard of the parish in which you had your last home or died – whether or not you were even a Christian! But this legal right does not extend to a memorial or headstone: that has to be paid for privately. There is no law which says your last resting place must be marked in some way. Sadly, many people lie in unmarked and untended graves.

But Church of England Law says that, if a headstone exists, it must fall within legal guidelines for the preservation of the dignity of graveyards. These guidelines are supervised by church consistory courts presided over by bishops' judges called diocesan chancellors, and cases are sometimes brought when local vicars refuse to allow headstone inscriptions using such homely but 'undignified' words as 'Dad', 'Mum' or 'Grandma'. There was one such case in the village of Freckleton, Lancashire, as recently as August 1994, when Judge John Bullimore, chancellor of the Blackburn diocese, upheld the local vicar's ruling that a sorrowing family could not use the words 'Dad' and 'Grandad' on the gravestone of an 83-year-old relative.

Even at the very end, we cannot escape the law.

INDEX

speeding 220–21
sports 257–64
squatters 290–93
Staughton, Lord Justice 26
Steel, Sir David 16
Steptoe, Dr Patrick 19
sterilisation 14–15
surrogacy 20–22
Swift, Mr Justice 259

Taylor, Lord 2
Taylor, John 4
Templeman, Lord 12
test-tube babies 19–20
Thatcher, Baroness 19, 129
Thorpe, Lord Justice 37
Thurnham, Peter 41
Timms, Chris 225–6
Tolstoy, Count Nikolai 321
Toyn, Judge 205
traffic lights 218–19

unborn child, legal rights of 25–8
unfair dismissal 177–87

Veale, Mr Justice 72
VDUs 146–7
visitors to private homes 202–5

Waite, Mr Justice 115
Wall, Mr Justice 124
Wallington, Mr Justice 125
Warnock, Baroness 19
Watts, Judge 97
wheel clamping 228–31
Widgery, Lord 226, 275
William, HRH Prince 55
Willis, Judge Stephen 44
wills 327–42
    intestacy 327–30
    law of 331–42
Wilson, Mr Justice 54
Wilson, Professor Alan 316
Wilson, Harold 140, 149
windscreen cleaners 219–20
Woolf, Mr Justice 196

Yeo, Tim 41